I0880830

Instigation to Crimes against Humanity

International Criminal Law Series

Editorial Board

Series Editor

M. Cherif Bassiouni (*USA/EGYPT*)

Distinguished Research Professor of Law Emeritus, President Emeritus, International Human Rights Law Institute, DePaul University College of Law; President, International Institute of Higher Studies in Criminal Sciences; Honorary President, Association Internationale de Droit Pénal; Chicago, USA

Kai Ambos (GERMANY)
Judge, District Court, Göttingen; Professor of Law and Head, Department for Foreign and International Criminal Law, Georg August Universität

Mahnoush Arsanjani (IRAN)
Member, Institut de Droit International; former Director, Codification Division, United Nations Office of Legal Affairs

Mohamed Chande Othman (TANZANIA)
Chief Justice, Court of Appeal of Tanzania

Eric David (BELGIUM)
Professor of Law, Faculty of Law, Free University of Brussels

Mireille Delmas-Marty (FRANCE)
Professor of Comparative Legal Studies and Internationalisation of Law, Collège de France

Adama Dieng (SENEGAL)
UN Secretary-General's Special Adviser on the Prevention of Genocide; former Registrar, International Criminal Tribunal for Rwanda; former Secretary General, International Commission of Jurists

Mark Drumbl (CANADA/USA)
Class of 1975 Alumni Professor of Law, Director, Transnational Law Institute, Washington and Lee University School of Law

Chile Eboe-Osuji (NIGERIA)
Judge, Trial Division, International Criminal Court; former Legal Adviser to the High Commissioner for Human Rights, Office of the High Commissioner for Human Rights

Geoff Gilbert (UK)
Professor of Law and Head, School of Law, University of Essex

Philippe Kirsch (BELGIUM/CANADA)
Ad hoc Judge, International Court of Justice; former President, International Criminal Court; Ambassador (Ret.) and former Legal Advisor, Ministry of Foreign Affairs of Canada

André Klip (THE NETHERLANDS)
Professor of Law, Department of Criminal Law and Criminology, Faculty of Law, Maastricht University

Erkki Kourula (FINLAND)
Judge and President of the Appeals Division, International Criminal Court

Motoo Noguchi (JAPAN)
Legal Adviser, Ministry of Justice of Japan; Visiting Professor of Law, University of Tokyo; former International Judge, Supreme Court Chamber, Extraordinary Chambers in the Courts of Cambodia

Diane Orentlicher (USA)
Professor of International Law, Co-Director, Center for Human Rights and Humanitarian Law, Washington College of Law, American University

Fausto Pocar (ITALY)
Judge and former President, International Criminal Tribunal for the Former Yugoslavia; President, International Institute of Humanitarian Law; Professor of International Law Emeritus, University of Milan

Leila Nadya Sadat (FRANCE/USA)
Henry H. Oberschelp Professor of Law, Director, Whitney R. Harris World Law Institute, Washington University School of Law

William Schabas (CANADA/IRELAND)
Professor of International Law, Department of Law, Middlesex University; Chairman, Irish Centre for Human Rights, National University of Ireland

Michael Scharf (USA)
John Deaver Drinko-Baker & Hostetlier Professor of Law, Director, Frederick K. Cox International Law Center, Case Western Reserve University School of Law

Ulrich Sieber (GERMANY)
Professor of Criminal Law, Director, Max Plank Institute for Foreign and International Criminal Law, University of Freiburg

Göran Sluiter (THE NETHERLANDS)
Professor of Law, Department of Criminal Law and Criminal Procedure, Faculty of Law, University of Amsterdam

Otto Triffterer (AUSTRIA)
Professor of International Criminal Law and Procedure, Faculty of Law, University of Salzburg

Françoise Tulkens (BELGIUM)
Vice-President, European Court of Human Rights

Xuimei Wang (CHINA)
Professor of International Criminal Law, College for Criminal Law Science, Beijing Normal University, Executive Director, ICC Project Office

Christine van den Wyngaert (BELGIUM)
Judge, Trial Division, International Criminal Court; former Judge, International Criminal Tribunal for the Former Yugoslavia; former *Ad hoc* Judge, International Court of Justice

Gert Vermeulen (BELGIUM)
Professor of Criminal Law, Director, Institute for International Research on Criminal Policy, Ghent University, Extraordinary Professor of Evidence Law, Maastricht University

Giuliana Ziccardi Capaldo (ITALY)
Professor of International Law, Faculty of Law, University of Salerno

VOLUME 3

The titles published in this series are listed at brill.com/icls

Instigation to Crimes against Humanity

The Flawed Jurisprudence of the Trial and Appeal Chambers of the International Criminal Tribunal For Rwanda (ICTR)

By

Avitus A. Agbor

MARTINUS NIJHOFF PUBLISHERS

LEIDEN · BOSTON
2013

Library of Congress Cataloging-in-Publication Data

Agbor, Avitus A., author.
Instigation to crimes against humanity : the flawed jurisprudence of the Trial and Appeal Chambers of the International Criminal Tribunal for Rwanda (ICTR) / By Avitus A. Agbor.
pages cm -- (International criminal law series ; 3)
Includes bibliographical references and index.
ISBN 978-90-04-25412-1 (hardback : alk. paper) -- ISBN 978-90-04-25413-8 (e-book) 1. International Criminal Tribunal for Rwanda. 2. International criminal courts--Rwanda. 3. Trials (Crimes against humanity)--Rwanda. 4. Trials (Genocide)--Rwanda. I. Title.
KZ1201.A12A33 2013
345'.02510264--dc23

2013038446

This publication has been typeset in the multilingual "Brill" typeface. With over 5,100 characters covering Latin, IPA, Greek, and Cyrillic, this typeface is especially suitable for use in the humanities. For more information, please see www.brill.com/brill-typeface.

ISSN 2213-2724
ISBN 978-90-04-25412-1 (hardback)
ISBN 978-90-04-25413-8 (e-book)

Copyright 2013 by Koninklijke Brill NV, Leiden, The Netherlands.
Koninklijke Brill NV incorporates the imprints Brill, Global Oriental, Hotei Publishing, IDC Publishers and Martinus Nijhoff Publishers.

All rights reserved. No part of this publication may be reproduced, translated, stored in a retrieval system, or transmitted in any form or by any means, electronic, mechanical, photocopying, recording or otherwise, without prior written permission from the publisher.

Authorization to photocopy items for internal or personal use is granted by Koninklijke Brill NV provided that the appropriate fees are paid directly to The Copyright Clearance Center, 222 Rosewood Drive, Suite 910, Danvers, MA 01923, USA.
Fees are subject to change.

This book is printed on acid-free paper.

To my parents, Pa Agbor Agbor Cuthbert John and Ma Mary Agbor, for the incessant and selfless sacrifices they continue to make for me; and to my beloved and wonderful sisters and brothers for the love we share.

CONTENTS

ACKNOWLEDGEMENT

When I embarked on this journey, I knew the easiest part of it would be writing an acknowledgment. As I approached its end, I made a flashback on how I navigated this path up to the point where I began to see the light at the end of the tunnel. A journey that was saturated with ups and downs, twists, speculations, challenges, appointments and disappointments, it became extremely difficult to express words of gratitude to those who were supportive.

To Professor Bonita Meyersfeld, many thanks to you for putting at my disposal your professional scholarship and research acumen. About three years ago, you inspired me to become a contributor and producer of legal literature, and not just a consumer. I remain grateful to you for the sublime supervision you provided me when I pursued my doctoral studies at the University of the Witwatersrand, Johannesburg, Republic of South Africa.

To my parents, Pa Agbor Agbor Cuthbert John and Ma Mary E. Agbor, I remain grateful to you all for the sacrifices you made in ensuring that I got educated at some of the best schools in the country. Whenever I look at the past, the meagreness of your resources, the never-ending family obligations and social demands, a word of thanks to both of you is very insufficient. I know in your thoughts and prayers, you have always wished that my efforts came to a successful end. This success, I say sincerely, is not mine. It is yours. The Good Lord has lengthened your sojourn on this earth so that you see this as your accomplishment.

I remain indebted to my uncle, Mr Eric Elad Enock, who, all through my academic career, has made me feel the breadth and depth of his magnanimity. Within the family circle, no issue of your siblings has been the greatest beneficiary of your practical benevolence, which, though unknown to you, boosted me when in the lowlights of academic troubles, and assured me that there is someone who cares. To my siblings, Beltus, Ernestine, Miriam, Irene, Emilia, Samuel, James and Anne-Marie, I am thankful to you all. You invested that trust in me that someday, you would have a doctor within your midst. That trust has not been betrayed. Despite the distance, the love is still strong, the support has always flowed, and the results have always been positive.

To Mr and Mrs Frederick Elad of Winchester Hills, Johannesburg, South Africa, I am thankful to you all for the support. I could not have thought of

South Africa as a research destination without you; and even though we had no formal discussion prior to me commencing this programme at Wits, you have been there for me all the times. You prayed for me all the time, at times putting the needs of your own children secondary to mine. I am very thankful to you and may God bless you exceedingly and abundantly.

To my own very dear friends, Mr and Mrs John Fankmeni of Bear, Delaware, United States, I am forever grateful to you all. When I made the decision to quit the United States to pursue this degree, you both offered me positive advice and support. You did this in absolute confidence that I was up to the task and it was the right thing to do. I will never forget the calls, the emails, the soft messages, the uplifting words and the counsel of you all when in tough moments. I am thankful to you all for your support.

In all the alliances I built and friendships that were broken in the pursuit of this, I have seen God in everything, whom I thank for the wisdom, spirit of endurance and humility, and bringing this project to a successful end is eloquent testimony of His unfettered favours shining incessantly in my life. There is no way I can be prouder than being a son of the Most High.

LIST OF STATUTES

Bill of Rights 1689 (England)

British India Act No. 30 of 1836 (United Kingdom)

Declaration of the Rights of Man and of the Citizen (France)
- Article 11

Draft Criminal Code (Law Com. No. 177) (United Kingdom)
- Clause 47

French Penal Code
- Article 265
- Article 266
- Article 267

German Penal Code 1871 (Germany)

Offences Against the Person Act 1861 (United Kingdom)
- Section 4

Rwandan Penal Code (Rwanda)

Smith Act 1940 (United States)

United States' Constitution
- First Amendment

Wireless Telegraphy Act 1949 (United Kingdom)
- Section 1(1)

LIST OF INTERNATIONAL INSTRUMENTS

African Charter on Human and Peoples' Rights
- Article 9
- Article 9(2)
- Article 27(2)
- Article 28

Allied Control Council Law No. 10
- Article II(1)
- Article II(1)(c)
- Article II(2)
- Article II(c)

Charter of the International Military Tribunal (IMT), Nuremberg
- Article 1
- Article 6(1)
- Article 6(a)
- Article 6(b)
- Article 6(c)
- Article 7
- Article 8
- Article 9
- Article 10
- Article 11

Charter of the International Military Tribunal for the Far East (IMTFE), Tokyo
- Article 1
- Article 5
- Article 5(c)

Convention on the Prevention and Punishment of the Crime of Genocide, 1948
- Article 2
- Article 2(a)
- Article 3
- Article 3(b)

- Article 3(c)
- Article 3(d)
- Article 3(e)

Draft Code of Crimes against the Peace and Security of Mankind 1996
- Article 2(3)(f)
- Article 18

Draft Code of Offences against the Peace and Security of Mankind 1954
- Article 2(13)(ii)

European Convention for the Protection of Human Rights and Fundamental Freedoms
- Article 10(1)
- Article 10(2)

Fourth Hague Convention 1907

Inter-American Convention on Human Rights
- Article 13
- Article 13(4)
- Article 13(5)

International Convention on the Elimination of All Forms of Racial Discrimination
- Article 5

International Covenant on Civil and Political Rights (ICCPR)
- Article 19
- Article 20

International Law Commission Draft Code of Crimes 1951
- Article 21

Rome Statute of the International Criminal Court
- Article 1
- Article 7
- Article 7(1)
- Article 7(k)
- Article 11(1)
- Article 25(3)

Statute of the International Criminal Tribunal for Rwanda (ICTR)
- Article 1
- Article 2
- Article 2(a)
- Article 2(3)
- Article 2(3)(a)
- Article 2(3)(b)
- Article 2(3)(c)
- Article 2(3)(d)
- Article 2(3)(e)
- Article 3
- Article 3(a)
- Article 4
- Article 6(1)
- Article 10
- Article 11
- Article 12(2)
- Article 15(3)
- Article 16(3)

Statute of the International Criminal Tribunal for the former Yugoslavia (ICTY)
- Article 2
- Article 3
- Article 4
- Article 5
- Article 5(1)
- Article 7(1)

Statute of the Special Court for Sierra Leone
- Article 2
- Article 2(i)
- Article 6(1)

United Nations Declaration on the Elimination of All Forms of Racial Discrimination
- Article 9

Universal Declaration of Human Rights
- Article 19

LIST OF CASES

Barbie Case, Jugement, Cour de Cassation, 20 Décembre 1985, *Bulletin des arrêts de la Cour de Cassation,* 1985.

Chelmsford Justices, ex p Amos [1973] Crim LR 437, DC.

Dargoljub Kunarac, Radomir Kovač & Zoran Vuković v The Prosecutor, Case No. IT-96-23 & 23/1-T (Appeal Chamber).

DPP v Armstrong [2000] Crim LR 379.

Invicta Plastics Ltd v Clare [1976] RTR 251, [1976] Crim LR 131.

James and Ashford (1985) 82 Cr App R 226.

Osland v R (1998) 73 ALJR 173.

R v Banks (1873) 12 Cox CC 393.

R v Buxton (1969) 85 LQR 252.

R v Cope (1921) 16 Cr App R 17.

R v Curr [1968] 2 QB 944, [1967] 1 All ER 478, CA.

R v El Faisal [2004].

R v Hendrickson and Tichner [1977] Crim LR 356.

R v Higgins (1801) 2 East 9.

R v Krause (1902) 66 JP 121.

R v Marlow [1997] Crim LR 897.

R v Most (1881) 7 QBD 244.

R v Nkosiyana 1966 (4) SA 655.

R v Prior [2004] Crim LR 849.

R v Ransford (1874) 13 Cox CC 9.

Race Relations Board v Applin [1973] QB 815.

Sivakumar v Canada (Minister of Employment and Immigration) [1994] FC 433.

The Hans Fritzsche Case.

The Julius Streicher Case.

The Prosecutor v Alfred Musema, Case No. ICTR-96-13.

The Prosecutor v André Ntagerura, Case No. ICTR-96-10A.

The Prosecutor v Anto Furundžija, Case No. IT-95-17/1.

The Prosecutor v Callixte Kalimanzira, Case No. ICTR-05-88.

The Prosecutor v Clément Kayishema, Case No. ICTR-95-1.

The Prosecutor v Clément Kayishema and Obed Ruzindana, Case No. ICTR-95-1.

The Prosecutor v Dargoljub Kunarac, Radomir Kovač and Zoran Vuković, Case No. IT-96-23 & 23/1-T (Trial Chamber).

The Prosecutor v Dario Kordić and Mario Čerkez, Case No. IT-95-14/2.

The Prosecutor v Duško Tadić, Case No. IT-94-1.

The Prosecutor v Eliézer Niyitegeka, Case No. ICTR-96-14.

The Prosecutor v Elizaphan Ntakirutimana, Case No. ICTR-96-10; ICTR-96-17.

The Prosecutor v Ephrem Setako, Case No. ICTR-04-81.

The Prosecutor v Fatmir Limaj, Haradin Bala and Isak Muslui, Case No. IT-03-66.

The Prosecutor v Ferdinand Nahimana, Case No. ICTR-96-11.

The Prosecutor v Ferdinand Nahimana, Jean-Bosco Barayagwiza and Hassan Ngeze, Case No. ICTR-99-52-T.

The Prosecutor v Gérard Ntakirutimana, Case No. ICTR-96-10; ICTR-96-17.

The Prosecutor v Georges Ruggiu, Case No. ICTR-97-32.

The Prosecutor v Georges Rutaganda, Case No. ICTR-96-3.

The Prosecutor v Hassan Ngeze, Case No. ICTR-97-27.

The Prosecutor v Hormisdas Nsengimana, Case No. ICTR-01-69.

The Prosecutor v Idelphonse Hategekimana, Case No. ICTR-00-55.

The Prosecutor v Ignace Bagilishema, Case No. ICTR-95-1-A.

The Prosecutor v Jean-Bosco Barayagwiza, Case No. ICTR-97-19.

The Prosecutor v Jean-Paul Akayesu, Case No. ICTR-96-4.

The Prosecutor v Jean de Dieu Kamuhanda, Case No. ICTR-99-54.

The Prosecutor v Jean Kambanda, Case No. ICTR-97-23.

The Prosecutor v Joseph Serugendo, Case No. ICTR-2005-84.

The Prosecutor v Juvénal Kajelijeli, Case No. ICTR-98-44A.

The Prosecutor v Laurent Semanza, Case No. ICTR-97-20.

The Prosecutor v Miladen Naletilić and Vinko Martinović, Case No. IT-98-34.

The Prosecutor v Mitar Vasiljević, Case No. IT-98-32-T.

The Prosecutor v Obed Ruzindana, Case No. ICTR-95-1; ICTR-96-10.

The Prosecutor v Paul Bisengimana, Case No. ICTR-00-60.

The Prosecutor v Simon Bikindi, Case No. ICTR-01-72.

The Prosecutor v Tharcisse Muvunyi, Case No. ICTR-00-55 (Retrial).

The Prosecutor v Zoran Kupreškić, Drago Josipović, Vladimir Šantić, Mirjan Kupreškić, Vlatko Kupreškić, and Dragan Papić, Case No. IT-95-16.

Zdravko Mucić, Hazim Delić, Esad Landžo, and Zejnil Delalić v The Prosecutor, Case No. IT-96-21 (Appeal Chamber).

FOREWORD

M. Cherif Bassiouni

Crimes against humanity, although older than the crime of genocide, which was codified in 1948, or modern humanitarian law, which was codified in the Geneva Conventions in 1954, is the least well defined because it has never been the subject of a comprehensive international treaty. Rather, crimes against humanity has evolved in customary international law and defined variously by the statutes and jurisprudence of different tribunals and institutions based on evolving conceptions of the crime. The multiple sources of crimes against humanity – whether in customary international law or in the Statutes and jurisprudence of the Tribunals – has allowed for the sometimes inconsistent and sometimes illogical application of the crime.

The illogical application of crimes against humanity is the topic of Avitus Agbor's important new contribution to the study of international criminal law. Agbor's study details the illogical application of instigation for crimes against humanity and its interplay with the jurisprudence on incitement to genocide, which will hopefully allow for their proper application by future tribunals and maturing tribunals such as the International Criminal Court (ICC).

To understand Agbor's important critique of incitement to crimes against humanity, it is necessary to trace the evolution of the notion of the crime itself, which was first enunciated during the First World War with regards to the treatment of Armenians by the Ottoman Empire. The notion of crimes against humanity, however, was only codified and criminalized in the Charter of the International Military Tribunal at Nuremberg, and in the Charter of the International Military Tribunal for the Far East in Tokyo after the end of the Second World War. During the Cold War, crimes against humanity, as with most of international criminal war, stagnated, and it was only with the establishment of the International Criminal Tribunal for the former Yugoslavia (ICTY) by Security Council Resolution 827 that the crime began to take on its modern form, which is still being resolved and to which this volume will undoubtedly contribute.

Nevertheless, differences persisted, especially as the definition of crimes against humanity adopted by the Security Council for the International Criminal Tribunal for Rwanda (ICTR) in Resolution 955 differed from that of the ICTY in subtle but important ways. In effect, while the substantive acts criminalized by the ICTR and ICTY mirrored each other exactly,[1] the circumstantial requirements for the application of the crime differed. While the ICTY Statute mandated that crimes against humanity must be committed within the context of an "armed conflict, whether international or internal in character", the ICTR Statute eliminated the nexus requirement to armed conflict and added the requirement that the criminal conduct occur within the context of a "widespread or systematic attack" and that it be based "on national, political, ethnic, racial or religious grounds".[2]

The differences between the two definitions allow for significant differences in jurisprudence. The ICTR definition, for instance, allows for the criminalization of particular conduct in times of peace or war, which is not technically permissible under the ICTY Statute, where it must be linked to an armed conflict. The ICTR Statute also adopted the requirement that the criminal act must occur within the context of a widespread or systematic attack, which effectively requires a state policy for its commission, an element lacking in the ICTY definition. Finally, the ICTR Statute required a discriminatory purpose for the act, an element also not required by the ICTY Statute.

Despite these subtle but essential differences between the two definitions, in practice, the ICTY and ICTR have treated the definitions of crimes against humanity in the respective Statutes as synonymous. This convergence has been the product of the shared Appeals Chamber of the two Tribunals, which has focused on the creation of a unified corpus of law rather than on the legal and technical differences between the definitions provided by the Security Council for the two Tribunals. Feeling themselves bound by the judgments of the Appeals Chamber, the Trial Chambers of the ICTY and ICTR have adopted a unified definition of crimes against humanity, in effect eliminating the war nexus requirement of the ICTY Statute and the discriminatory purpose requirement of the ICTR Statute, while adopting the widespread and systematic requirement outlined contained in the ICTR definition. This final combined definition was effectively adopted by the Rome Statute of the International Criminal Court, and

[1] They are murder; extermination; enslavement; deportation; imprisonment; torture; rape; persecutions on political, racial and religious grounds; and other inhumane acts.

[2] Both maintained the essential aspect that the attack be upon a civilian population.

probably represents the most widely recognized enunciation of crimes against humanity today.[3]

Nevertheless, the jurisprudence of the ICTR and ICTY has been problematic with regards to the requirements for incitement under article 6(1) of the Statute of the ICTR versus the provision for genocide under article 2(3)(c), an issue that Agbor has honed in on in this book. Under article 6(1) of the Statute of the ICTR, "A person who planned, instigated, ordered, committed or otherwise aided and abetted in the planning, preparation or execution of a crime referred to in Articles 2 to 4 [genocide, crimes against humanity and war crimes, respectively] of the present Statute, shall be individually responsible for the crime." Article 2(3)(c) criminalizes "Direct and public incitement to commit genocide". As Agbor points out, article 6(1) clearly provides for the prosecution of individuals for incitement to commit crimes against humanity, something it has not, in fact, done.

As Agbor points out, the jurisprudence of the ICTR has established that for article 6(1) the perpetrator must make a "substantial contribution" towards the commission of the ultimate crime, which in effect means that an individual can only be convicted for the commission of the act under that article of the Statute. This is problematic insofar as the same underlying act can qualify as both genocide and a crime against humanity for extermination, and yet the ICTR has only ever treated that underlying act of incitement under article 2(3)(c) for genocide, and not once under article 6(1) for crimes against humanity.[4]

This bifurcation, as Agbor describes, also has the unfortunate effect that it is impossible for the ICTR to enter a conviction for incitement to commit crimes against humanity even though the underlying acts are the same, a violation of both the wording and purpose of article 6(1), which is to ensure that all phases (whether planning, preparation or execution) are within the purview of the court. As Agbor rightly points out, this has "stagnated the evolution of the jurisprudence on instigation to commit crimes against humanity".

---

[3] The Rome Statute of the ICC did, however, add the requirement that the accused have knowledge of the widespread or systematic act.

[4] It should be noted that incitement to genocide under article 2(3)(c) contains the additional requirement that the accused make a direct and public incitement, as well as the general proviso that the accused have the requisite specific intent to destroy, in whole or in part, the protected group. In most circumstances the evidentiary showing for incitement to crimes against humanity is therefore lower than for genocide, which would logically lead to a greater likelihood of conviction under article 6(1) for crimes against humanity than under article 2(3)(c) for genocide. The opposite is true in practice, an illogical outcome.

While the ICTR is scheduled to cease operations in December 2014, the principles Agbor outlines in this book will survive that date. By refocusing on the object and purpose of the incitement provision in article 6(1) of the ICTR Statute, it is hoped that incitement to commit crimes against humanity will re-emerge in the jurisprudence of the ICC and the Residual Mechanism to the ICTR and the ICTY, as well as in the customary definitions of the crime and any future statute on crimes against humanity.

M. Cherif Bassiouni
DePaul University College of Law,
United States of America

PREFACE

In the decades after attaining independence from its colonial masters, Rwanda's two principal ethnic groups, the Hutus and the Tutsis, suffered worsening tensions, which often resulted in the perpetration of atrocities, especially gross violations of human rights. Peace agreements brokered by the international community did not ease these ethnic tensions. In April 1994, the ethnic crisis took a different dimension following the assassination of the Presidents of Rwanda and Burundi. In the aftermath of this assassination, genocidal and other inhumane acts were committed by the Hutus. They targeted the Tutsis because of their ethnicity and Hutu-moderates because of their tolerant political views. In about a hundred days, close to a million Tutsis and Hutu-moderates were massacred. The planning, preparation and execution of these atrocities were done by almost everyone within the Hutu majority: the leadership (both civilian and military), businessmen, the clergy, artists, professors, journalists, militias, the commoners, and other civil society actors.

The Rwandan Patriotic Front (RPF) under the leadership of General Paul Kagame overthrew the Rwandan Armed Forces (RAF) and brought the genocide to an end. In an effort to build a government of national unity, the Government of Rwanda under the leadership of President Paul Kagame requested the United Nations Security Council to establish a tribunal for the trial of persons who bear responsibility for the atrocities committed in Rwanda. In response to this request, the United Nations Security Council passed Resolution 955 (8 November 1994) creating the second United Nations' *ad hoc* international criminal tribunal, the International Criminal Tribunal for Rwanda (ICTR). Annexed to Resolution 955 was the Statute of the ICTR.

The Statute gave the Tribunal jurisdiction over three crimes: genocide, crimes against humanity and violations of Article 3 common to the Geneva Conventions and of Additional Protocol II. Amongst other things, it also defined on which individuals it would impose criminal responsibility.

The definition of genocide and the punishable acts as contained in the Statute of the ICTR (Article 2) were simply imported from the United Nations' Convention on the Prevention and Punishment of the Crime of Genocide, 1948 (Article III). One of these punishable acts is direct and public incitement to commit genocide (Article 2(3)(c) of the Statute of the

ICTR). As seen in Article 6(1) of the Statute of the ICTR, there are five different modes of participation that would lead to the imposition of criminal responsibility: planning, instigating, ordering, committing or otherwise aiding and abetting. Instigation is one of these modes of participation.

An examination of the jurisprudence of both the Trial and Appeal Chambers of the ICTR reveals that there is an overlap between direct and public incitement to commit genocide under Article 2(3)(c) and instigation as a mode of participation under Article 6(1).

The Trial and Appeal Chambers have contributed enormously to the development of the jurisprudence of direct and public incitement to commit genocide under Article 2(3)(c). Now settled as an inchoate crime in international criminal law, criminal responsibility is imposed irrespective of whether the direct and public incitement successfully results in the commission of genocide.

On the other hand, instigation is one of the modes of participation that would lead to the imposition of criminal responsibility. Participation under Article 6(1) is not limited to any particular crime, but extends to all the crimes over which the ICTR has jurisdiction – genocide, crimes against humanity and violations of Article 3 common to the Geneva Conventions and of Additional Protocol II. The jurisprudence of the Trial and Appeal Chambers on Article 6(1) states that criminal responsibility can only be imposed where it is proved that the accused's mode of participation substantially contributed to the commission of the crime. Therefore, instigation, which is one of the modes of participation, must be shown to have substantially contributed to the commission of the crime for criminal responsibility to be imposed.

In my opinion, this requirement of substantial contribution for the imposition of criminal responsibility is wrong. It emanates from a poor understanding of Article 6(1) and the construction of the words therein. It is a judicial invention which does not square with established principles of criminal responsibility in general and inchoate crimes in particular.

This book critiques the jurisprudence of the ICTR on instigation as a mode of participation under Article 6(1). Instigation is a recognised mode of participation in international crimes. Under the common law system, it is also an inchoate crime. International instruments and the jurisprudence of the Trial and Appeal Chambers have recognised the inchoate nature of incitement. However, in the construction of Article 6(1) wherein instigation features as a mode of participation, the Trial and Appeal Chambers erred. In this book, I illustrate that a correct construction and understanding of Article 6(1) shows its inchoate and bifurcated character: first, any of the modes of participation must lead to any of the stages of any of the crimes (planning, preparation or execution). These modes of participation are not limited to any particular crime. Therefore, if instigation leads to the planning or preparation of any of the crimes, that renders it inchoate (which is understood to mean a criminal activity that is incomplete, or is still at its initial stage). Secondly, the imposition of criminal responsibility is bifurcated. In other words, it must go through two stages: first, there must be a mode of participation, and second, it must lead to any of the stages of the crimes. Thirdly, the substantial contribution requirement does not square with a strict construction of Article 6(1). In articulating the different stages that a mode of participation must lead to, it states 'planning, preparation or execution' of any of the crimes. The use of a disjunctive word 'or' rather than a conjunctive word 'and' suggests that any of the modes of participation that leads to any of these stages (planning, preparation or execution) of any of these crimes (genocide, crimes against humanity, violations of Article 3 common to the Geneva Conventions and of Additional Protocol II) would suffice. Therefore, to require that there must be a substantial contribution to the commission of a crime before criminal responsibility can be imposed under Article 6(1) is a clear limitation to the last stage of the crime, which is execution (or commission).

As evidenced by the cases tried at the Tribunal, Article 2(3)(c) (the inchoate crime of direct and public incitement to commit genocide) and Article 6(1) (the imposition of criminal responsibility), do overlap. In other words, incitement that qualifies as direct and public incitement to commit genocide under Article 2(3)(c) may as well qualify as instigation to any of the crimes over which the ICTR has jurisdiction under Article 6(1). From the delivery of its first judgment in the case of *The Prosecutor v Jean-Paul Akayesu*,[1] the Trial Chambers did not recognise the confluence between these two Articles. However, in the case of *The Prosecutor v Callixte Kalimanzira*,[2] the Trial Chambers made this observation, and outlined a set of guidelines on how to resolve cases of overlap. I call these the 'Kalimanizira Principles'. Though a colossal step in fixing this problem, the guidelines are faulted because they repeat the same mistakes made by previous Trial Chambers: first, they limit instigation only to genocide even under Article 6(1); second, they still hold that criminal responsibility can be imposed under Article 6(1) only when it is proved that the mode of participation substantially contributed to the commission of the crime.

---

[1] Judgment, Case No. ICTR-96-4. T. Ch. I, 2 September 1998.

[2] Judgment, Case No. ICTR-05-88-T, T. Ch. III, 22 June 2009.

While it resonates with conventional wisdom today that incitement, synonymous with instigation, is limited to the crime of genocide, I examine and critique the jurisprudence of both the Trial and Appeal Chambers of the ICTR and argue that instigation is a mode of participation in crimes against humanity following a strict construction of Article 6(1). Furthermore, incitement that qualifies as 'direct and public incitement' to commit genocide under Article 2(3)(c) may also qualify as instigation to commit genocide, crimes against humanity, or both under Article 6(1). Third, 'direct and public incitement' to commit genocide under Article 2(3)(c) is limited to the crime of genocide, and must fulfil the caveats of 'direct' and 'public'. Meanwhile, instigation under Article 6(1) does not need to meet any requirement as long as it leads to the 'planning, preparation or execution' of any of the crimes over which the ICTR has jurisdiction.

In addition to this critique, this book recognises the dramatic turn that occurred in the definition of crimes against humanity, and further argues that the introduction of the definitional elements of an attack that is widespread or systematic, directed against any civilian population on any of the enlisted discriminatory grounds ought to highlight the indispensability of group involvement in the planning, preparation or commission of crimes against humanity. As discussed in the subsequent chapters, crimes against humanity became recognised in international criminal law following the Charter of the International Military Tribunal (IMT) for Nuremberg. Beyond this instrument, it suffered numerous variations in its definitions, especially those advanced by the United Nations Security Council creating first the International Criminal Tribunal for the former Yugoslavia and secondly, the ICTR.[3] As would be noted in the discussions below, the Statute of the ICTY required any of the enlisted acts to be committed within an armed conflict, whether international or internal. On the other hand, the Statute of the ICTR requires that the enlisted acts be committed as part of an attack that is either widespread or systematic, directed against any civilian population and based on any of the stipulated discriminatory grounds: race, ethnicity, nationality, politics or religion. The introduction of these novel elements into the definition of crimes against humanity does not only vary in substance what are crimes against humanity: it evokes the necessity of a group of individuals, which highlight the sui generis nature of crimes against humanity as group crimes. These elements form part of

[3] For a detailed discussion on the historic evolution of the crime of crimes against humanity in international law, see M. Bassiouni, *Crimes against Humanity: Historical Evolution and Contemporary Application* (Cambridge University Press 2011).

the critique levied against the approach taken by the Trial and Appeal Chambers of the ICTR.

The poor construction of Article 6(1) has resulted in huge controversies about instigation as a mode of participation in crimes over which the ICTR has jurisdiction under Article 6(1). More specifically, instigation, which is one of the modes, overlaps with the wording of Article 2(3)(c) which deals with the inchoate crime of direct and public incitement to commit genocide. The substantial contribution requirement is a judicial invention which does not align squarely with established principles of criminal responsibility for inchoate crimes. It is the unfortunate outcome of a poor construction of Article 6(1) and has orchestrated a confused understanding of instigation as a mode of participation. It has blurred and obfuscated instigation as a mode of participation in crimes against humanity; stagnated the evolution of the jurisprudence on instigation to commit crimes against humanity; and above all, propelled international criminal law on an ambitious and controversial mission from which it must retreat.

CHAPTER ONE

INTRODUCTION

Events that occurred in Rwanda in 1994 resulted in the establishment of the United Nations Security Council's second *ad hoc* international criminal tribunal, the ICTR.[1] Empowered to try 'persons responsible for genocide and other serious violations of international humanitarian law committed in the territory of Rwanda and Rwandan citizens responsible for genocide and other such violations committed in the territory of neighbouring states, between 1 January 1994 and 31 December 1994',[2] the ICTR has jurisdiction over three crimes: genocide,[3] crimes against humanity,[4] and violations of Article 3 Common to the Geneva Conventions and of Additional Protocol II.[5]

The definition of criminal responsibility under the Statute of the ICTR is not so different from the definition of previous international instruments.[6] Instigation as one of the modes leading to the imposition of criminal responsibility under Article 6(1) of the Statute was not novel. As far back as the Charter of the International Military Tribunal (hereinafter referred to as the IMT), Nuremberg, criminal responsibility was imposed on those who, *inter alia*, instigated any of the crimes over which the Nuremberg Tribunal had jurisdiction.[7] The Statute of the ICTY which immediately preceded the Statute of the ICTR recognised instigation as a mode of participation that would lead to the imposition of criminal responsibility.[8] Under the Statute of the ICTR, criminal responsibility is imposed on an individual

[1] United Nations Security Council Resolution 955, U. N. SCOR, 3453rd meeting, U.N. Doc. S/RES/955 (1994) of 8 November 1994.

[2] Statute of the ICTR, Article 1.

[3] Statute of the ICTR, Article 2.

[4] Statute of the ICTR, Article 3.

[5] Statute of the ICTR, Article 4.

[6] Statute of the International Criminal Tribunal for the former Yugoslavia (hereinafter referred to as the ICTY), annexed to United Nations Security Council Resolution 827, U. N. SCOR, 3217th meeting, U.N. Doc. S/RES/827 (1993), Article 7(1).

[7] These crimes were crimes against peace, war crimes and crimes against humanity, expressly contained in the Charter of the IMT, Nuremberg, Articles 6(a), (b), and (c) respectively.

[8] Statute of the ICTY, Article 7(1).

who, *inter alia*, instigated any of the crimes over which the Tribunal has jurisdiction.[9]

To have a better picture of the evolution of instigation to crimes against humanity, it is necessary to look at the jurisprudence of the Nuremberg Tribunal, given the fact that crimes against humanity as a crime and instigation as a mode of participation were both given legislative birth at Nuremberg.[10]

Of the numerous individuals docked for trial for the atrocities of the Nazi Regime at Nuremberg,[11] two individuals incurred criminal responsibility for participation through instigation: Hans Fritzsche, Minister

---

[9] Statute of the ICTR, Article 6(1). The other modes of participation contained therein include those who planned, ordered, committed or otherwise aided and abetted in the planning, preparation or execution of any of the crimes over which the Tribunal has jurisdiction (see Article 6(1)).

[10] See the Charter of the IMT, Nuremberg, Article 6(c).

[11] Some of these individuals were Hermann Goering, Rudolf Hess, Joachim von Ribbentrop (Hitler's Foreign Minister), Robert Ley (Leader of the German Labour Front), Field Marshal Wilhelm Keitel (Chief, Hitler's Military Staff), Julius Streicher (who was the Nazi leader in Franconia, and also the editor and publisher of the distasteful anti-Semitic newspaper *Der Sturmer*); Ernst Kaltenbrunner (following Heinrich Himmler's suicide, he was the senior surviving official of the SS and Gestapo); Alfred Rosenberg (Minister of German-occupied eastern territories and official ideologist of the Nazi Regime); Hans Frank (who was the Civilian Governor-General of occupied Poland), Wilhelm Frick (the Minister of the Interior and subsequently appointed the Protector of Bohemia and Moravia). The selection of the first ten names was based on the wide publicity they had in almost every household in Europe. These individuals were state actors who had occupied influential posts of responsibility in the Nazi Regime. Then, the list was extended to include leaders of criminal groups or organizations, which included officials like Adolf Hitler, the *Führer* (whose death had not been officially confirmed but would be added if there was any information to the contrary); Hjalmar H.G. Schacht, who, prior to the war, was head of Reichsbank and Minister of Economics, did handle the financing necessary to expand war production); Arthur Seyss-Inquart, an Austrian Nazi who later became Commander-in-Chief of the German Navy from 1943–1945, and was named in Hitler's will as President and Supreme Commander in the Reich; Walter Funk who succeeded Schacht as head of the Reichsbank and Minister of Economics; Albert Speer, who was Hitler's favourite architect and later became Minister of Armament and Munitions; Grand-Admiral Karl Doenitz, Gustav Krupp, Fritz Sauckel, who was the primary figure in the foreign forced labour program, Alfred Jodl, who was Chief of Operations on Hitler's Military Staff, Franz von Papen, who was the Reich Chancellor in 1932, Vice Chancellor in the Hitler Cabinet from 1933–1934 and subsequently Ambassador to Austria and Turkey, Constantin von Neurath, who was Ribbentrop's predecessor as Former Minister, and later Reich Protector of Bohemia and Moravia, Hans Fritzsche, who was the highest subordinate of Goebbels at the Propaganda Ministry, Grand Admiral Erich Raeder, who was the Commander in Chief of the German Navy until his retirement in 1943, and Baldur von Schirach, who was the Nazi Youth Leader, added because of his 'vicious indoctrination' of the youths. Telford Taylor, *The Anatomy of the Nuremberg Trials: A Personal Memoir* (Alfred A. Knopf, Inc. 1992); Richard Overy, *Interrogations: The Nazi Elite in Allied Hands, 1945* (Penguin Group 2001).

of Propaganda,[12] and Julius Streicher, who became a *Gauleiter*[13] and owned and published *Der Stürmer*.[14] *Der Stürmer* was an anti-Semitic journal that was created for, and dedicated mostly to the publication of anti-Semitic materials.[15] The purpose of this was to engage the broader German public into perpetrating and/or tolerating atrocities against the Jews, and he used his publications as a means of inciting them towards that goal.[16]

The contents of Streicher's publications aroused interest in the scholarship for the kind of effect he generated through his regular anti-Semitic publications. Issue after issue, Julius Streicher scapegoated the Jews for Germany's economic problems. Through his publications, he instigated Germans to believe not just in racial superiority, but also that the elimination of Jews was the sole and permanent solution to the 'Jewish problem'.

As discussed later, the Nuremberg Tribunal examined a collection of Julius Streicher's publications and assessed their impact on the atrocities perpetrated against the Jews. In its seminal judgment, the Tribunal, finding Julius Streicher guilty, sentenced him to death by hanging.

About fifty years after the Nuremberg Tribunal handed down this judgment, events in Rwanda and the activities of some Rwandan journalists would make the ICTR a focal point on instigation as a mode of participation in international criminal law. Three individuals (journalists) stood trial for instigating the atrocities committed in Rwanda: Ferdinand Nahimana,[17]

---

12 The Propaganda Ministry was given broad jurisdiction by a decree issued by the German Fuhrer on June 30, 1933, which stipulated that 'the Reich Minister of Public Enlightenment and propaganda has jurisdiction over the whole field of spiritual indoctrination if the nation, of propagandizing the State, of cultural and economic propaganda, of enlightenment of the public at home and abroad. Furthermore, he is in charge of the administration of all institutions serving those purposes.' *Affidavits at Nuremberg Trials*, para. 2030-PS; Donna E. Arzt, 'Nuremberg, Denazification and Democracy: The Hate Speech Problem at the International Military Tribunal' (1995) Vol. XII 3 *N. Y. L. Sch. J. Hum. Rts* 689, 689–758.

13 *Gauleiter* was a political rank in Germany, which meant a party leader of a regional branch of the NSDAP (commonly known as Nazi Party). See Randall L. Bytwerk, *Julius Streicher: Nazi Editor of the Notorious Anti-Semitic Newspaper Der Stürmer* (Cooper Square Press 2001).

14 *'Der Sturmer'* means *'The Stormer'*. The banner slogan on the paper was 'The Jews are Our Misfortune'. D.A. Sprecher, *Inside the Nuremberg Trial: A Prosecutor's Comprehensive Account* (University Press of America 1999) 515; Richard Breitman, *The Architect of Genocide: Himmler and the Final Solution* (The Bodley Head 1991) 46–65, 85–104.

15 Bytwerk (n. 13).

16 Ibid.

17 *The Prosecutor v Ferdinand Nahimana*, Amended Indictment, Case No. ICTR-96-11, OTP, 15 November 1999, Count 3, Paras. 4.1–6.27.

Jean-Bosco Barayagwiza[18] and Hassan Ngeze.[19] These three individuals were indicted separately.[20] However, the prosecution subsequently filed a motion to try them jointly.[21] The underlying reasons for this were first, for the most part, they participated through a common medium: the media. Second, the prosecution had the same witnesses to testify, and to cause them to make different trips for the different trials would be time-consuming and eventually prolong the trial. Trial Chamber I approved the prosecutor's motion on joinder of trial.[22] The judgments rendered by both the Trial[23] and Appeals[24] Chambers are in one document naming all three defendants/appellants.

Commonly known as 'The Media Trial',[25] the three Rwandan journalists stood trial for numerous crimes. Amongst them were the crime of genocide,[26] direct and public incitement to commit genocide[27] and crimes against humanity.[28] The voluminous judgment rendered at the end of their trial stated the overall impact of their publications and broadcasts on the Hutu population and how they contributed to the perpetration of atrocities against the Tutsis and Hutu-moderates. The Trial Chamber found that there was a direct causal relationship between statements made over the media and the commission of genocide in Rwanda. Citing the Nuremberg Tribunal's judgment on Julius Streicher and situating the context (political and cultural) in which those ethnically sensitive and charged broadcasts and publications were made,[29] these three individuals were all found guilty

[18] *The Prosecutor v Jean-Bosco Barayagwiza*, Amended Indictment, Case No. ICTR-97-19, OTP, 14 April 2000, Count 4, Paras. 5.1–7.13.

[19] *The Prosecutor v Hassan Ngeze*, Amended Indictment, Case No. ICTR-97-27, OTP, 10 November 1999, Count 4, Paras. 5.1–7.15.

[20] *The Prosecutor v Ferdinand Nahimana, Jean-Bosco Barayagwiza, Hassan Ngeze*, Judgment Summary, Case No. ICTR-99-52-T, T. Ch. I, 3 December 2003, Para. 5.

[21] See Prosecutor's Motion for Joinder of Trials of *The Prosecutor v Jean-Bosco Barayagwiza*, *The Prosecutor v Ferdinand Nahimana* and *The Prosecutor v Hassan Ngeze* of 10 April 2000.

[22] See Decision on the Prosecutor's Motion for Joinder and Decision on Barayagwiza's Extremely Urgent Motion for Lack of Jurisdiction and for Waiver of Time Limits Under Rule 72(A) and (F) of the Rules, *The Prosecutor v Jean-Bosco Barayagwiza* ICTR-97-19-I.

[23] *Nahimana* et al (n. 21) para. 5.

[24] *Ferdinand Nahimana, Jean-Bosco Barayagwiza and Hassan Ngeze v The Prosecutor*, Appeal Judgment, Case No. ICTR-99-52-A, Appeal Chamber, 28 November 2007.

[25] See generally Allan Thompson (ed), *The Media and the Rwanda Genocide* (Pluto Press 2007).

[26] *Nahimana* et al (n. 20) para. 5.

[27] Ibid.

[28] Ibid.

[29] *The Prosecutor v Ferdinand Nahimana, Jean-Bosco Barayagwiza and Hassan Ngeze*, Judgment, Case No. ICTR-99-52-T, T. Ch. I, 3 December 2003, Para. 981.

and convicted of direct and public incitement to commit genocide and other crimes.[30]

Individuals like Julius Streicher and the three Rwandan journalists who reach out to, and influence, others to perpetrate the material elements of a crime, take the guise of remote operatives. They instigate these crimes because they desire to have them committed. With the media at their disposal, they use them to influence the commission of crimes. Bassiouni calls such individuals the 'moral authors' of crimes, meaning those individuals who encourage, motivate, or influence the minds of others so that an intended crime is committed by such persons without them perpetrating any of the elements (*actus reus*) of the planned crimes.[31]

Though a major step in the evolution of the jurisprudence on instigation in international criminal law, the judgments of the Trial and Appeals Chambers of the ICTR in 'The Media Trial' are disappointing in respect of instigation to commit crimes against humanity. Despite the fact that compelling evidence was tendered during their trial and dotted by exhibits of both radio broadcasts and newspaper publications,[32] the opportunity to formulate comprehensively and postulate the principles of instigation under Article 6(1) as a mode of participation to commit crimes against humanity was squandered. The testimonies analysed in the judgment disclose the existence of a criminal conspiracy to commit these crimes. The use of the media to instigate the commission of crimes was clearly established. However, despite the overwhelming proof of a causal relationship between use of media to instigate and the commission of crimes against humanity, instigation was limited to only direct and public incitement to commit genocide under Article 2(3)(c) and to genocide under Article 6(1) of the Statute of the ICTR. Therefore, although crimes against humanity were committed, the accused were not held accountable for these crimes. The Trial Chamber's judgment therefore suggests that these three instigators selected to instigate only the crime of genocide. I argue that this position is indefensible and that the accused instigated crimes, including crimes against humanity, which substantively fall within the jurisdiction of the ICTR.

---

30 *Nahimana* et al (n. 20) Section IV (detailing the verdict of the Trial Chamber against each of the accused individuals).

31 Cherif M. Bassiouni, *Crimes against Humanity in International Criminal Law* (Kluwer Law International 1999) 248.

32 *Nahimana* et al (n. 29) paras. 949–1046.

Therefore, 'The Media Trial' was a great opportunity for the Trial Chamber to make enormous contributions to instigation as a mode of participation to the planning, preparation or commission of crimes against humanity under Article 6(1) of the Statute. Unfortunately, the purport of Article 6(1) was not grasped, and even though there was clearly a joint criminal enterprise in which these instigators got involved and instigated others to commit the crimes, the Trial Chamber's judgment did not acknowledge this in respect of crimes against humanity. Despite the compelling evidence of a causal link between the instigation and the crimes committed, the Trial Chamber took a parochial approach in understanding and construing instigation as a mode of participation, limiting it to, and finding them guilty for direct and public incitement to commit genocide under Article 2(3)(c) and instigation to genocide under Article 6(1) of the Statute.[33]

In addition to this poor construction of Article 6(1), there was a confluence between instigation to commit a crime under Article 6(1) and Article 2(3)(c). The use of the media to instigate the commission of these crimes earned a conviction for direct and public incitement to commit genocide under Article 2(3)(c) and instigation as a mode of participation (to the crime of genocide) under Article 6(1).[34] However, the Trial Chamber in 'The Media Trial' failed to identify the confluence of instigation under these two Articles. It therefore could not develop any set of guidelines on how to construe instigation under separate Articles.

The outcome of this has been the stagnation of the jurisprudence on instigation to commit crimes against humanity. As I have stated before, and argue in this book, this is a position that runs contrary to both the spirit and wording of Article 6(1).[35]

However, in the recent case of *The Prosecutor v Callixte Kalimanzira*,[36] the Trial Chamber formally recognised this confluence, and developed the 'Kalimanzira Principles' on how to construe instigation under Article 6(1)

---

33 A perusal of the Amended Indictment of Ferdinand Nahimana discloses that the factual allegations used to found a charge of direct and public incitement to genocide under Article 2(3)(c) were used to found a charge of genocide though the word instigation was not used as a mode of participation. See *Nahimana* (n. 17) paras. 4.1–6.27.

34 Examples are Ferdinand Nahimana, Jean-Bosco Barayagwiza and Hassan Ngeze, all convicted of genocide in which they participated through instigation as well as for the charge of direct and public incitement to commit genocide. See *Nahimana* et al (n. 20) Section IV 'Verdict'.

35 Instigation is a mode of participation in the planning, preparation or execution of any of the crimes over which the ICTR has jurisdiction.

36 *The Prosecutor v Callixte Kalimanzira*, Judgment, Case No. ICTR-05-88-T, T. Ch. III, 22 June 2009.

and Article 2(3)(c).[37]A major development though, a critical look at the 'Kalimanzira Principles' reveals two significant flaws: first, the Trial Chamber still repeated the 'substantial contribution' requirement as earlier cases did, which is to the effect that criminal responsibility under Article 6(1) can be imposed only where it is proved that the mode of participation substantially contributed to the commission of the crime. Furthermore, the Trial Chamber in *Kalimanzira* limited instigation even under Article 6(1) to the crime of genocide only.[38] Instigation therefore is a legal puzzle to the ICTR. These two flaws are discussed in detail in Chapter Five (below).

With this background, I am motivated to contribute to international criminal law scholarship by solving this puzzle. I do this by examining instigation as a mode of participation under the ICTR. I also look at the confluence, and review the 'Kalimanzira Principles', articulating guidelines on how instigation can be resolved when there is a confluence between Article 6(1) and Article 2(3)(c) of the Statute.

As stated earlier, the Statute of the ICTR introduced new elements in its definition of crimes against humanity. Looking at these definitional elements in Chapter Four (below), I argue that they require the existence of a joint criminal enterprise, which, however, existed in Rwanda prior to, and during the genocide. The joint criminal enterprise, as discussed in Chapter Five (below), comprised of different persons who agreed to play various roles. Their goal was to formulate a plan on how to eliminate the Tutsis and Hutu-moderates. It was a criminal conspiracy in which instigators participated by instigating the commission of crimes. Within the framework of a joint criminal enterprise, crimes were instigated. Legal practitioners distinguish and qualify these crimes as either genocide, crimes against humanity or violations of Article 3 Common to the Geneva Conventions and of Additional Protocol II. Within this framework of a joint criminal enterprise, specific acts targeted specific individuals: they were targeted based on either their ethnicity (as in the case of Tutsis), or their political opinions (as in the case of Hutu-moderates). The killing of a Tutsi family because they were Tutsi qualifies as a genocidal act punishable under the Statute of the ICTR. That same killing qualifies as a crime against humanity because it was perpetrated within the framework of a widespread or systematic attack, against a civilian population. Therefore, crimes against humanity and genocide, except for their definitional differences, are very much alike.

[37] Ibid para. 516.

[38] Ibid.

As a corollary, instigation to genocide may as well qualify as instigation to crimes against humanity. The definitional differences aside, responsibility must be imposed on every instigator for every crime committed given the fact that they instigated crimes to be committed: they knew these crimes would be committed when they instigated the principal offenders, and finally, these crimes were committed with genocidal intent and as part of a framework in which an attack was launched against a civilian population on the discriminatory grounds.

I critique the Trial and Appeal Chambers jurisprudence on instigation, arguing that instigation as a mode of participation as stipulated under Article 6(1) extends to all crimes over which the ICTR has jurisdiction. Therefore, limiting incitement to the inchoate crime of direct and public incitement to commit genocide is a parochial understanding of Article 6(1), and an incorrect application of its wording. The requirement of a 'substantial contribution' as an indispensable condition for the imposition of criminal responsibility does not square with the letter of Article 6(1). I examine the letter of Article 6(1), the jurisprudence of both the Trial and Appeal Chambers and the unprecedented definition of crimes against humanity as expressed in Article 3 of the Statute of the ICTR, and the definitional elements which suggest the existence of a joint criminal enterprise for the planning, preparation or execution of crimes against humanity. I argue that given the wording of Article 6(1) and the definitional elements of crimes against humanity, the Trial and Appeal Chambers' requirement of a substantial contribution for criminal responsibility to be imposed is wrong. Any of the modes of participation, as long as it led to any of the stages of any of the crimes, should lead to the imposition of criminal responsibility.

This work is particularly relevant given the fact that instigation features as a mode of participation under the Rome Statute of the ICC.[39] In addition, and similar to the Statute of the ICTR, the inchoate crime of direct and public incitement to genocide is specifically made punishable under the same Rome Statute of the ICC.[40] It therefore becomes an urgent necessity

---

[39] See Article 25(3)(b) of the Rome Statute of the International Criminal Court, U. N. Doc. A/CONF.183/9 (1998), reprinted in 37 I.L.M. 999 (1998) (hereinafter referred to as the Rome Statute of the ICC). The Rome Statute of the ICC does not use the word 'instigate'. Rather, it makes use of words which are synonymous with instigation: '...solicits or induces....' (see Rome Statute of the ICC, Article 25(3)(b)).

[40] See Article 25(3)(e) of the Rome Statute of the ICC. It is interesting to observe the words used here: 'In respect of the crime of genocide, directly and publicly incites others to commit genocide.' This is not so different from other international instruments because it is limited to the crime of genocide, and such incitement must be made directly and publicly.

to avoid the mistakes of the Trial and Appeal Chambers of the ICTR by fixing the construction of the wording of the Rome Statute of the ICC.

The Trial and Appeal Chambers' jurisprudence on instigation is a valuable contribution to international law. Therefore, one can envisage the heavy reliance on this jurisprudence by legal scholars and practitioners in order to define the evolution of some concepts in international criminal law. One of such concepts is instigation as a mode of participation, which, unfortunately, has been erroneously construed by the Trial and Appeal Chambers. This critical appraisal of the jurisprudence of the Trial and Appeal Chambers heralds the need for scrutiny, so that a flawless, lucid and consistent jurisprudence on instigation as a mode of participation in serous international crimes is built by successive international criminal institutions.

CHAPTER TWO

A SYNOPSIS OF THE PROBLEMATIC JURISPRUDENCE OF THE TRIAL AND APPEAL CHAMBERS OF THE ICTR

2.1 Introduction

Most legal systems recognise three different kinds of individuals who commit crimes. The first are principal offenders. With the requisite *mens rea*, they commit the material elements (*actus reus*) of a crime.[1]

The second are those who aid and abet the commission of a crime, which falls under the rules of accessorial liability.[2] There are some key distinctions between principal offenders and those who aid and abet the commission of a crime. First, the former requires the perpetration of the *actus reus* with the requisite *mens rea* of the crime; while the latter is limited to rendering any assistance that facilitates the perpetration of such a crime. Secondly, the imposition of criminal responsibility for those who aid and abet the commission of a crime usually depends on whether the principal offender

[1] They also take full responsibility where the resultant crime is perpetrated through an 'innocent agent' or 'innocent instrument' (such as an infant, a lunatic, an animal, or any entity that lacks the requisite *mens rea* of such a crime). For discussions on 'innocent agency' and 'innocent instrumentality', see David Ormerod, *Smith and Hogan Criminal Law* (12th edn., Oxford University Press 2008) 181–82; Joshua Dressler, *Understanding Criminal Law* (5th edn., LexisNexis 2009) 468–69 respectively. See also Michael J. Allen and Simon Cooper, *Elliott & Wood's Cases and Materials on Criminal Law* (9th edn., Sweet & Maxwell 2006) 364. This discussion on the different modes of participation in criminal activities is approached differently by the major legal systems in the world. However, much of the analysis is borrowed from the common law principles because, as evidenced in the judgments of both the Trial and Appeal Chambers of the International Criminal Tribunal for Rwanda, the analysis of the different modes of participation (especially instigation as stipulated under Article 6(1) of the Statute of the ICTR) was influenced by both the common law (since the Statute of the International Criminal Tribunal for Rwanda was crafted on common law principles) and civil law (the applicable legal system in Rwanda at the time of the genocide). As would be seen in the discussions below, the jurisprudence of the Trial and Appeal Chambers reflects much analysis of, and dependence on the common law principles. This discussion therefore does not attempt to postulate the universality of the principles relating to the imposition of criminal responsibility, but to identify and build on the approach(es) used by the Trial and Appeal Chambers of the ICTR and how the resultant construction of instigation as a mode of participation was flawed.

[2] Ormerod (n. 1) 182; Dressler (n. 1) 468; Allen and Cooper (n. 1) 364.

actually committed the crime. Criminal law further classifies co-offenders as principal offenders (in some jurisdictions, they are called principals in the first degree). They are those who, with the necessary mental element (*mens rea*), partake in the commission of a crime by committing any of the material elements (*actus reus*) of that crime. While a co-offender must partake in committing any of the *actus reus* of the crime, aiding and abetting requires some assistance to facilitate in the commission of the crime. It does not require the person rendering the assistance to commit any of the elements of the *actus reus* of the crime, otherwise, he or she becomes liable as a co-offender.

The third are those who instigate others to commit a crime.[3] Tagged as 'moral authors'[4] of crimes, this last category is usually problematic to criminal justice systems for some reasons. First, instigators are usually distant from the crime scene. In other words, they operate remotely. This makes it difficult to draw a precise line as to when an instigator commenced his or her act of instigation, and when the principal perpetrator commits the crime. Secondly, in cases of multiple instigators, it is difficult to determine with exactitude whose act of instigation actually influenced the mind of the principal perpetrator. Thirdly, where an individual embarking on a criminal enterprise with the requisite *mens rea* of that crime is subsequently instigated to commit that crime, it becomes difficult to ascertain whether such instigation played a role in the perpetration of the crime. In other words, how can we determine whether the instigation was substantial or the operative cause in the commission of the crime?

International criminal law recognises instigation as well as other modes of participation.[5] Participation in a criminal activity in international

---

[3] Instigation as a form of participation under common law systems is synonymous with incitement, encouragement. As an inchoate offence, it need not result in the commission of the crime instigated. The offence is instigated is committed and punishable once the instigator urges, solicits, encourages or persuades another to commit a crime. Instigation may take the forms of words, threats, gestures, promises, etc. Ormerod (n. 1) 438; Allen and Cooper (n. 1) 482–88. See also Russell Heaton, *Criminal Law Textbook* (Oxford University Press 2004) 433–36.

[4] Bassiouni uses the concept of 'moral author' without hinging its understanding to the moral content of a crime. It refers to 'the type of perpetrator who, having the requisite mental element, sets in motion events leading to the commission of the crime, but does not perform the *actus reus* or who does not otherwise aid or abet in the classical meaning of these terms under generally accepted principles of criminal law.' Cherif M. Bassiouni, *Crimes against Humanity in International Criminal Law* (Kluwer Law International 1999) 248.

[5] Rome Statute of the International Criminal Court, U. N. Doc. A/CONF.183/9 (1998), reprinted in 37 I.L.M. 999 (1998) (hereinafter referred to as the Rome Statute of the ICC), Article 25(3), serves as the starting point. Prior to the Rome Statute of the ICC,

criminal law ranges from planning, ordering, instigating, executing or perpetrating any internationally recognised crime. These traditional modes of participation are also recognised in customary international law. Furthermore, they have received expression in international instruments since the Charter of the IMT, Nuremberg.[6]

Instigation is one of these recognised modes of participation in international criminal law. Recognised since the Charter of the Nuremberg Tribunal, it has consistently featured in international instruments.[7]

An example of an international instrument is the Statute of the ICTR. The Statute of the ICTR recognises instigation as a mode of participation in the crimes over which the ICTR has jurisdiction.[8]

A noticeable feature of the Statute of the ICTR is the inclusion of direct and public incitement to commit genocide.[9] Incorporated from the United

---

international instruments recognised instigation as a mode of participation. Examples include the Statute of the Special Court for Sierra Leone (hereinafter referred to as the SCSL), annexed to the Agreement between the United Nations and the Government of Sierra Leone on the Establishment of a Special Court for Sierra Leone pursuant to United Nations Security Council Resolution 1315, U. N. SCOR, 4186th meeting, U.N. Doc. S/RES/1315 (2000), Article 6(1); Statute of the ICTR, annexed to United Nations Security Council Resolution 955, U. N. SCOR, 3453rd meeting, U.N. Doc. S/RES/955 (1994), Article 6(1); Statute of the ICTY, annexed to United Nations Security Council Resolution 827, U. N. SCOR, 3217th meeting, U.N. Doc. S/RES/827 (1993), Article 7(1); the Draft Code of Crimes against the Peace and Security of Mankind, 1996, adopted by the International Law Commission, 48th Session, 1996, submitted to the United Nations General Assembly as part of the ILC's Report covering the work of the session (hereinafter referred to as the Draft Code of Crimes against the Peace and Security of Mankind, 1996), Article 2(3)(f); the Draft Code of Offences against the Peace and Security of Mankind, 1954, adopted by the International Law Commission, 6th Session, 1954, submitted to the United Nations General Assembly as part of the ILC's Report covering the work of the session (hereinafter referred to as the Draft Code of Offences against the Peace and Security of Mankind, 1954), Article 2(13)(ii); the Charter of the International Military Tribunal for the Far East (hereinafter referred to as the IMTFE), Tokyo, Article 5; the Allied Control Council Law No. 10, Article II(2); and the Charter of the IMT, Nuremberg, Article 6(c).

6 Rome Statute of the ICC, Article 25(3); Statute of the SCSL, Article 6(1); Statute of the ICTR, Article 6(1); Statute of the ICTY, Article 7(1); the Draft Code of Crimes against the Peace and Security of Mankind, 1996, Article 2(3)(f); the Draft Code of Offences against the Peace and Security of Mankind, 1954, Article 2(13)(ii); the Charter of the IMTFE, Tokyo, Article 5; the Allied Control Council Law No. 10, Article II(2).

7 Charter of the IMT, Nuremberg, Article 6(c). International instruments which have recognised instigation as a mode of participation include the following: Rome Statute of the ICC, Article 25(3); Statute of the SCSL, Article 6(1); Statute of the ICTR, Article 6(1); Statute of the ICTY, Article 7(1); the Draft Code of Crimes against the Peace and Security of Mankind, 1996, Article 2(3)(f); the Draft Code of Offences against the Peace and Security of Mankind, 1954, Article 2(13)(ii); the Charter of the IMTFE, Tokyo, Article 5; the Allied Control Council Law No. 10, Article II(2).

8 Statute of the ICTR, Article 6(1).

9 Statute of the ICTR, Article 2(3)(c).

Nations' Convention on the Prevention and Punishment of the Crime of Genocide (hereinafter referred to as the Genocide Convention),[10] direct and public incitement to commit genocide is of an inchoate character; and responsibility for it would be imposed irrespective of whether the incitement is successful or unsuccessful in leading to the commission of genocide.[11] Direct and public incitement to commit genocide is one of the punishable acts imported from the Genocide Convention.[12]

The Statute of the ICTR and the Genocide Convention share a key similarity in that they contain a list of inchoate crimes related to genocide that are punishable. These inchoate crimes are conspiracy to commit genocide,[13]direct and public incitement to commit genocide,[14] and attempt to commit genocide.[15] These two instruments also make complicity in genocide punishable.[16] However, there is a major distinguishing feature between these two instruments (the Genocide Convention and the Statute of the ICTR): while the former simply defines genocide and the different punishable acts, the latter does the same but goes further to articulate a definition on the imposition of individual criminal responsibility. This is expressed in Article 6(1) of the Statute of the ICTR, which states as follows:

> A person who planned, instigated, ordered, committed or otherwise aided and abetted in the planning, preparation or execution of a crime referred to in articles 2 to 4 [genocide, crimes against humanity and violations of Article 3 common to the Geneva Conventions and of Additional Protocols II] of the present Statute, shall be individually responsible for the crime.

---

[10] *Convention on the Prevention and Punishment of the Crime of Genocide*, United Nations General Assembly Resolution 260(III), U.N. GAOR, 3rd Session, 179th meeting, U.N. Doc. A/RES/260A (1948).

[11] *The Prosecutor v Callixte Kalimanzira*, Judgment, Case No. ICTR-05-88-T, T. Ch. III, 22 June 2009, Para. 515; *The Prosecutor v Simon Bikindi*, Judgment, Case No. ICTR-01-72, T. Ch. III, 2 December 2008, Para. 419; *Ferdinand Nahimana, Jean-Bosco Barayagwiza and Hassan Ngeze v The Prosecutor*, Appeal Judgment, Case No. ICTR-99-52-A, Appeal Chamber, 28 November 2007, Paras. 678–79; *The Prosecutor v Juvénal Kajelijeli*, Judgment, Case No. ICTR-96-44-T, T. Ch. II, 1 December 2003, Para. 855; *The Prosecutor v Eliézer Niyitegeka*, Judgment, Case No.ICTR-96-14-T, T. Ch.I, 16 May 2003, Para. 431; *The Prosecutor v Alfred Musema*, Judgment, Case No.ICTR-96-13-T, T. Ch. I, 27 January 2003, Para. 120; *The Prosecutor v Georges Rutaganda*, Judgment, Case No.ICTR-96-3-T, T. Ch. I, 6 December 1999, Para. 38; and, *The Prosecutor v Jean-Paul Akayesu*, Judgment, Case No.ICTR-96-4, T. Ch. I, 2 September 1998, Para. 562.

[12] See the Statute of the ICTR, Article 2(3)(c); the Genocide Convention, Article 3(c).

[13] See the Statute of the ICTR, Article 2(3)(b); the Genocide Convention, Article 3(b).

[14] See the Statute of the ICTR, Article 2(3)(c); the Genocide Convention, Article 3(c).

[15] See the Statute of the ICTR, Article 2(3)(d); the Genocide Convention, Article 3(d).

[16] See the Statute of the ICTR, Article 2(3)(e); the Genocide Convention, Article 3(e).

In addition to the inchoate crime relating to direct and public incitement to commit genocide under Article 2(3)(c), Article 6(1) of the Statute of the ICTR mentions five modes of participating in the planning, preparation or execution of any of the crimes over which the ICTR has jurisdiction. These modes of participation have been recognised in most international instruments prior to the Statute of the ICTR.[17]

On the other hand, the Genocide Convention does not make mention of any of these modes of participation. It simply defines the crime of genocide and its punishable acts.[18] Furthermore, the Genocide Convention is limited to the crime of genocide. It was the first international instrument in which the crime of genocide was defined and specific and accessorial acts related to genocide made punishable.[19]

Given the illustration above, I argue that this key distinction between the Statute of the ICTR and the Genocide Convention has provided fertile ground upon which the wording of Article 6(1) was erroneously interpreted by the prosecutors and the Trial and Appeal Chambers of the ICTR.

Under Article 6(1) of the Statute of the ICTR, instigation is one of the modes of participation that would lead to the imposition of criminal responsibility for any of the crimes over which the ICTR has jurisdiction (genocide, crimes against humanity and violations of Article 3 common to the Geneva Conventions and of Additional Protocol II).[20] On the other hand, Article 2(3)(c) of the Statute of the ICTR like the Genocide Convention, makes direct and public incitement to commit genocide punishable.[21] As has been developed by the Trial and Appeal Chambers of the ICTR, Article 2(3)(c) of the Statute of the ICTR is an inchoate crime: responsibility would be imposed where it is proved that the incitement was direct, public and to the crime of genocide.[22] The same analysis has not occurred regarding crimes other than genocide, and specifically, there is no

---

[17] See Rome Statute of the ICC, Article 25(3); Statute of the SCSL, Article 6(1); Statute of the ICTR, Article 6(1); Statute of the ICTY, Article 7(1); the Draft Code of Crimes against the Peace and Security of Mankind, 1996, Article 2(3)(f); the Draft Code of Offences against the Peace and Security of Mankind, 1954, Article 2(13)(ii); the Charter of the IMTFE, Tokyo, Article 5; the Allied Control Council Law No. 10, Article II(2).

[18] Genocide Convention, Articles 2 and 3.

[19] See generally the Genocide Convention.

[20] Statute of the ICTR, Article 6(1).

[21] Statute of the ICTR, Article 2(3)(c).

[22] *Kalimanzira* (n. 11) para. 515; *Bikindi* (n. 11) para. 419; *Nahimana* et al (n. 11) paras. 678–79; *The Prosecutor v Joseph Serugendo*, Judgment, Case No. ICTR-2005-84, T. Ch.I, 12 June 2006, Para. 9; *Kajelijeli* (n. 11) para. 855; *Niyitegeka* (n. 11) para. 431; *Musema* (n. 11) para. 120; *Rutaganda* (n. 11) para. 38; *Akayesu* (n. 11) para. 562.

understanding of the inchoate nature of instigating others to commit crimes against humanity. My concern is that the failure to analyse instigation to commit crimes against humanity is not based on sound legal principles but rather on a failure by the prosecutors at the ICTR to apply the provisions of the Statute of the ICTR.

Article 6(1) of the Statute of the ICTR states different modes of participation in any of the following crimes: genocide, crimes against humanity and violations of the Geneva Conventions. Criminal responsibility will be imposed if any of these modes led to the planning, preparation or execution of any of the crimes over which the ICTR has jurisdiction, namely, genocide, crimes against humanity and violations of Article 3 common to the Geneva Conventions and of Additional Protocol II.[23] In addition, the Statute of the ICTR makes direct and public incitement to commit genocide a punishable crime.[24]

Given the wordings of both Articles 6(1) and 2(3)(c) and the jurisprudence of the Trial and Appeal Chambers of the ICTR in construing and applying them to the cases they have tried, some observations can be made, which reflect a poor understanding and illogical construction of these two Articles.

The Trial and Appeal Chambers of the ICTR, following the *raison d'être* of the inclusion of direct and public incitement to commit genocide in the Genocide Convention, have consistently construed its application in the cases it has tried as an inchoate crime that was created as a result of the role instigators play in the perpetration of genocide.[25] The Trial and Appeal Chambers have therefore not departed from the rationale and logic the drafters of the Genocide Convention had in mind when they created the inchoate crime of direct and public incitement to commit genocide. However, they have progressively built on the jurisprudence of this inchoate crime by finding and giving meanings to the words 'direct', 'public', and 'incitement'.[26] In this area of the law, the Trial Chambers, bereft of any guidelines as to construing the words of the Statute of the ICTR, and tasked with interpreting its words as well as building the jurisprudence on

---

[23] Statute of the ICTR, Articles 2–4 respectively.

[24] Statute of the ICTR, Article 2(3)(c).

[25] *Nahimana* et al (n. 11) para. 678; *The Prosecutor v Ferdinand Nahimana, Jean-Bosco Barayagwiza and Hassan Ngeze*, Judgment, Case No.ICTR-99-52-T, T. Ch. I, 3 December 2003, Para. 978; *Akayesu* (n. 11) para. 551.

[26] *Kalimanzira* (n. 11) para. 515; *Bikindi* (n. 11) para. 419; *Nahimana* et al (n. 11) paras. 678–79; *Serugendo* (n. 22) para. 9; *Kajelijeli* (n. 11) para. 855; *Niyitegeka* (n. 11) para. 431; *Musema* (n. 11) para. 120; *Rutaganda* (n. 11) para. 38; *Akayesu* (n. 11) para. 562.

incitement, ought to be given credit for the consistency that has been shown in defining and applying the meanings of the words 'direct', 'public', and 'incitement' in the inchoate crime of direct and public incitement to commit genocide under Article 2(3)(c) of the Statute of the ICTR.

However, the differences between the application of instigation as a mode of participation under Article 6(1) and direct and public incitement to commit genocide under Article 2(3)(c) have not been understood by the Trial and Appeal Chambers. As a result of this, the jurisprudence on instigation as a mode of participation under Article 6(1) remains underdeveloped. Furthermore, the poverty in understanding and construing the applicability of Article 6(1) has resulted in the imposition of a substantial contribution requirement: that for criminal responsibility to be imposed under Article 6(1), it must be proved that the accused's mode of participation substantially contributed to the commission of any of the crimes over which the ICTR has jurisdiction.[27]

I contend that this is incorrect. First, given the fact that the ICTR prosecutors limited instigation to genocide, I argue that this does not square with the wording of Article 6(1). Article 6(1) has a bifurcated character. It states that criminal responsibility shall be imposed on a person who 'planned, instigated, ordered, committed or otherwise aided and abetted in the planning, preparation or execution of a crime....' The stipulated modes of participation must result in any of the three stages (namely, planning, preparation or execution). For criminal responsibility to be imposed, it must be proved that first, an accused participated through any of the statutorily defined modes, and second, that such a mode of participation led to the planning, preparation or execution of any of the crimes over which the ICTR has jurisdiction. The bifurcated character of Article 6(1) further reveals its inchoate character. By including the stages of planning and preparation, criminal responsibility therefore ought not to be imposed only when and where such a mode of participation actually leads to the commission of a crime. Therefore, where an instigator's words led to the

---

27 *The Prosecutor v Idelphonse Hategekimana*, Judgment, Case No. ICTR-00-55, T. Ch. II, 6 December 2010, Para. 644; *Kalimanzira* (n. 11) para. 512; *Kajelijeli* (n. 11) para. 759; *The Prosecution v Laurent Semanza*, Judgment, Case No. ICTR-97-20, T. Ch. II, 15 May 2003, Para. 379; *The Prosecutor v Elizaphan Ntakirutimana and Gérard Ntakirutimana*, Judgement, Case No.ICTR-96-17-T, T. Ch. I, 21 February 2003, Para. 787; *Clément Kayishema and Obed Ruzindana v The Prosecutor*, Judgement, Case No. ICTR-95-1A, Appeal Chamber, 1 June 2001, Paras. 186; *The Prosecutor v Ignace Bagilishema*, Judgement, Case No. ICTR-95-1-A, T. Ch. I, 7 June 2001, Paras. 30, 33; *Musema* (n. 11) para. 115; *Rutaganda* (n. 11) para. 43; *The Prosecutor v Clément Kayishema and Obed Ruzindana*, Judgment, Case No.ICTR-95-1-T, T. Ch. I, 21 May 1999, Paras. 199–207; *Akayesu* (n. 11) para. 477.

planning or preparation of any of the crimes over which the ICTR has jurisdiction, criminal responsibility ought to be imposed under Article 6(1). Instigation under Article 6(1) must neither be direct nor public. It must only lead to any of the stages of any of the crimes.

The inclusion of these three stages (planning, preparation or execution) in the Statute of the ICTR suggests that an accused's mode of participation must lead to any (and not all) of them for criminal responsibility to be imposed.[28] This is further corroborated by the use of a disjunctive word 'or', rather than a conjunctive 'and'.[29] Therefore, the Trial and Appeal Chambers' requirement that criminal responsibility can be imposed only where it is proved that the accused's mode of participation substantially contributed to the commission of a crime is incorrect as it focuses on the last stage of the crime (execution) whereas the Statute articulates the stages of planning and preparation, all in the disjunctive and not in the conjunctive.

Article 2(3)(c) is limited to the inchoate crime of direct and public incitement to commit genocide. In respect of the crime of genocide, therefore, Articles 2(3)(c) and 6(1) overlap. For there to be criminal responsibility under Article 2(3)(c), it must be proved that there was incitement, which was both direct and public and to the crime of genocide only.[30] On the other hand, Article 6(1) is not restrictive or limited in its application. Instigation as one of the modes of participation must lead to any of the stages (planning, preparation or execution) of *any* of the crimes over which the ICTR has jurisdiction. These crimes are genocide, crimes against humanity and violations of Article 3 common to the Geneva Conventions and of Additional Protocol II. The application of Article 6(1) is not limited to any one of these crimes but applies to all of them. Therefore, criminal responsibility would arise under Article 6(1) if an accused person, through instigation (as a mode of participation), caused the planning, preparation or execution of any of the above-mentioned crimes.

With the phrasing and construction of both Articles 6(1) and 2(3)(c) of the Statute of the ICTR, there are instances where these two Articles overlap. This confluence existed since the ICTR's first case of *The Prosecutor v Jean-Paul Akayesu*,[31] but went unnoticed in the numerous cases that have been tried. In these cases, words by the accused that amounted to

---

28 Statute of the ICTR, Article 6(1).

29 Ibid.

30 *Kalimanzira* (n. 11) para. 515; *Bikindi* (n. 11) para. 419; *Nahimana* et al (n. 11) paras. 678–79; *Serugendo* (n. 26) para. 9; *Kajelijeli* (n. 11) para. 855; *Niyitegeka* (n. 11) para. 431; *Musema* (n. 11) para. 120; *Rutaganda* (n. 11) para. 38; *Akayesu* (n. 11) para. 562.

31 *Akayesu* (n. 11).

instigation were limited by both the prosecutors and Trial Chambers to the inchoate crime of direct and public incitement to commit genocide under Article 2(3)(c). It is my argument that these same factual allegations of the accused persons directly and publicly inciting others to commit genocide ought to qualify as instigation under Article 6(1), and if it led to any of the stages of any of the crimes over which the ICTR has jurisdiction, then, criminal responsibility ought to be imposed on such accused persons.[32] However, in the recent case of *The Prosecutor v Callixte Kalimanzira*,[33] the Trial Chamber recognised this confluence and articulated a set of guidelines on how to approach cases where there is a confluence between instigation under Article 6(1) and direct and public incitement to commit genocide under Article 2(3)(c) – the 'Kalimanzira Principles'.[34] Though the 'Kalimanzira Principles' are a significant step forward on how to resolve such complex situations in the future, I argue that to some extent, they are fundamentally flawed as they repeat the substantial cause requirement for criminal responsibility under Article 6(1).

The above analyses therefore suggest that instigation that is direct, public, and to commit the crime of genocide can also lead to the imposition of criminal responsibility under Article 6(1) because instigation to genocide is clearly contemplated in and covered under Article 6(1). The troubling issue here is whether factual allegations that lead to a charge of direct and public incitement to commit genocide can still be used to impose criminal responsibility for instigation to genocide under Article 6(1). Per the jurisprudence of the ICTR, this is permissible.[35] Commonly referred to as 'cumulative convictions' in which the same set of facts are used to lay charges for different crimes, the Trial and Appeal Chambers have established rules that make this permissible.[36]

32 *Kalimanzira* (n. 11) para. 515; *Bikindi* (n. 11) para. 419; *Nahimana* et al (n. 11) paras. 678–79; *Serugendo* (n. 26) para. 9; *Kajelijeli* (n. 11) para. 855; *Niyitegeka* (n. 11) para. 431; *Musema* (n. 11) para. 120; *Rutaganda* (n. 11) para. 38; *Akayesu* (n. 11) para. 562.

33 *Kalimanzira* (n. 11).

34 *Kalimanzira* (n. 11) para. 516.

35 *Alfred Musema v The Prosecutor*, Judgment, Case No. ICTR-96-13A, Appeal Chamber, 16 November 2001, Para. 363, in which the Appeal Chamber of the ICTR applied the test and logic as developed and implemented by the ICTY Appeal Chamber in the case of *Zdravko Mucić, Hazim Delić, Esad Landžo, Zejnil Delalić v The Prosecutor*, Judgment, Case No. IT-96-21, Appeal Chamber, 20 February 2001, Para. 380 (known as *Mucić* et al but commonly referred to as the '*Čelebići Case*').On this issue, *Musema* was preceded by *Akayesu* (n. 11), paras. 462–70, where the Trial Chamber discussed and evaluated its permissibility by looking at the ICTY Trial Chamber's jurisprudence in the case of *The Prosecutor v Dusko Tadić*, Judgment, Case No. IT-94-1, T. Ch., 7 May 1997. See *Akayesu* (n. 11) para. 463.

36 *Musema* (n. 35) para. 363; *Akayesu* (n. 11) para. 463. See also cases decided by both the Trial and Appeal Chambers of the ICTY such as the '*Čelebići Case*' (n. 35);*Tadić*(n. 35).

In my view, the Trial and Appeal Chambers of the ICTR have not construed Article 6(1) correctly. The ICTR Trial and Appeal Chambers have required that there must be a substantial contribution for criminal responsibility to be imposed. In other words, the mode of participation (namely planning, ordering, instigating, committing or aiding and abetting) must substantially contribute to the commission of the crime. For the reasons discussed below, this is an incorrect requirement. Furthermore, no individual has been indicted for instigating crimes against humanity despite the fact that a logical construction of Article 6(1) indicates clearly that instigation as a mode of participation in the planning, preparation or execution of crimes against humanity. The Office of the Prosecution, the Trial and Appeal Chambers, through indictments and judgments, have limited instigation to the inchoate crime of direct and public incitement to commit genocide. Today, in legal parlance and the repertoire of instigation, academic writers as well as civil society actors are quick to construe instigation only in the context of direct and public incitement to commit genocide.[37]

This construction of Article 6(1) is problematic, and has stagnated the jurisprudence on instigation as a mode of participation under Article 6(1). With three crimes over which the ICTR has jurisdiction, I choose crimes against humanity to examine how Article 6(1) could be used to advance the jurisprudence of instigation as a mode of participation. I do so for several reasons. First, of the three crimes over which the ICTR has jurisdiction, it is the oldest.[38] Secondly, the definition of crimes against humanity per the

---

[37] See Gerald Caplan, 'Rwanda: Walking the Road to Genocide' in Allan Thompson (ed), *The Media and the Rwanda Genocide* (Pluto Press 2007) 20–37; Alison Des Forges, 'Call to Genocide: Radio in Rwanda, 1994' Allan Thompson (ed), *The Media and the Rwanda Genocide* (Pluto Press 2007) 41–54; Mary Kimani, 'RTLM: the Medium that Became a Tool for Mass Murder' Allan Thompson (ed), *The Media and the Rwanda Genocide* (Pluto Press 2007) 110–24; Charles Mironko, 'The Effect of RTLM's Rhetoric of Ethnic Hatred in Rural Rwanda' in Allan Thompson (ed), *The Media and the Rwanda Genocide* (Pluto Press 2007) 125–35; Thomas Kamilindi, 'Journalism in a Time of Hate Media' Allan Thompson (ed), *The Media and the Rwanda Genocide* (Pluto Press 2007) 136–42; Jean-Pierre Chrétien, 'RTLM Propaganda: the Democratic Alibi' Allan Thompson (ed), *The Media and the Rwanda Genocide* (Pluto Press 2007) 55–61; Darryl Li, 'Echoes of Violence: Considerations on Radio and Genocide in Rwanda' Allan Thompson (ed), *The Media and the Rwanda Genocide* (Pluto Press 2007) 90–109; Simone Monasebian, 'The Pre-Genocide Case Against Radio-Télévision Libre des Milles Collines' Allan Thompson (ed), *The Media and the Rwanda Genocide* (Pluto Press 2007) 308–29; Charity Kagwi-Ndungu, 'The Challenges in Prosecuting Print Media for Incitement to Genocide' Allan Thompson (ed), *The Media and the Rwanda Genocide* (Pluto Press 2007) 330–42; Jean-Marie Biju-Duval, '"Hate Media"– Crimes Against Humanity and Genocide: Opportunities Missed by the ICTR' Allan Thompson (ed), *The Media and the Rwanda Genocide* (Pluto Press 2007) 343–61.

[38] The three crimes over which the ICTR has jurisdiction are genocide, crimes against humanity and violations of Article 3 common to the Geneva Conventions and of Additional

Statute of the ICTR is unprecedented as it introduced new elements which, hitherto, did not feature in any international instrument.[39] These new elements require that an act must be committed as part of a widespread or systematic attack directed against any civilian population and on any of the prohibited discriminatory grounds (namely, national, political, ethnic, racial or religious).[40] This was a new formulation of the definition of crimes against humanity, introducing key elements that were not contained even in the first United Nations *Ad Hoc* Tribunal, the ICTY: the definition of crimes against humanity required that the enlisted acts to be committed within an armed conflict, internal or international (these definitional differences are examined later in this book). Third, the *actus reus* of the crimes of genocide and crimes against humanity are not mutually exclusive. I argue that a genocidal act may well qualify as a crime against humanity. Based on the doctrine of 'cumulative convictions' (discussed later in Chapter Five), a killing would qualify as a genocidal act if it was perpetrated with the intent to destroy a people, in part or in whole.[41] It would also qualify as a crime against humanity if it were perpetrated as part of a widespread or systematic attack directed against any civilian population on any of the prohibited discriminatory grounds (namely, national, political, ethnic, racial or religious).[42]

As discussed before, the Trial and Appeal Chambers of the ICTR have construed Article 2(3)(c) of the Statute of the ICTR to be an inchoate crime:

Protocol II. The crime of crimes against humanity predates the other two as it was given positive formulation by the Charter of the Nuremberg Tribunal. Genocide, both as a word and concept did not exist prior to 1945, and only became a crime in 1948 following the United Nations General Assembly Resolution 260 (III)A on 9 December 1948 (and went into force on 12 January 1951). Violations of Article 3 common to the Geneva Conventions and of Additional Protocol II as a crime over which the ICTR has jurisdiction did not also exist in any international instrument prior to the Statute of the ICTR (though its constituent crimes are simply a catalogue and an amalgamation of war crimes contained in the various Geneva Conventions).

39 The definitional elements of an attack that is widespread or systematic in nature, and directed against any civilian population on any of the discriminatory grounds had never featured in any international instrument prior to the Statute of the ICTR. See the Statute of the ICTR, Article 3. Even though the first United Nations *ad hoc* Tribunal, the ICTY, was created by the same institution (the United Nations Security Council), in less than a period of two years, this same body gave two fundamentally different formulations on the meaning of crimes against humanity. The Statute of the ICTY, which precedes that of the ICTR, defines crimes against humanity as '…the following crimes when committed in armed conflict, whether international or internal in character, and directed against any civilian population….' (Statute of the ICTY, Article 5).

40 Statute of the ICTR, Article 3.

41 Statute of the ICTR, Article 2(2)(a).

42 Statute of the ICTR, Article 3(a).

therefore, criminal responsibility for direct and public incitement to commit genocide is punishable irrespective of whether such incitement actually led to the commission of genocide.[43] In construing the wording of Article 2(3)(c), the Trial Chamber in the case of *Akayesu*[44] accepted the logical analysis postulated by the delegates to the Genocide Convention, who argued that it would be difficult to engage a huge number of people to perpetrate genocidal acts without the involvement of those who directly and publicly incite them to commit such acts.[45] In every case involving a charge of direct and public incitement to commit genocide, the Trial and Appeal Chambers have consistently stated the inchoate nature of Article 2(3)(c) of the Statute of the ICTR.[46]

However, as examined in this book, the jurisprudence on instigation indicates that the use of the word 'inchoate' seems to have been a misnomer for a few reasons. First, as it exists in legal parlance, the word 'inchoate' means something that is still at the initial, embryonic stage.[47] It is used in criminal jurisprudence to refer to crimes that are still at the preparatory stages, not completely developed or materialised.[48] Three crimes that are commonly referred to as inchoate crimes are attempt, conspiracy, and incitement.[49] As argued in this book, the imposition of criminal responsibility for an inchoate crime does not depend on whether the contemplated crime has been committed or not.[50] Once the ingredients of the inchoate crime are proved, criminal liability will be imposed.[51] For example: in the inchoate crime of attempt to murder, an accused will incur criminal responsibility if, with the requisite *mens rea*, he or she goes beyond mere preparation to kill another, but is intercepted by an act or omission independent of his or her volition which makes it impossible for him or her to commit the crime of murder.[52] In such a case, he or she will be charged with attempted

---

[43] *Kalimanzira* (n. 11) para. 515; *Bikindi* (n. 11) para. 419; *Nahimana* et al (n. 11) paras. 678–79; *Kajelijeli* (n. 11) para. 855; *Niyitegeka* (n. 11) para. 431; *Musema* (n. 11) para. 120; *Rutaganda* (n. 11) para. 38; *Akayesu* (n. 11) para. 562.

[44] *Akayesu* (n. 11).

[45] *Akayesu* (n. 11).

[46] See generally the following cases: *Kalimanzira* (n. 11) para. 515; *Bikindi* (n. 11) para. 419; *Nahimana* et al (n. 11) paras. 678–79; *Kajelijeli* (n. 11) para. 855; *Niyitegeka* (n. 11) para. 431; *Musema* (n. 11) para. 120; *Rutaganda* (n. 11) para. 38; *Akayesu* (n. 11) para. 562.

[47] Ormerod (n. 1). See also Allen and Cooper (n. 1) 433; Heaton (n. 3) 401–02; Dressler (n. 1) 379–80; Philip Asterley Jones and Richard Card, *Cross and Jones' Introduction to Criminal Law* (8th edn., Butterworths 1976) 333.

[48] Ibid.

[49] Ibid.

[50] Ibid.

[51] Ibid.

[52] Ibid.

murder. In the case of conspiracy, the accused persons will be charged with criminal conspiracy if they had reached an agreement to commit a crime, for example, to rob a bank.[53] In these hypothetical cases, criminal responsibility is imposed because the accused persons have committed the ingredients (*actus reus*) of the inchoate crimes in question. If they actually committed the crimes, then, criminal responsibility will be imposed for the crimes. So, if the accused succeeded in committing murder, he or she will be charged with the full offence of murder and not with attempted murder. The same applies to the case of the two conspirators to rob a bank: they will be charged with bank robbery rather than conspiracy to rob a bank.[54]

These analyses are very important because they illuminate the fine distinctions that exist in criminal law, especially when the notion of inchoate crimes is used, and more importantly, when such inchoateness is lost. The inchoateness of crimes is lost when the full crime is committed, and criminal responsibility for the completed crimes ought to be incurred.[55] This basic principle is necessary because later (in Chapter Five below), I question the prosecutorial approach of indicting individuals for the inchoate crime of direct and public incitement to commit genocide when genocide was committed in Rwanda.

The second reason I castigate this substantial contribution requirement is based on the synonymous usage of incitement and instigation. The Trial and Appeal Chambers have held instigation to be synonymous with incitement.[56] If this is true, then, I argue that instigation under Article 6(1) is an inchoate crime as much as direct and public incitement to commit genocide under Article 2(3)(c) of the Statute of the ICTR. And if criminal responsibility for an inchoate crime such as direct and public incitement to commit genocide under Article 2(3)(c) would be incurred *irrespective* of whether such incitement successfully led to the commission of the crime of genocide, it corroborates the argument that the requirement of a 'substantial contribution' to the commission of a crime through any of the enlisted modes (namely, planning, instigating, ordering, committing or otherwise aided and abetted) before criminal responsibility can be imposed under Article 6(1) is completely wrong.

Third, this lends support to the argument that though the drafters of the Genocide Convention included the crime of direct and public incitement

53 Ibid.
54 Ibid.
55 Ibid.
56 *Kalimanzira* (n. 11) para. 511; *Akayesu* (n. 11) para. 481.

to commit genocide, their intention was not merely to make such an inchoate crime punishable: it was to expand the scope of criminal responsibility to include even those who directly and publicly incite the commission of genocide. A thorough perusal of the preparatory works of the Genocide Convention reveals that direct and public incitement to commit genocide (as well as other inchoate crimes and forms of complicity) was included in order to expand the scope of criminal responsibility for those who take part in the planning, preparation or commission of the heinous crime of genocide.[57]

The unfortunate outcome of this jurisprudential mixture is the narrow construction of instigation under Article 6(1). As evidenced by the cornucopia of social science writers who narrowly construe instigation or incitement to be limited to genocide only (direct and public incitement to commit genocide, especially following the Trial Chamber's landmark verdict in *The Prosecutor v Jean-Bosco Barayagwiza, Ferdinand Nahimana and Hassan Ngeze*),[58] it is very disappointing and embarrassing to observe that even legal scholars of the stature and calibre of William A. Schabas and Guénaël Mettraux who have a deep understanding of criminal law, failed to address this issue, treating instigation under Article 6(1) in just a few lines.[59]

In this book, I examine and critique the jurisprudence of the Trial and Appeal Chambers on instigation, arguing that their construction of Article 6(1) has been erroneous. The outcome of this is the imposition of the requirement that the accused's mode of participation must substantially contribute to the commission of any of the crimes over which the ICTR has jurisdiction. The result is that the Trial and Appeal Chambers of the ICTR have looked at instigation under Article 2(3)(c) as a standalone crime only in the context of genocide. Although instigation to commit crimes against humanity by definition should similarly be a standalone crime, the Trial and Appeal Chambers have consistently failed to address it as such. The result is that the legal nature of instigation as a mode of participation under Article 6(1) requires that the instigation must substantially contribute to the commission of the crime for criminal responsibility to be imposed. I argue that this is incorrect because Article 6(1), unlike Article 2(3)(c), is

---

[57] *Akayesu* (n. 11) para. 551; Summary Records of the Meetings of the Sixth Committee of the General Assembly, 21 September–10 December 1948, Official Records of the General Assembly, Statements by Mr Morozov, p 241.

[58] *Nahimana* et al (n. 25).

[59] William A. Schabas, *The UN International Criminal Tribunals: The Former Yugoslavia, Rwanda and Sierra Leone* (Cambridge University Press 2006); Guénaël Mettraux, *International Crimes and the ad hoc Tribunals* (Oxford University Press 2005).

not limited to any specific crime. I also argue that despite the limited approach taken by the Office of the Prosecutors and the Trial and Appeal Chambers, incitement that qualifies as direct and public incitement to commit genocide under Article 2(3)(c) also qualifies as instigation under Article 6(1) and would lead to the imposition of criminal responsibility if such instigation resulted in the planning, preparation or execution of any of the crimes over which the ICTR has jurisdiction, including crimes against humanity.

The substantial contribution requirement is not only inconsistent with Article 6(1) of the Statute of the ICTR, it also does not reflect the Rwandan realities. Given the widespread nature of crimes during the genocide and the systematic character of their planning, preparation and execution, the atrocities in Rwandan reveal the existence of a joint criminal enterprise. In such cases, criminal responsibility ought to be attributed to each individual who participated through any mode of criminal participation, namely, planning, ordering, instigating, committing or aiding and abetting. Requiring that criminal responsibility can be imposed only when such a mode of participation substantially contributes to the commission of a crime neither squares with the letter of Article 6(1) nor is it in accordance with the jurisprudence on assigning guilt in cases of joint criminal enterprises.[60]

2.2 Synoptic Statement of the Problematic Jurisprudence of the Trial and Appeal Chambers of the ICTR

As discussed earlier, instigation features under both Article 6(1) and Article 2(3)(c). Article 6(1) defines the imposition of criminal responsibility in the following words:

> A person who planned, instigated, ordered, committed or otherwise aided and abetted *in the planning, preparation or execution of a crime* referred to in articles 2 to 4 [genocide, crimes against humanity and violations of Article 3 common to the Geneva Conventions and of Additional Protocol II] of the present Statute, shall be individually responsible for the crime.[61]

On the other hand, Article 2(3) of the Statute of the ICTR makes punishable genocide-related acts. Article 2(3) states as follows:

---

[60] Ormerod (n. 1) 206–21, 402–16; Heaton (n. 3) 386–91.

[61] Emphasis added.

> The following acts shall be punishable....
> c) Direct and public incitement to commit genocide....

The approach of the Office of the Prosecutor and the Trial and Appeal Chambers in addressing both Article 6(1) and Article 2(3)(c) has been problematic. The problem is attributable, in part, to the poor understanding and construction of Article 6(1), and in part, to a failure to take on cases where there is limited precedent.

The first problem arising from Article 6(1) is that the Trial and Appeal Chambers have required that criminal responsibility can only be imposed if it is proved that the accused's mode of participation (instigation being one of them) substantially contributed to the commission of a crime.[62] I argue that this is wrong. Any of the enlisted modes of participation (instigation included) must lead to any of the stages (planning, preparation or execution) of any of the crimes over which the ICTR has jurisdiction (genocide, crimes against humanity and violations of Article 3 common to the Geneva Conventions and of Additional Protocol II).[63] These stages are planning, preparation or execution. The Statute, in enlisting these different stages, evaded the use of a conjunctive 'and' to mean that such a mode of participation must go through all the stages, from planning, preparation to execution. Rather, it used a disjunctive 'or', which, when logically construed, means that a mode of participation must lead to any of the stages. To require that there must be a substantial contribution to the commission of any of the crimes before criminal responsibility can be imposed limits the Tribunal's focus to execution. Therefore, it is incorrect to require substantial contribution to an outcome; the activity of instigation in and of itself constitutes a prosecutable crime.

This poverty in construing Article 6(1) has affected the development of the jurisprudence on instigation as a mode of participation in the planning, preparation or execution of the crimes over which the ICTR has jurisdiction under Article 6(1) and specifically in respect of crimes against humanity. The Office of the Prosecutor, the Trial and Appeal Chambers have limited instigation to Article 2(3)(c) which, in itself, is an inchoate crime. Criminal responsibility for the crime of direct and public incitement to

---

[62] *Hategekimana* (n. 27) para. 644; *Kalimanzira* (n. 11) para. 512; *Kajelijeli* (n. 11) para. 759; *Semanza* (n. 18) para. 379; *Ntakirutimana and Ntakirutimana* (n. 27) para. 787; *Kayishema and Ruzindana* (n. 27) (AC) para. 186; *Bagilishema* (n. 27) paras. 30, 33; *Musema* (n. 11) para. 115; *Rutaganda* (n. 11) para. 34; *Kayishema and Ruzindana* (n. 27) (TC) paras. 199-207; *Akayesu* (n. 11) para. 477.

[63] Statute of the ICTR, Article 6(1).

commit genocide will be imposed irrespective of whether such direct and public incitement successfully led to the commission of the crime of genocide.[64] Without departing from the intention of the drafters of the Genocide Convention who appreciated the role of instigators in the perpetration of genocide, the Trial and Appeal Chambers have played an invaluable role in developing the jurisprudence on the inchoate crime of direct and public incitement to commit genocide.[65] The problem that has arisen from this practice is that instigation as a mode of participation in the planning, preparation or execution of other crimes as contemplated under Article 6(1) on the definition of criminal responsibility has been unaddressed. In every case involving instigation, the Trial and Appeal Chambers limited it to the standalone crime of direct and public incitement to commit genocide under Article 2(3)(c). With no individual indicted for instigation to crimes against humanity, and numerous individuals indicted for direct and public incitement to genocide, the question arises as to whether the imposition of criminal responsibility for the inchoate crime of direct and public incitement to genocide automatically bars the imposition of criminal responsibility under Article 6(1) for instigation.

The nature of Article 6(1) (which contains a broad definition of the imposition of criminal responsibility) is distinct from that of Article 2(3)(c) (which is limited to the crime of direct and public incitement to commit genocide). Direct and public incitement to commit genocide is inchoate in character.[66] Article 6(1) is also inchoate in character. So, direct and public incitement to commit genocide that is punishable under Article 2(3)(c) should also lead to the imposition of criminal responsibility under Article 6(1) if such instigation (which must not necessarily be direct and public) led to either the planning, preparation or execution of any of the crimes over which the ICTR has jurisdiction. By analogy therefore, instigation that qualifies under Article 2(3)(c) also qualifies for the imposition of criminal

64 *Kalimanzira* (n. 11) para. 515; *Bikindi* (n. 11) para. 419; *Nahimana* et al (n. 11) paras. 678–79; *Serugendo* (n. 26) para. 9; *Kajelijeli* (n. 11) para. 855; *Niyitegeka* (n. 11) para. 431; *Musema* (n. 11) para. 120; *Rutaganda* (n. 11) para. 38; *Akayesu* (n. 11) para. 562.

65 In the cases they have tried, they have identified the inchoate nature of the crime of direct and public incitement to genocide for which an accused would incur responsibility irrespective of whether such direct and public incitement actually led to the commission of genocide. Secondly, they have construed the words 'direct', 'public' and 'incitement' as contained in Article 2(3)(c). See *Kalimanzira* (n. 11) para. 515; *Bikindi* (n. 11) para. 419; *Nahimana* et al (n. 11) paras. 678–79; *Serugendo* (n. 26) para. 9; *Kajelijeli* (n. 11) para. 855; *Niyitegeka* (n. 11) para. 431; *Musema* (n. 11) para. 120; *Rutaganda* (n. 11) para. 38; *Akayesu* (n. 11) para. 562.

66 *Kalimanzira* (n. 11) para. 515; *Bikindi* (n. 11) para. 419; *Nahimana* et al (n. 11) paras. 678–79; *Serugendo* (n. 26) para. 9; *Kajelijeli* (n. 11) para. 855; *Niyitegeka* (n. 11) para. 431; *Musema* (n. 11) para. 120; *Rutaganda* (n. 11) para. 38; *Akayesu* (n. 11) para. 562.

responsibility under Article 6(1) if such instigation led to either the planning, preparation or execution of genocide, crimes against humanity or violations of Article 3 common of the Geneva Conventions and of Additional Protocol II. I argue that this is the correct application of these two Articles. With this approach, there is the possibility of a confluence between Articles 2(3)(c) and 6(1): instigation may well qualify under both Articles.

Although this confluence has existed in cases as early as *Akayesu*,[67] the overlap between these articles went unnoticed until in the recent case of *Kalimanzira*[68] where the Trial Chamber developed and outlined a set of guidelines (the 'Kalimanzira Principles') on how to resolve cases of a confluence.[69] The 'Kalimanzira Principles', though a major step in this direction, are fundamentally flawed because they are partly formulated upon the erroneous construction of Article 6(1), insisting as previous Trial Chambers have, that criminal responsibility can be imposed under Article 6(1) only when it can be shown that the accused's mode of participation substantially contributed to the commission of the crime.[70] In addition, they limit incitement to the crime of genocide only.

This poses a problem for future cases of instigation especially to crimes against humanity. The jurisprudence of the ICTR on instigation as a mode of participation obscures rather than illuminates aspects of instigation to crimes against humanity.[71] Recognising the contribution the Trial and Appeal Chambers of the ICTR have made towards developing the jurisprudence on the inchoate crime of direct and public incitement to commit genocide, it is difficult to deny that they did nothing to develop instigation as a mode of participation to commit crimes against humanity under Article 6(1), and this jurisprudential inertia is partly attributable to their myopic perception and erroneous construction of Article 6(1). I outline this problem, and argue in this book that the nature of instigation as a mode of participation in the planning, preparation or execution of crimes against humanity has been insufficiently and inconsistently addressed by the

---

[67] *Akayesu* (n. 11).

[68] *Kalimanzira* (n. 11).

[69] *Kalimanzira* (n. 11) para. 516.

[70] *Hategekimana* (n. 27) para. 644; *Kalimanzira* (n. 11) para. 512; *Kajelijeli* (n. 11) para. 759; *Semanza* (n. 27) para. 379; *Ntakirutimana and Ntakirutimana* (n. 27) para. 787; *Kayishema and Ruzindana* (n. 27) (AC) para. 186; *Bagilishema* (n. 27) paras. 30, 33; *Musema* (n. 11) para. 115; *Rutaganda* (n. 11) para. 34; *Kayishema and Ruzindana* (n. 27) (TC) paras. 199–207; *Akayesu* (n. 11) para. 477.

[71] The Statute of the ICTR makes instigation a mode of participation in any of the crimes over which the ICTR has jurisdiction. See the Statute of the ICTR, Article 6(1).

prosecutors, the Trial and Appeal Chambers of the ICTR. The result is that the jurisprudence of instigation as a mode of participation in the planning, preparation or execution of crimes against humanity as developed by the Trial and Appeal Chambers is unclear, undeveloped and unreliable. It is the objective of this book to clarify the status of instigation as a mode of participation that would lead to the imposition of criminal responsibility under Article 6(1) and how future trials by different institutions should construe and apply the law in this regard.

2.3 Central Arguments

As aforementioned, instigation features as a mode of participation that would lead to the imposition of criminal responsibility. The wording of Article 6(1) reads as follows:

> A person who planned, instigated, ordered, committed or otherwise aided and abetted *in the planning, preparation or execution of a crime* referred to in articles 2 to 4 of the present Statute, shall be individually responsible for the crime.[72]

Article 2(3)(c) makes direct and public incitement to commit genocide punishable. It is a crime by, and in itself.[73]

The jurisprudence of the Trial and Appeal Chambers establishes that for criminal responsibility to be imposed under Article 6(1), it must be proved that the accused's mode of participation substantially contributed to the commission of the crime.[74] However, given the inchoate character of direct and public incitement to commit genocide under Article 2(3)(c), criminal

---

72 Emphasis added.

73 The Statute of the ICTR as well as the Genocide Convention use the descriptive phraseology 'the following acts shall be punishable'. See the Statute of the ICTR, Article 2(3); and the Genocide Convention, Article III. Furthermore, the approach of the Office of the Prosecutors as well as the jurisprudence of the Trial and Appeal Chambers of the ICTR establish this owing to the fact that individuals were indicted for, and subsequently tried and convicted of direct and public incitement to genocide. These two international instruments and the jurisprudence of the ICTR support the view that direct and public incitement to commit genocide is a crime, and does not depart from the intention of the drafters of the Genocide Convention. See *Akayesu* (n. 11) para. 551.

74 *Hategekimana* (n. 27) para. 644; *Kalimanzira* (n. 11) para. 512; *Kajelijeli* (n. 11) para. 759; *Semanza* (n. 27) para. 379; *Ntakirutimana and Ntakirutimana* (n. 27) para. 787; *Kayishema and Ruzindana* (n. 27) (AC) para. 186; *Bagilishema* (n. 27) paras. 30, 33; *Musema* (n. 11) para. 115; *Rutaganda* (n. 11) para. 34; *Kayishema and Ruzindana* (n. 27) (TC) paras. 199–207; *Akayesu* (n. 11) para. 477.

responsibility would be incurred by an individual irrespective of whether genocide is committed or not.[75]

Based on this jurisprudence, I make the following arguments. The first argument centres on the requirement that the accused's mode of participation must substantially contribute to the commission of the crime for criminal responsibility to be imposed.[76] In Chapter Five, I critique this requirement by strictly construing Article 6(1). To buttress this argument, I look at the bifurcated and inchoate character of Article 6(1). I also highlight the inclusion of the three different stages of the crimes (planning, preparation or execution) and the use of a disjunctive word ('or') rather than a conjunction ('and') to suggest that any of the modes of participation, if it leads to any of the stages of the crime (namely, planning, preparation or execution), would lead to the imposition of criminal responsibility under Article 6(1).

The atrocities in Rwanda were not accidental. They were the final outcome of a long history of bigotry and inflated ethnic tensions preceded by internecine clashes.[77] The atrocities that occurred in Rwanda in 1994 were well-planned: they required the involvement of civil and military officials, the broader Hutu community as well as key civil society actors.[78] The massive scales of the perpetration and victimisation revealed an attack that was widespread and systematic. Furthermore, they indicate the existence of a joint criminal enterprise.[79] There was a criminal conspiracy to which

---

[75] *Kalimanzira* (n. 11) para. 515; *Bikindi* (n. 11) para. 419; *Nahimana* et al (n. 11) paras. 678–79; *Serugendo* (n. 26) para. 9; *Kajelijeli* (n. 11) para. 855; *Niyitegeka* (n. 11) para. 431; *Musema* (n. 11) para. 120; *Rutaganda* (n. 11) para. 38; *Akayesu* (n. 11) para. 562.

[76] *Hategekimana* (n. 27) para. 644; *Kalimanzira* (n. 11) para. 512; *Kajelijeli* (n. 11) para. 759; *Semanza* (n. 27) para. 379; *Ntakirutimana and Ntakirutimana* (n. 27) para. 787; *Kayishema and Ruzindana* (n. 27) (AC) para. 186; *Bagilishema* (n. 27) paras. 30, 33; *Musema* (n. 11) para. 115; *Rutaganda* (n. 11) para. 34; *Kayishema and Ruzindana* (n. 27) (TC) paras. 199–207; *Akayesu* (n. 11) para. 477.

[77] Virginia Morris and Michael P. Scharf, *The International Criminal Tribunal for Rwanda* Vol. 1 (Transnational Publishers, Inc. 1998) 47–59. See generally Christian P. Sherrer, *Genocide and Crisis in Central Africa: Conflict Roots, Mass Violence, and Regional War* (Praeger 2002); Edward L. Nyankanzi, *Genocide: Rwanda and Burundi* (Schenkam Books 1998); Linda Melvern, *Conspiracy to Murder: The Rwandan Genocide* (Verson 2004); Telford Taylor, *The Anatomy of the Nuremberg Trials: A Personal Memoir* (Alfred A. Knopf, Inc. 1992); Richard Overy, *Interrogations: The Nazi Elite in Allied Hands, 1945* (Penguin Group 2001).

[78] Ibid.

[79] As discussed below in Chapter Five (below), a joint criminal enterprise exists where several persons act with a common purpose. See Ormerod (n. 1) 182. It is important to note that this is a topic which has drawn the attention of many academics in this discipline, and their writings, for the most part, have been influenced by the jurisprudence of the *ad hoc* Tribunals (the ICTY and the ICTR). However, it is important to note that the contents of their works focus on identifying ways to draw lines on which individuals to hold

many individuals subscribed. These individuals played different roles at different times. In cases of a joint criminal enterprise, criminal responsibility is evenly distributed amongst persons who partook in the crimes. The rationale behind this allocation of criminal responsibility is that it is usually difficult to accurately point fingers at who actually committed the crime(s) and therefore, it is necessary to have some type of catchall net of liability. Secondly, in joint criminal enterprise was established to further a criminal conspiracy, therefore, collective responsibility is taken for every act or omission that is perpetrated as part of that criminal conspiracy.[80] This was the approach taken by the prosecutors at Nuremberg: they considered the Nazi Regime to be a criminal conspiracy (many individuals had agreed to commit the crimes), and eased their task by identifying key individuals and organisations that played a part in furthering the actualisation of the criminal conspiracy.[81] They all bore responsibility for the crimes committed as part of, or in furtherance of the criminal conspiracy.[82]

---

responsible for crimes committed as a result of a joint criminal enterprise. My approach is significantly different: while acknowledging the need to know which persons to hold accountable, the issue under consideration in this book is the imposition of criminal responsibility for a mode of participation: instigation. I engage this doctrine as an answer to the 'how' question: in other words, how the modes of participation contributed to the different stages of the different crimes over which the ICTR has jurisdiction. The 'how' approach within the framework of a joint criminal enterprise focuses on the roles played by different persons at different times leading to the commission of the crimes. See generally Allison Marston Danner and Jenny S. Martinez, 'Guilty Associations: Joint Criminal Enterprise, Command Responsibility, and the Development of International Criminal Law' (2005) Vol. 93, 1 *California Law Review* 75–169; Antonio Cassese, 'The Proper Limits of Individual Responsibility under the Doctrine of Joint Criminal Enterprise' (2007) Vol. 5, 1 *J Int Criminal Justice* 109–133; Elies van Slierdregt, 'Joint Criminal Enterprise as a Pathway to Convicting Individuals for Genocide' (2007) Vol. 5, 1 *J Int Criminal Justice* 184–207; Harmen van der Wilt, 'Joint Criminal Enterprise Possibilities and Limitations', (2007) Vol. 5, 1 *J Int Criminal Justice* 91–108; Jens David Ohlin, 'Three Conceptual Problems with the Doctrine of Joint Criminal Enterprise' (2007) Vol. 5, 1 *J Int Criminal Justice* 69–90; Kai Ambos, 'Joint Criminal Enterprise and Command Responsibility', (2007) Vol. 5, 1 *J Int Criminal Justice* 159–183; Kai Hamdorf, 'The Concept of a Joint Enterprise and Domestic Modes of Liability for Parties to a Crime: A Comparison of German and English Law' (2007) Vol. 5, 1 *J Int Criminal Justice* 208–226; Rebecca L. Haffajee, 'Prosecuting Crimes of Rape and Sexual Violence at the ICTR: The Application of Joint Criminal Enterprise Theory' (2006) 29 *Harv. J. L. & Gender* 201–221; Steven Powles, Joint Criminal Enterprise–Criminal Liability by Prosecutorial Ingenuity and Judicial Creativity' (2004) 2 *J. Int'l Crim. Just.* 606–619; Verena Han, 'The Development of the Concept of Joint Criminal Enterprise at the International Criminal Tribunal for the Former Yugoslavia' (2005) 5 *Int'l Crim. L. Rev.* 167–201.

[80] Ormerod (n. 1) 206–21, 402–16; Dressler (n. 1) 465–502; Heaton (n. 3) 386–91.

[81] Nina H.B. Jorgensen, *The Responsibility of States for International Crimes* (Oxford University Press Inc. 2000).

[82] Ibid.

One of the crimes over which the ICTR has jurisdiction is the crime of crimes against humanity.[83] The Statute of the ICTR gave it a definition which, hitherto, did not exist in international law.[84] A critical analysis of these definitional elements, per the jurisprudence of the ICTR and writings of legal scholars, reveals that crimes against humanity require group (or collective) participation.[85] For an attack to meet the definitional requirements of crimes against humanity as stipulated in the Statute of the ICTR, there must be at least group involvement in the conception, preparation and execution.

I argue that with these definitional elements, a joint criminal enterprise is necessary for the planning, preparation or execution of crimes against humanity. In such a joint criminal enterprise, different persons would definitely play different roles including but not limited to 'ordering, planning, instigating, committing or aiding and abetting' the crimes.[86] These roles would be played at different times: some at the planning, preparation or execution stages. Article 6(1) contains the traditional modes of participation in criminal law, which, as it requires, must lead to any of the stages of any of the crimes for criminal responsibility to be imposed. It therefore becomes irrational to require that criminal responsibility can be imposed under Article 6(1) only when it is proved that the accused's mode of participation substantially contributed to the commission of a crime.[87] Within the context of a joint criminal enterprise, different roles were played by different persons at different times. The fact that the crimes were committed is illustrative of the actualisation of the criminal conspiracy, and to require a substantial contribution is to insinuate that in addition to partaking in the joint criminal enterprise, the accused's mode of participation must be proved to have led to the crime. Article 6(1) requires simply that a mode of participation leads to any of the stages of any of the crimes. Its wording recognises the possibility of the existence of a joint criminal

---

83 Statute of the ICTR, Article 3.

84 The definitional elements of an attack, which must be widespread or systematic in pattern, directed against any civilian population on any of the discriminatory grounds had never featured in any international instrument.

85 See generally Mettraux (n. 59).

86 These different modes of participation are contained in Article 6(1) of the Statute of the ICTR.

87 *Hategekimana* (n. 27) para. 644; *Kalimanzira* (n. 11) para. 512; *Kajelijeli* (n. 11) para. 759; *Semanza* (n. 27) para. 379; *Ntakirutimana and Ntakirutimana* (n. 27) para. 787; *Kayishema and Ruzindana* (n. 27) (AC) para. 186; *Bagilishema* (n. 27) paras. 30, 33; *Musema* (n. 11) para. 115; *Rutaganda* (n. 11) para. 34; *Kayishema and Ruzindana* (n. 27) (TC) paras. 199–207; *Akayesu* (n. 11) para. 477.

enterprise and the different modes of involvement by different persons at different times. To require a substantial contribution to the commission of a crime before criminal responsibility can be imposed, I argue, is delimiting Article 6(1) to only the final stage of the crimes, and this is untenable given both the wording of Article 6(1) and the existence of a joint criminal enterprise in Rwanda within which the planning, preparation and execution of these crimes took place.

The third argument addresses the inchoateness of Article 2(3)(c) within the context of Rwanda during the genocide. The jurisprudence of both the Trial and Appeal Chambers establishes Article 2(3)(c) as an inchoate crime: responsibility would be imposed whether or not the incitement led to the commission of genocide.[88] However, the word 'inchoate' in criminal law is used for a specific set of crimes which are at their initial or incomplete stages. As discussed below in Chapter Three, inchoate crimes are crimes that are not yet completely executed. The imposition of criminal responsibility for such crimes is different.[89] In inchoate crimes such as attempt, conspiracy and incitement, responsibility is incurred once the accused person, with the required mental element, performs any of the ingredients of the*actus reus*. For example, in the inchoate crime of attempted murder, an accused would be criminally responsible if he or she went beyond mere preparation and embarked on the commission of the crime of murder.[90] In the inchoate crime of conspiracy to rob a bank, an accused person would be criminally responsible if he or she, with the required mental element, reached an agreement with another to rob a bank.[91] In the case of incitement to murder, criminal responsibility would be imposed on an individual who intentionally reaches out to another influencing, encouraging or soliciting him or her to commit murder.[92] In all these cases, criminal responsibility is imposed once any of the elements of the *actus reus* is committed even though the commission of the ultimate crime has not been completed. However, the inchoateness of these crimes would be lost when the crime is committed. In the inchoate crime of attempt to murder, if the individual were to actually perpetrate the act of killing, he or she would be responsible for murder and not attempted murder. In conspiracy to rob a bank, once

[88] *Kalimanzira* (n. 11) para. 515; *Bikindi* (n. 11) para. 419; *Nahimana* et al (n. 11) paras. 678–79; *Kajelijeli* (n. 11) para. 855; *Niyitegeka* (n. 11) para. 431; *Musema* (n. 11) para. 120; *Rutaganda* (n. 11) para. 38; *Akayesu* (n. 11) para. 562.

[89] Ormerod (n. 1) 379–470; Dressler (n. 1) 379; Allen and Cooper (n. 1) 438–502.

[90] Ormerod (n. 1) 380–98; Dressler (n. 1) 379–419; Allen and Cooper (n. 1) 438–63.

[91] Ormerod (n. 1) 399–437; Dressler (n. 1) 429–64; Allen and Cooper (n. 1) 43–82.

[92] Ormerod (n. 1) 438–44; Dressler (n. 1) 421–28; Allen and Cooper (n. 1) 482–88.

the parties to the agreement go beyond the agreement and commit any of the *actus reus* of the crime they agreed to commit (bank robbery), both would be responsible as joint or co-offenders or principal and accessory (depending on what roles they both played in the commission of the crimes).[93] In incitement to murder, the inciter is criminally responsible irrespective of whether the ultimate crime of murder is committed or not.[94]

In Rwanda, as evidenced by the indictments, some individuals directly and publicly incited others to commit the crime of genocide (and other atrocities committed therein).[95] Genocide was committed in Rwanda.[96] The argument I raise on this is whether it was correct to indict, try, convict and punish individuals for direct and public incitement to commit genocide. This is because the crime of genocide *includes* the element of incitement. Incitement to genocide falls within the same criminal definition as genocide; whereas incitement to murder is categorically distinct from the definition of the crime of murder. As in the hypothetical cases discussed in the preceding paragraph, the inchoateness of Article 2(3)(c) ought to have been lost or ushered into abeyance because the crime they incited (genocide only for the purposes of Article 2(3)(c)) was actually committed. The Trial and Appeal Chambers have recognised the inchoate character of the crime of direct and public incitement to commit genocide.[97] Inchoate crimes lose their inchoateness when the ultimate crime is committed.

[93] Ormerod (n. 1) 399–437.

[94] Ormerod (n. 1) 178–209, 399–437.

[95] *The Prosecutor v Callixte Kalimanzira*, Amended Indictment, Case No. ICTR-2005-88-I, OTP, 21 July 2005, Count 3, Paras. 18–27; *The Prosecutor v Joseph Serugendo*, Corrigendum of Indictment, Case No. ICTR-2005-84-I, OTP, 21 July 2005, Count 4, Paras. 51–73; *The Prosecutor v Simon Bikindi*, Amended Indictment, Case No. ICTR-2001-72-I, OTP, 15 June 2005, Count 4, Paras. 31–41; *The Prosecutor v Tharcisse Muvunyi*, Amended Indictment, Case No. ICTR-2000-55A-T, OTP, 23 December 2003 (a retrial on the lone charge of direct and public incitement to commit genocide); *The Prosecutor v Eliézer Niyitegeka*, Amended Indictment, Case No. ICTR-96-14-T, OTP, 25 November 2002, Count 4, Paras. 5.1–6.71; *The Prosecutor v Juvénal Kajelijeli*, Amended Indictment, Case No. ICTR-98-44A-I, OTP, 25 January 2001, Count 4, Paras. 2.1–4.18; *The Prosecutor v Jean-Bosco Barayagwiza*, Amended Indictment, Case No. ICTR-97-19, OTP, 14 April 2000, Count 4, Paras. 5.1–7.13; *The Prosecutor v Ferdinand Nahimana*, Amended Indictment, Case No. ICTR-96-11, OTP, 15 November 1999, Count 3, Paras. 4.1–6.27; *The Prosecutor v Hassan Ngeze*, Amended Indictment, Case No. ICTR-97-27, OTP, 10 November 1999, Count 4, Paras. 5.1–7.15; *The Prosecutor v Georges Henri Yvon Joseph Ruggiu*, Amended Indictment, Case No. ICTR-97-32-I, OTP, 10 December 1998, Count 2, Paras. 3.1–5.12; and, *The Prosecutor v Jean-Paul Akayesu*, Amended Indictment, Case No. ICTR-96-4-I, OTP, June 1997, Count 4, Paras. 14–15.

[96] Morris and Scharf (n. 77) 48–67.

[97] *Kalimanzira* (n. 11) para. 515; *Bikindi* (n. 11) para. 419; *Nahimana* et al (n. 11) paras. 678–79; *Serugendo* (n. 26) para. 9; *Kajelijeli* (n. 11) para. 855; *Niyitegeka* (n. 11) para. 431; *Musema* (n. 11) para. 120; *Rutaganda* (n. 11) para. 38; *Akayesu* (n. 11) para. 562.

Therefore, imposing criminal responsibility on individuals for the inchoate crime of direct and public incitement to commit genocide when the crime of genocide was actually committed does not reflect an understanding of the nature of inchoate crimes in criminal law in general. Even if this practice was demanded by the necessity to build the jurisprudence on this inchoate crime, it should not have blurred the construction of instigation as a mode of participation in any of the crimes under Article 6(1).

Instigation as a mode of participation under Article 6(1) need not be direct or public and is not limited to the crime of genocide.[98] Instigation, like every other mode of participation articulated in Article 6(1), must lead to either the planning, preparation or execution of any of the crimes over which the ICTR has jurisdiction.[99] In Rwanda, some individuals directly and publicly incited others to commit the crime of genocide. Though it remains debatable as to the exact reasons underlying this prosecutorial practice, criminal responsibility ought to be imposed upon such individuals under Article 6(1) because instigation is a mode of participation, and it led to either the planning, preparation or execution of the crime of genocide.

However, even if the Trial and Appeal Chambers correctly construed direct and public incitement to commit genocide as an inchoate crime which does not require the successful commission of genocide for criminal responsibility to be imposed, I argue that it would have been much better and correct for them to use same facts amounting to direct and public incitement to commit genocide to impose criminal responsibility under Article 6(1) for crimes against humanity.

2.4 Conclusion

In the above discussion, I have stated the current problem in this area of the law: the erroneous construction of instigation as a mode of participation in crimes against humanity under Article 6(1) and how it becomes a legal puzzle in cases where there is a confluence between instigation as a mode of participation under Article 6(1) and direct and public incitement

[98] Article 6(1) stipulates the different modes of participating in the crimes over which the ICTR has jurisdiction.

[99] These crimes are genocide (Article 2), crimes against humanity (Article 3) and violations of Article 3 common to the Geneva Conventions and of Additional Protocol II (Article 4).

to commit genocide being an inchoate crime under Article 2(3)(c). I also outlined my key arguments why I consider that the Trial and Appeal Chambers of the ICTR have erred in their construction of Article 6(1) generally, and instigation as one of its modes in particular.

The purpose of this exercise, as mentioned earlier, is to fix this area of the law by identifying errors and lapses in the current jurisprudence on instigation and making it better by analysing the wording of Article 6(1). This is done through a strict construction of Article 6(1), an examination of the cases which the Trial Chambers of the ICTR have adjudicated, and consultation of academic writers on the subject of instigation.

CHAPTER THREE

THE JURISPRUDENCE OF THE ICTR ON INSTIGATION AS A MODE OF PARTICIPATION

3.1 Introduction

The Statute of the ICTR defines the imposition of criminal responsibility as follows:

> A person who planned, instigated, ordered, committed or otherwise aided and abetted in the planning, preparation or execution of a crime referred to in articles 2 to 4 [genocide, crimes against humanity and violations of Article 3 common to the Geneva Conventions and of Additional Protocol II] of the present Statute, shall be individually responsible for the crime.[1]

Five traditional modes of participation (planned, instigated, ordered, committed or aided and abetted) are contained therein, which, if connected to any of the stages (planning, preparation or execution) of any of the crimes over which the ICTR has jurisdiction (genocide, crimes against humanity and violations of Article 3 common to the Geneva Conventions and of Additional Protocol II), would lead to the imposition of criminal responsibility.

Instigation is one of the traditional modes of participation, which, as it exists in most jurisdictions, is an inchoate crime.[2] However, this same mode of participation, instigation, features again in the Statute of the ICTR. Article 2(3) of the Statute of the ICTR states as follows:

> ...the following acts shall be punishable...
> c. direct and public incitement to commit genocide.

[1] United Nations Security Council Resolution 955, U. N. SCOR, 3453rd meeting, U.N. Doc. S/RES/955 (1994) of 8 November 1994, to which was annexed the Statute of the ICTR, Article 6(1).

[2] See the discussion below on inchoate crimes. See generally David Ormerod, *Smith and Hogan Criminal Law* (12th edn., Oxford University Press 2008) 438–40; Joshua Dressler, *Understanding Criminal Law* (5th edn., LexisNexis 2009) 379–465; Michael J. Allen and Simon Cooper, *Elliott & Wood's Cases and Materials on Criminal Law* (9th edn., Sweet & Maxwell 2006) 438–99; Russell Heaton, *Criminal Law Textbook* (Oxford University Press 2004) 401–39.

As discussed in the Chapters below, the Trial and Appeal Chambers of the ICTR have developed the jurisprudence on these two Articles. They have outlined the elements of both Articles: what must be proved for criminal responsibility to be imposed under Article 6(1) and Article 2(3)(c). Though the words instigation and incitement have been used in the different Articles, the jurisprudence of the Trial Chambers of the ICTR has established that these two words are synonymous with each other, and can therefore be used interchangeably to connote the same meaning.[3]

In this Chapter (as well as other portions of this book), I make interchangeable use of these two words as I examine the evolution and ingredients of instigation as an inchoate crime. Beyond defining their synonymous usage, the Trial and Appeal Chambers have stated that criminal responsibility can be imposed under Article 6(1) only where it is proved that the accused's mode of participation 'substantially contributed' to the commission of a crime.[4] On the other hand, direct and public incitement to commit genocide under Article 2(3)(c) has been recognised as an inchoate crime: criminal responsibility will be imposed irrespective of whether such direct and public incitement to commit genocide successfully led to the commission of genocide.[5] In other words, in respect of genocide, there need be no actual connection between the instigation to commit genocide and an actual or possible act of genocide.

---

[3] *The Prosecutor v Callixte Kalimanzira*, Judgment, Case No. ICTR-05-88-T, T. Ch. III, 22 June 2009, Para. 511; *The Prosecutor v Jean-Paul Akayesu*, Judgment, Case No.ICTR-96-4, T. Ch.I, 2 September 1998, Para. 481.

[4] *The Prosecutor v Idelphonse Hategekimana*, Judgment, Case No. ICTR-00-55, T. Ch. II, 6 December 2010, Para. 644; *Kalimanzira* (n. 3) para. 512; *The Prosecutor v Juvénal Kajelijeli*, Judgment, Case No.ICTR-96-44-T, T. Ch. II, 1 December 2003, Para. 759; *The Prosecution v Laurent Semanza*, Judgment, Case No.ICTR-97-20, T. Ch. II, 15 May 2003, Para. 379; *The Prosecutor v Gérard Ntakirutimana and Elizaphan Ntakirutimana*, Judgement, Case No. ICTR-96-17-T, T. Ch. I, 21 February 2003, Para. 787; *Clément Kayishema and Obed Ruzindana v The Prosecutor*, Judgement, Case No. ICTR-95-1A, Appeal Chamber, 1 June 2001, Paras. 186; *The Prosecutor v Ignace Bagilishema*, Judgement, Case No.ICTR-95-1-A, T. Ch. I, 7 June 2001, Paras. 30, 33; *The Prosecutor v Alfred Musema*, Judgment, Case No. ICTR-96-13-T, T. Ch. I, 27 January 2003, Para. 115; *The Prosecutor v Georges Rutaganda*, Judgment, Case No.ICTR-96-3-T, T. Ch. I, 6 December 1999, Para. 34; *The Prosecutor v Clément Kayishema and Obed Ruzindana*, Judgment, Case No.ICTR-95-1-T, T. Ch. I, 21 May 1999, Paras. 199–207; *Akayesu* (n. 3) para. 477.

[5] *The Prosecutor v Tharcisse Muvunyi*, Judgment, Case No. ICTR-00-55A-T, T. Ch. III, 11 February 2010, Paras. 24–25; *Kalimanzira* (n. 3) para. 510; *The Prosecutor v Simon Bikindi*, Judgment, Case No. ICTR-01-72, T. Ch. III, 2 December 2008, Para. 419; *Ferdinand Nahimana, Jean-Bosco Barayagwiza and Hassan Ngeze v The Prosecutor*, Judgment, Case No. ICTR-99-52-A, Appeal Chamber, 28 November 2007, Paras. 678–79; *The Prosecutor v Ferdinand Nahimana, Jean-Bosco Barayagwiza and Hassan* Ngeze, Judgment, Case No. ICTR-99-52-T, T. Ch. I, 3 December 2003, Paras. 678, 720; *Kajelijeli* (n. 4) para. 855; *The Prosecutor v Eliézer Niyitegeka*, Judgment, Case No.ICTR-96-14-T, T. Ch. I, 16 May 2003, Para. 431; *Musema* (n. 4) para. 120; *Rutaganda* (n. 4) para. 38; *Akayesu* (n 3) para. 562.

To some extent, the construction of Article 2(3)(c) is correct. However, as I discuss in Chapter Five (below), the construction of Article 6(1) leading to the imposition of the substantial contribution requirement is wrong. Before I critique the jurisprudence of both the Trial and Appeal Chambers' construction of Article 6(1), it is important to examine instigation as a mode of participation under Article 6(1). As will be seen in the discussions below, the Trial and Appeal Chambers have limited instigation to the inchoate crime of direct and public incitement to commit genocide. Furthermore, even when the factual allegations comprising direct and public incitement to commit genocide could be used to impose criminal responsibility under Article 6(1) (because instigation is a mode of participation), the Trial and Appeal Chambers did not engage a thorough reading of Article 6(1). Their imposition of a substantial contribution requirement for criminal responsibility to be incurred under Article 6(1) is the unfortunate outcome of an incorrect construction of Article 6(1) in particular, and an understanding of instigation as a mode of participation in general.

In this Chapter, I look at instigation as a mode of participation that has been recognised in every international instrument prior to, under and after the Statute of the ICTR. I examine its nature as an inchoate crime and how it has evolved since the judgment of IMT, Nuremberg, in the Julius Streicher Case. I study every case that has been tried by the ICTR to select those in which instigation featured as a charge against the accused. I then identify, put together and analyse the ingredients of instigation as a mode of participation as developed by both the Trial and Appeal Chambers. Finally, I look at a recurrent theme of debate that was raised by most of the persons accused of direct and public incitement to commit genocide: the free speech argument.

3.2 Instigation as an Inchoate Crime Under Common Law

Generally speaking, in criminal law, different individuals play different roles at different times in the commission of a crime.[6] These roles may be at the initial (such as planning or preparatory) or final stage (such as perpetration of the crime) of the criminal activity. Criminal law punishes not only those who perpetrate the material elements of a crime. It also punishes those who engage in criminal conduct at the preparatory or initial stage of the planned offence.

[6] Ormerod (n. 2) 379; Dressler (n. 2) 379–465; Allen and Cooper (n. 2) 438–99; Heaton (n. 2) 401–39.

Consequently, it is the policy of criminal justice not to limit its focus on completed crimes. Some crimes are committed by the mere fact that their perpetration is planned. Such acts or omissions are made crimes even at the developmental stages, without requiring their complete commission for criminal responsibility. In jurisprudential terminology, these are called inchoate crimes.[7] This means they are crimes which are still at the conceptual, beginning or incipient stages. They are incomplete. They are still being developed, and the accused has not completed the commission of the ultimate crime. They therefore fall short of the complete crime. They are 'incomplete' because they have not been fully developed or completely committed to satisfy the *actus reus* of the contemplated crime.[8] The initial conduct, however, is criminal.

Three kinds of crimes fall under this genre: attempt, conspiracy and instigation. As inchoate crimes, they need not result in any tangible or visible harm: for example, in the inchoate crime of conspiracy, it is sufficient that the accused agreed with another person to commit a crime.[9]

Penalising such preparatory or initial acts as crimes poses difficulties, especially in drawing with precision at what point an inchoate crime is committed. The final commission of a crime is usually preceded by planning and preparation. Some of these stages require no physical act at all. An example is the inchoate crime of conspiracy, which is committed once an agreement to commit a crime is reached.[10] In the inchoate crime of instigation, it is complete once the instigator reaches another persuading or encouraging him or her to commit a crime.[11] However, in the inchoate crime of attempt, not every act done by the defendant would qualify as an attempt.[12] The law makes a distinction between acts that are merely preparatory and acts that unequivocally convey the irrevocability of the defendant's intention to bring to fruition the crime contemplated or planned.

The behaviour covered by inchoate crimes is diverse. Acts range from purely harmless acts such as an agreement in the case of conspiracy to mere words of encouragement as would happen in the case of instigation.

---

[7] Ormerod (n. 2) 178–325; Dressler (n. 2) 379–465; Allen and Cooper (n. 2) 438–99; Heaton (n. 2) 401–39.

[8] Ormerod (n. 2) 379; Dressler (n. 2) 379–465; Allen and Cooper (n. 2) 438–99; Heaton (n. 2) 401–39.

[9] Ormerod (n. 2) 399–402; Dressler (n. 2) 379–465; Allen and Cooper (n. 2) 438–99; Heaton (n. 2) 415.

[10] Ormerod (n. 2) 399–437; Dressler (n. 2) 429–64; Allen and Cooper (n. 2) 463–82; Heaton (n. 2) 415.

[11] Ormerod (n. 2) 379, 387; Dressler (n. 2) 421–28; Allen and Cooper (n. 2) 482–88.

[12] Ormerod (n. 2) 389–90; Dressler (n. 2) 379–401; Allen and Cooper (n. 2) 438–63.

Numerous reasons have been advanced for the criminalisation of such conduct. However, the defendant's demonstration through his or her actions of the willingness to commit a substantive crime is one reason advanced by criminologists, lawyers and other policy makers.

Lastly, inchoate crimes always relate to a substantive crime. They are not crimes *per se*. In other words, there is nothing like the crime of attempt, instigation, or conspiracy. An accused is often charged for the crime of attempted murder, an instigation to commit murder, or conspiracy to murder.[13]

Instigation (or incitement) is an inchoate crime in criminal law. Most legal systems define and characterise it as an inchoate crime. An example of this is English Law. International Criminal Law is not different. Its inclusion as a mode of participation in the Charter of the IMT, Nuremberg, as well as subsequent international instruments, has not been a novel creation.[14]

Criminal responsibility is incurred once the instigator reaches out to another, irrespective of whether the person instigated performs an act in

13 Liability for inchoate crimes is independent of accessorial liability. Accessorial liability is often derived from the commission of the full crime by the principal offender, whereas inchoate crimes are completed and can be prosecuted before the commission of any full crime. This distinction highlights a few differences. First, when it comes to participation in a criminal activity, some defences avail to the defendant who demonstrates a change in mind before the commission of the criminal act; while inchoate liability is complete with the act of attempt, incitement and conspiracy, and withdrawal from the criminal act can only be a mitigating factor in sentencing. This chapter looks at one of the inchoate crimes, instigation, and how it has been recognised as a mode of incurring criminal responsibility in international criminal law.

14 See the Rome Statute of the ICC, U. N. Doc. A/CONF.183/9 (1998), reprinted in 37 I.L.M. 999 (1998), Article 25(3), serves as the starting point. Prior to the Rome Statute of the ICC, international instruments recognised instigation as a mode of participation. Examples include the Statute of the Special Court for Sierra Leone, annexed to the Agreement between the United Nations and the Government of Sierra Leone on the Establishment of a Special Court for Sierra Leone pursuant to United Nations Security Council Resolution 1315, U. N. SCOR, 4186th meeting, U.N. Doc. S/RES/1315 (2000), Article 6(1); Statute of the ICTR, Article 6(1); Statute of the ICTY, annexed to United Nations Security Council Resolution 827, U. N. SCOR, 3217th meeting, U.N. Doc. S/RES/827 (1993), Article 7(1); the Draft Code of Crimes against the Peace and Security of Mankind, 1996, adopted by the International Law Commission, 48th Session, 1996, submitted to the United Nations General Assembly as part of the ILC's Report covering the work of the session (hereinafter referred to as the Draft Code of Crimes against the Peace and Security of Mankind, 1996), Article 2(3)(f); the Draft Code of Offences against the Peace and Security of Mankind, 1954, adopted by the International Law Commission, 6th Session, 1954, submitted to the United Nations General Assembly as part of the ILC's Report covering the work of the session (hereinafter referred to as the Draft Code of Offences against the Peace and Security of Mankind, 1954), Article 2(13)(ii); the Charter of the IMTFE, Tokyo, Article 5; the Allied Control Council Law No. 10, Article II(2); and the Charter of the IMT, Nuremberg, Article 6(c).

furtherance of the instigation. As a result, instigation exists in common law as a specific-intent crime, and is completed upon the communication of the solicitation to another.[15]

A person cannot be guilty of the crime of instigation unless he intentionally commits the *actus reus* of the crime: that is, he intentionally invites, requests, counsels, motivates, influences, or encourages another to commit a crime with the specific intent that the other person completes the target crime.

There is no requirement that the instigator should have any prior or personal relationship with the person instigated. No instigation occurs if the instigator intends to commit the crime himself, but requests the assistance of another person. The crime of instigation is predicated upon the influence exerted by a person on another, causing him or her to commit a crime. Where both individuals plan the commission of a crime, it does not amount to instigation. No ingredient of the target crime must be committed by the instigator. Otherwise, that person becomes an accessory or principal offender (because that person would have committed a material ingredient or *actus reus* of the crime).

A person is guilty of the crime of instigation if his or her purpose is to promote or facilitate the commission of a substantive crime by another; and with such purpose, he or she commands, encourages, requests or instigates another person to engage in conduct that would constitute the crime, an attempt to commit it or would establish the other person's complicity in its commission or attempted commission.

The relationship between the instigator and the instigated party need not be that of accomplice to perpetrator.

3.2.1 Actus Reus *of Instigation*

The concept of inchoate crimes is well-developed in common law systems and instigation is recognised as an inchoate crime. To better understand instigation as a mode of participation and an inchoate crime, it is important to examine it under English criminal law as the Trial and Appeal Chambers have done. In *R v Nkosiyana*, Holmes JA defined an instigator as someone 'who reaches and seeks to influence the mind of another to the commission of a crime.'[16] He further acknowledged that such approach to

15 Ormerod (n. 2) 438–40; Dressler (n. 2) 421–29; Allen and Cooper (n. 2) 482–488.

16 Holmes, JA in *R v Nkosiyana* 1966 (4) SA 655 at 658, AD.

influence the mind of another may take different forms such as suggestion, proposal, request, exhortation, gesture, argument, persuasion, inducement, goading or the arousal of cupidity. In *R v Marlow*,[17] the court opined that this 'gamut of words' omits 'encourage' which it thought 'represents as well as any modern word can the concept involved'; and further added a proviso that the encouragement involved must be a clear positive step 'aimed at inciting another to commit a crime.' Not every encouragement necessarily amounts to incitement.

Instigation can be made through threats, pressure or persuasion;[18] and may be implied or express. Advertising an article for sale, as well as its potential to do what would amount as a crime, is incitement.[19] On the other hand, a man who manufactures an article which can be used only to commit a crime does not amount to incitement.[20]

Instigation to commit a crime is criminal, irrespective of whether it is successful in persuading another to commit or attempt to commit, the crime. In *R v Higgins*,[21] Lord Kenyon said

> But it is argued, that a mere intent to commit evil is not indictable, without an act done; but is there not an act done, when it is charged that the defendant solicited another to commit a felony? The solicitation is an act: and the answer given at the Bar is decisive, that it would be sufficient to constitute an overt act of high treason.[22]

In *Marlow*,[23] the accused published a book on the cultivation and production of cannabis. Witnesses testified that they were influenced by reading the book. The crime of incitement was committed once the book was published and read by anyone irrespective of whether he or she was influenced by it or not. The evidence was relevant only to establish the book's persuasive quality and, probably, though remotely, the author's intention.

The act instigated must be one which, when done, would amount to a crime by the person instigated. Instigation to commit an *actus reus* of a crime is a crime. If a man threatens another man with a fatal weapon if he

---

17 [1997] Crim LR 897.

18 *Race Relations Board v Applin* [1973] QB 815 at 827, CA, Civil Div., per Lord Denning MR, followed in *Invicta Plastics Ltd v Clare* [1976] RTR 251, [1976] Crim LR 131.

19 *Invicta Plastics* (n. 18) (indication that 'Radatex' may be used to detect police radar traps is instigation to commit a crime under s. 1 (1) of the English Wireless Telegraphy Act 1949).

20 *R v James and Ashford* (1985) 82 Cr App Rep 226, 232, distinguishing it from *Invicta Plastics* (n. 18).

21 (1801) 2 East 5.

22 Ibid 170.

23 *R v Marlow* (n. 17).

does not commit sodomy (in a context where sodomy is unlawful), that would amount to instigation. The major test is the effect of the accused's act on the person who commits the crime. There must be, or must have been, some degree of influence on the mind of the person perpetrating the crime.

The essence of instigation is that someone reaches out to influence the mind of another. The instigation must be communicated to the person,[24] but this seems to be of less importance[25] since the failure of communication may still give rise to an attempt to instigate.[26] If the crime instigated is actually committed, then, the defendant becomes a participant in the crime and is indictable.

Today, advances in technology, especially in digital communication systems, make it possible for individuals to disseminate different kinds of literature to multitudes of people across the world. Criminal law does not place any limitation as to the number of persons to be instigated (although this is implied in international criminal law where the inchoate crime of direct and public incitement to commit genocide requires the 'public' element to be satisfied by the number of persons incited).[27] It is therefore logical to say that an individual who publishes a newspaper advertisement or some other media broadcast can commit the crime of instigation. In *R v El Faisal*,[28] convictions for soliciting murder were upheld where the defendant encouraged the audience to kill Jews and 'unbelievers'.

Lastly, there is no requirement that the communication with another must be successful in persuading that person to commit the crime. There is instigation where the instigator completes his or her communication, and it is irrelevant whether such a communication is effective in persuading the person instigated to commit the crime. Lord Kenyon's ruling in the case of *R v Higgins*[29] suggests that solicitation itself is an act sufficient to attract criminal responsibility. In *Marlow*,[30] the crime of instigation involved the publication of a book about the cultivation and production of cannabis, the court held that the crime of instigation was committed once the book

---

24 *R v Banks* (1873) 12 Cox CC 393 (where a letter suggesting the murder of an unborn child was intercepted, it was held to amount to an attempt to instigate under the English Offences Against the Person Act, 1861, s. 4 (repealed)).

25 *R v Ransford* (1874) 13 Cox CC 9.

26 A crime at common law: *Chelmsford Justices, ex p Amos* [1973] Crim LR 437, DC; *Cope* (1921) 16 Cr App R 17.

27 *Muvunyi* (n. 5) para. 27; *Kajelijeli* (n. 4) para. 851; *Akayesu* (n. 3) para. 555.

28 [2004] EWCA Crim 343.

29 *R v Higgins* (n. 21).

30 *R v Marlow* (n. 17).

was published and read by anyone, holding that it was immaterial whether anyone was influenced by the book or not.[31] It is also a logical sequence that the offence would be committed where the person instigated is a police officer involved in the suppression of the type of crime instigated.[32]

3.2.2 Mens Rea *of Instigation*

The *mens rea* of instigation is two-fold: first, the inciter must intend the consequences specified in the *actus reus* of the crime instigated. The essence of instigation is the accused's intention to bring a criminal result through the act or omission of some other person. It is therefore insufficient that the accused merely engages in some communication, and this communication is understood. The second element of the *mens rea* requires that it must be proved that the accused knew of, had reason to know, or deliberately closed his or her eyes to all the circumstances of the act instigated. I now turn to discuss each manifestation of *mens rea*.

3.2.2.1 *Intention*

It must be proved that the accused knew, or had reason to know, all the circumstances of the act instigated which are elements of the crime in question. He or she must intend the consequences of the *actus reus* of the crime. If the accused should instigate someone to inflict grievous bodily harm on another, the defendant is not guilty of instigation to murder. However, both the accused and the person will be guilty of murder if death should result from the infliction of the intended grievous bodily harm because it is foreseeable that grievous bodily harm may result in death. The rationale of instigation is to bring to fruition a criminal result by the criminal act of another. In *Marlow*,[33] the court made use of the word 'aim', suggesting that it must be the accused's purpose that the crime be committed. The accused does not need to know that his advice would be followed by the person instigated; but that the commission of a crime will be the probable outcome of it being followed. There must be an element of persuasion or pressure.[34] If defendant sells a pistol to a person, knowing that such a person intends to kill another, it would be difficult not to convict the

31 See the definition in *R v Most* (1881) 7 QBD 244, 258 per Huddleston B.

32 *DPP v Armstrong* [2000] Crim LR 379; *R v Krause* (1902) 66 JP 121.

33 *R v Marlow* (n. 17).

34 Ormerod (n. 2) 438–41; Dressler (n. 2) 421–24; Allen and Cooper (n. 2) 482–88. See also *R v Hendrickson and Tichner* [1977] Crim LR 356. cf *R v Buxton* (1969) 85 LQR 252 at 256.

accused of murder if such a person actually kills. However, the accused cannot be convicted of instigation to murder if the person does not perpetrate the crime.[35]

Intention in this context is not limited to direct intention only. It includes even oblique intention. It is therefore sufficient that the accused knew not necessarily that his advice would be heeded, but that if it was, then, the commission of the crime would be certain.[36] Therefore, a much different result would not have been expected in *Marlow*.[37]

3.2.2.2 *Knowledge of Circumstances*

The second element of *mens rea* requires that among the circumstances of which the accused must be proved to know, had reason to know, or deliberately closed his eyes to, is the *mens rea* of the person instigated. If an accused should believe that the person instigated does not have the necessary *mens rea* for the crime in question, and he or she intends to commit the crime through an innocent agent, then, the accused would be guilty as the principal or abettor if the *actus reus* of the crime is completed, but not guilty of instigation. In *R v Curr*,[38] the accused was acquitted of instigating women to commit crimes under the Family Allowances Act 1945 because it was not proved that the women had the guilty knowledge necessary to constitute that crime. If an accused urges a person to accept the gift of a wrist watch which is in fact a stolen wrist watch, the accused is not guilty of instigating such a person to handling stolen goods if the person was not aware that the gift is stolen.

Although the accused must intend the person to act with the requisite *mens rea* of the crime instigated, it is not necessary that he or she should have the *mens rea* of that crime. If the accused instigates another to steal property belonging to a third party, it is no defence that the accused intended to ensure that the victim would get his or her property back again, that is, that the accused did not have the intent to permanently deprive the victim of his property which is an element of the *mens rea* of the crime of theft. It is enough that the accused intends the person instigated to have

---

35 cf *R v James and Ashford* (n. 20) 232.

36 On this view, see English Law Commission, *Assisting and Encouraging Crime* (Consultation Paper No 131, 1993) 129–33; Canadian Law Reform Commission, *Secondary Liability: Participation in Crime and Inchoate Offences* (Canada Working Paper No 29, 1982) 30–31, which made reference to 'intent (direct or indirect)' as the relevant *mens rea*.

37 *R v Marlow* (n. 17).

38 [1968] 2 QB 944, [1967] 1 All ER 478, CA.

the intent. This principle, however, was overlooked in *R v Shaw*[39] where the accused instigated another to obtain property by deception from their employer. The accused was held not guilty of instigation to obtain if his purpose was, as he said, to demonstrate the insecurity of the employer's system and he did not intend the employer to suffer any permanent loss. The accused intended the person instigated to commit the crime and it should have been no answer that he intended to tell him afterwards that it was in a good cause.

The crime of instigation is complete once the instigator communicates to another person his or her intention. Withdrawal plays no role on criminal liability: it merely goes to mitigate the punishment. In *R v Prior*,[40] the defendant's phone calls in which he offered to sell drugs to an undercover police officer amounted to instigation despite the defendant's subsequent withdrawal of the offer in the course of the same phone call.

Having examined the basic principles of instigation as an inchoate crime in English Law, it is important to now examine it under International Criminal Law.

3.3 Instigation as a Mode of Participation in International Criminal Law

Prior to 1945, numerous concepts did not exist in international (criminal) law. Since 1945, a wide range of concepts and crimes have been given birth to by different international instruments. Examples include crimes against humanity, genocide and direct and public incitement to genocide.

However, as discussed above, instigation existed as an inchoate crime prior to 1945 (though not in international law). In 1945, it was recognised as a mode of participation, and since then, international instruments have continually articulated instigation as a mode of participation that would lead to the imposition of criminal responsibility. Its inclusion in the Statute of the ICTR was therefore not an unprecedented exercise, and as will be shown below, subsequent international instruments have stipulated instigation as a mode of participation.

---

39 [1994] Crim LR 365. cf the English Draft Criminal Code (Law Com. No. 177) cl 47: 'A person is guilty of incitement to commit an offence or offences if (a) he incites another to do or cause to be done an act or acts which, if done, will involve the commission of the offence by the other; and (b) he intends or believes that the other, if he acts as incited, shall or will do so with the fault required for the offence or offences.'

40 [2004] 6 Archbold News 1.

3.3.1 *The Nuremberg Charter and the Julius Streicher Legacy*

The Charter of the IMT, Nuremberg, was established for the 'just and prompt trial and punishment of the major war criminals of the European Axis.'[41] It created and defined three crimes over which the Tribunal would have jurisdiction, namely: crimes against peace,[42] war crimes[43] and crimes against humanity.[44] The Charter defined the imposition of criminal responsibility in the following words: 'leaders, organizers, instigators and accomplices participating in the formulation or execution of a common plan or conspiracy to commit any of the foregoing crimes'.[45]

As discussed earlier, two individuals were indicted for participating through instigation: they were Hans Fritzsche (Minister of Propaganda)[46] and Julius Streicher. The former, Hans Fritzsche, the Nazi Minister of Propaganda, was acquitted[47] (though later convicted by the national courts following Allied Control Council Law No. 10).[48]

Julius Streicher, a *Gauleiter*,[49] was owner and publisher of *Der Sturmer*,[50] an anti-Semitic magazine. He was a German who subscribed to the views, policies and plans of the Nazi regime. His greatest service to the Nazi regime was his journalistic skills. From 1923, Julius Streicher was publisher,

---

41 Charter of the IMT, Nuremberg, Article 1.

42 Charter of the IMT, Nuremberg, Article 6(a).

43 Charter of the IMT, Nuremberg, Article 6(b).

44 Charter of the IMT, Nuremberg, Article 6(c).

45 Ibid.

46 The Propaganda Ministry was given broad jurisdiction by a decree issued by the German Fuhrer on 30 June 1933, which stipulated that 'the Reich Minister of Public Enlightenment and propaganda has jurisdiction over the whole field of spiritual indoctrination if the nation, of propagandizing the State, of cultural and economic propaganda, of enlightenment of the public at home and abroad. Furthermore, he is in charge of the administration of all institutions serving those purposes.' *Affidavits at Nuremberg Trials*, para. 2030-PS; Donna E. Arzt, 'Nuremberg, Denazification and Democracy: The Hate Speech Problem at the International Military Tribunal' (1995) Vol. XII 3 *N. Y. L. Sch. J. Hum. Rts.* 689, 689–758.

47 Randall L. Bytwerk, *Julius Streicher: Nazi Editor of the Notorious Anti-Semitic Newspaper Der Stürmer* (New York: Cooper Square Press 2001); Dennis Showalter, *Jews, Nazis, and the Law: The Case of Julius Streicher 1997*, in the Museum of Tolerance on-line library at <<http://motlc.wiesenthal.com/site/pp.asp?c=gvKVLcMVIuG&b=395155>>.

48 Detailed Biographical Time-lines and Trial History of the Nuremberg Defendants.

49 *Gauleiter* was a political rank in Germany, which meant a party leader of a regional branch of the NSDAP (commonly known as Nazi Party): see Bytwerk (n. 47); Telford Taylor, *The Anatomy of the Nuremberg Trials: A Personal Memoir* (Alfred A. Knopf, Inc. 1992) 78–115; Richard Overy, *Interrogations: The Nazi Elite in Allied Hands, 1945* (Penguin Group 2001).

50 '*Der Sturmer*' means 'The Stormer'. The banner slogan on the paper was 'The Jews are Our Misfortune'. D.A. Sprecher, *Inside the Nuremberg Trial: A Prosecutor's Comprehensive Account* (University Press of America 1999) 515; Bytwerk (n. 47); Richard Breitman, *The Architect of Genocide: Himmler and the Final Solution* (The Bodley Head 1991) 46–65, 85–104.

editor-in-chief, and eventual owner of the nationally-distributed anti-Semitic magazine, *Der Sturmer*, along with a few other local journals. Numerous publications of *Der Sturmer* were saturated with deplorable cartoons, gory tales of alleged ritual murders, instructions for anti-Jewish campaigns and lists of Jewish dentists, doctors, and shopkeepers who Aryans were advised to avoid.[51]

At the Nuremberg Tribunal, the prosecution assembled Julius Streicher's speeches and publications as evidence to illustrate the intensity of his portrayal of Jews as the major source of evil, and his insistence on the necessity of their extermination. The prosecution characterised his crimes as amounting to 'the removal of opposition through anti-Jewish propaganda and incitement', which it divided into four parts: first, the anti-Jewish boycott of 1933, directed personally by Julius Streicher, second, *Der Sturmer*'s 'ritual murder' propaganda, third, the anti-Jewish demonstrations and last, his perversion of youth.[52]

The Nuremberg Tribunal examined the nature and contents of his publications, especially within the context of Nazi Germany where persecution of Jews was the official policy of the Nazi Regime. He was convicted of participating in the atrocities of the Nazi Regime through instigation, and was sentenced to death by hanging.[53] The pivotal judgment of the Nuremberg Tribunal in the *Streicher Case* stipulated that:

> In his speeches and articles, week after week, month after month, he infected the German mind with the virus of anti-Semitism, and incited the German people to active persecution.... But it was not only in Germany that this defendant advocated his doctrines. As early as1938 he began to call for the extermination of the Jewish race.... With knowledge of the extermination of the Jews in the Occupied Eastern Territories, this defendant continued to write and publish his propaganda of death....[54]

The Charter of the IMT, Nuremberg, and its judgment handed in the *Julius Streicher Case* provide both a legislative[55] and judicial[56] framework upon

---

51 Ibid.

52 Arzt (n. 46) 745.

53 Ibid.

54 Bytwerk (n. 47).

55 Rome Statute of the ICC, Article 25(3); the Statute of the SCSL, Article 6(1); the Statute of the ICTR, Article 6(1); the Statute of the ICTY, Article 7(1); the Draft Code of Crimes against the Peace and Security of Mankind, 1996, Article 2(3)(a)-(g); the Draft Code of Offences against the Peace and Security of Mankind, 1954, Article 2(13); Allied Control Council Law No. 10, Article II(2); and the Charter of the IMTFE, Tokyo, Article 5.

56 See generally the jurisprudence of the Trial Chambers in the cases *Nahimana* et al (n. 5) (TC) para. 981; *Akayesu* (n. 3) para. 550.

which subsequent international instruments and judicial analyses on instigation as a mode of participation have been built. As stated in the judgment, Julius Streicher's mode of participation was through instigation: 'infected the German mind with the virus of anti-Semitism, and incited the German people to active persecution.... With knowledge of the extermination of the Jews... this defendant [Julius Streicher] continued to write and publish his propaganda of death....'

3.3.2 *Post-Nuremberg Developments*

Beyond Nuremberg, numerous developments have occurred in international criminal law. These developments, occurring at different times and triggered by different situations, have not deviated from recognising instigation as a form of participation.

The Allied Control Council Law No. 10 was another international instrument that succeeded the Charter of the IMT, Nuremberg. It was enacted and promulgated on 20 December 1945 by the Allied Powers. It was a uniform piece of legislation applied across Germany. This piece of uniform legislation was called Control Council Law No. 10. It exercised jurisdiction over 'war criminals and similar offenders other than those dealt with by the International Military Tribunal'.[57] Crimes against peace, war crimes and crimes against humanity were 'recognized'[58] crimes over which Control Council Law No. 10 would have jurisdiction. Criminal responsibility was imposed on

> Any person without regard to nationality or the capacity in which he acted, is deemed to have committed a crime as defined in paragraph 1 of this Article, if he was (a) a principal or (b) was an accessory to the commission of any such crime or ordered or abetted the same or (c) took a consenting part therein or (d) was connected with plans or enterprises involving its commission or (e) was a member of any organization or group connected with the commission of any such crime or (f) with reference to paragraph 1 (a) if he held a high political, civil or military (including General Staff) position in Germany or in one of its Allies, co-belligerents or satellites or held high position in the financial, industrial or economic life of any such country.[59]

Though the word 'instigation' did not feature in the definition of criminal responsibility, it could be discerned from the inclusion of accessorial

[57] Preamble to the Control Council Law No. 10.
[58] Allied Control Council Law No. 10, Article II(1).
[59] Allied Control Council Law No. 10, Article II(2).

liability under Article II(2)(b) above. Hans Fritzsche, acquitted by the Nuremberg Tribunal, was however, convicted and sentenced to a term of imprisonment for having participated (through instigation) in the atrocitiesover which the Allied Control Council Law No. 10 had jurisdiction.

The Charter of the IMTFE, Tokyo, crafted and implemented by the Americans for 'the just and prompt trial and punishment of the major war criminals in the Far East',[60] imposed criminal responsibility on 'leaders, organizers, instigators and accomplices participating in the formulation or execution of a common plan or conspiracy to commit any of the foregoing crimes [crimes against peace, conventional war crimes and crimes against humanity] are responsible for all acts performed by any person in execution of such plan.'[61]

In 1948, the United Nations General Assembly adopted the Convention on the Prevention and Punishment of the Crime of Genocide (hereinafter referred to as the Genocide Convention).[62] The Genocide Convention defined the crime of genocide.[63] It also articulated other punishable acts.[64] Amongst these was direct and public incitement to commit genocide.[65]

The International Law Commission[66] produced drafts of two international instruments: the Draft Code of Offences against the Peace and Security of Mankind in 1954[67] and the Draft Code of Crimes against the Peace and Security of Mankind in 1996. In the 1954 Draft Code, criminal

---

60 The Charter of the IMTFE, Tokyo, Article 1.

61 The Charter of the IMTFE, Tokyo, Article 5.

62 *Convention on the Prevention and Punishment of the Crime of Genocide*, United Nations General Assembly Resolution 260(III), U.N. GAOR, 3rd Session, 179th meeting, U.N. Doc. A/RES/260A (1948).

63 Genocide Convention, Article 2(2).

64 These are genocide, conspiracy to commit genocide, direct and public incitement to commit genocide, attempt to commit genocide and complicity in genocide. See the Genocide Convention, Article 3(a)–(e).

65 Genocide Convention, Article 3(c).

66 The International Law Commission was created by the United Nations for the purpose of promoting 'the progressive development of international law and its codification'. See the United Nations General Assembly Resolution 174(II), U.N. GAOR, 2nd Session, 123rd meeting, U.N. Doc. A/RES/174(II) of 21 November 1947. United Nations General Assembly Resolution 177(II) mandated the International Law Commission to formulate 'the principles of international law recognised' in the Charter of the IMT, Nuremberg, and 'in the judgment of the Tribunal': see the United Nations General Assembly Resolution 177(II), U.N. GAOR, 2nd Session, 123rd meeting, U.N. Doc. A/RES/177(II) of 21 November 1947.

67 The International Law Commission adopted this text at its sixth session in 1954, which was submitted to the United Nations General Assembly as a part of the Commission's report covering the work of that session (at para. 54). The report, which also contains commentaries on the draft articles, appears in *Yearbook of the International Law Commission, 1954*, Vol. II.

responsibility would be incurred by those who, *inter alia*, 'direct incitement to commit any of the offences defined in the preceding paragraphs of this article'.[68]

The 1996 Draft Code of Crimes against the Peace and Security of Mankind[69] also imposed criminal responsibility on any individual who 'directly and publicly incites another to commit such a crime which in fact occurs'.[70]

From the above, it is evident that instigation remained a recognised mode of participation in international criminal law since 1945. Though only one individual had been convicted of participating through this mode, international instruments continuously recognised instigation as a mode of participation in international criminal law.[71] Therefore, as discussed below, even the Statutes of the two United Nations' *ad hoc* Tribunals are not different as they also recognise instigation as a mode of participation in committing the crimes over which the *ad hoc* Tribunals have jurisdiction.

3.3.3 *The United Nations'* Ad Hoc *Tribunals*

Events in the former Yugoslavia and Rwanda at different times led to two important international instruments recognising, *inter alia*, instigation as a form of participation. The first United Nations Security Council *ad hoc* Tribunal, the ICTY, was created.[72] Its Statute imposes criminal responsibility on a 'person who planned, instigated, ordered, committed or otherwise aided and abetted in the planning, preparation or execution of a crime'[73] over which the Tribunal has jurisdiction.[74] About a year later, a second *ad hoc*

---

68 Article 2(13)(ii).

69 The text of this Draft Code was adopted by the International Law Commission at its 48th session in 1996. It was submitted to the general assembly as a part of the Commission's report covering the work of that session (at para. 50). The report, which also contains commentaries on the draft articles, appears in *Yearbook of the International Law Commission, 1996*, Vol. II (Part Two).

70 Article 2(3)(f).

71 See the Rome Statute of the ICC, Article 25(3); the Statute of the SCSL, Article 6(1); the Statute of the ICTR, Article 6(1); the Statute of the ICTY, Article 7(1); the Draft Code of Crimes against the Peace and Security of Mankind, 1996, Article 2(3)(f); the Draft Code of Offences against the Peace and Security of Mankind, 1954, Article 2(13)(ii); the Charter of the IMTFE, Article 5; the Allied Control Council Law No. 10, Article II(2); and the Charter of the IMT, Nuremberg, Article 6(c).

72 United Nations Security Council Resolution 827, U.N. SCOR, 3217th meeting, U. N. Doc. S/RES/827 (1993) of 25 May 1993.

73 The Statute of the ICTY, Article 7(1).

74 These crimes are Grave Breaches of the Geneva Conventions of 1949 (Article 2), Violations of the laws or customs of war (Article 3), Genocide (Article 4), and Crimes against Humanity (Article 5).

Tribunal was created, the ICTR. Like the first, an individual incurs criminal responsibility if that person 'planned, instigated, ordered, committed or otherwise aided and abetted in the planning, preparation or execution of a crime'[75] over which the Tribunal (ICTR) has jurisdiction.[76]

3.3.4 *The Rome Statute of the International Criminal Court*

The Rome Statute of the ICC gives a more expansive version on the imposition of criminal responsibility. It states that

> In accordance with this Statute, a person shall be criminally responsible and liable for punishment for a crime within the jurisdiction of the Court if that person:
> a. Commits such a crime, whether as an individual, jointly with another or through another person, regardless of whether that other person is criminally responsible;
> b. Orders, solicits or induces the commission of such a crime which in fact occurs or is attempted;
> c. For the purpose of facilitating the commission of such a crime, aids, abets or otherwise assists in its commission or its attempted commission, including providing the means for its commission;
> d. In any other way contributes to the commission or attempted commission of such a crime by a group of persons acting with a common purpose. Such contribution shall be intentional and shall either:
> i. Be made with the aim of furthering the criminal activity or criminal purpose of the group, where such activity or purpose involves the commission of a crime within the jurisdiction of the Court; or
> ii. Be made in the knowledge of the intention of the group to commit the crime;
> e. In respect of the crime of genocide, directly and publicly incites others to commit genocide...[77]

---

[75] The Statute of the ICTR, Article 6(1). See the Statute of the ICTY, Articles 2–5 respectively.

[76] These crimes are Genocide (Article 2), Crimes against Humanity (Article 3), and Violations of Article 3 Common to the Geneva Conventions and of Additional Protocol II. See the Statute of the ICTR, Articles 2–4 respectively.

[77] Article 25(3) of the Rome Statute of the ICC (sub-article punishes 'direct and public incitement to genocide' as an inchoate crime). The word 'instigation' does not feature in the Rome Statute of the ICC as it did in the Statute of the ICTR. However, as discussed earlier, the words 'solicit', 'incitement', 'instigation', and 'inducement' are synonymous with each other. Given the fact that the jurisprudence of the ICC is still to be developed especially on these different modes of participation, it would be interesting to see how much reliance is made on the jurisprudence of the ICTR as well as to what extent such jurisprudence will be critiqued. For comments on the Rome State of the ICC, see generally: Otto Triffterer, *Commentary on the Rome Statute of the International Criminal Court: Observers' Notes, Article*

3.3.5 *The Statute of the Special Court for Sierra Leone (SCSL)*

The Statute of the SCSL[78] imposes individual criminal responsibility on a person who 'planned, instigated, ordered, committed or otherwise aided and abetted in the planning, preparation or execution of a crime'[79] over which the Court had jurisdiction.[80]

Given the above international instruments, it is settled in international criminal law that instigation is a mode of participation that will lead to the imposition of criminal responsibility.[81] I now examine the ingredients of instigation as a mode of participation in International Criminal Law.

3.4 The Ingredients of Instigation

As discussed earlier, instigation appears under Articles 6(1) and Article 2(3)(c) of the Statute of the ICTR. While the former is of general application (it is not limited to any particular crime), the latter is of limited application (instigation under Article 2(3)(c) must be direct, public, and to commit the crime of genocide for there to be criminal responsibility under Article 2(3)(c)).

The Statute of the ICTR, like other international legal instruments preceding it, does not define the meaning of instigation. However, the basic understanding of instigation as an inchoate crime as it exists under common law can serve as the point of departure in applying a meaning to it as it appears in the Statute of the ICTR.

---

by Article (2nd edn., Hart Publishing 2008); Antonio Cassese, Paola Gaeta and John R.W.D. Jones, *The Rome Statute of the International Criminal Court: A Commentary* (Oxford University Press 2002).

78 Established by agreement between the Government of Sierra Leone and the United Nations. See United Nations Security Council Resolution 1315, U.N. SCOR, 4186th meeting, U.N. Doc. S/RES/1315 (2000) of 14 August 2000.

79 The Statute of the SCSL, Article 6(1).

80 The Special Court had jurisdiction over the following crimes: crimes against humanity (Article 2), Violations of Article 3 Common to the Geneva Conventions and Additional Protocols II (Article 3), Other Serious Violations of International Humanitarian Law (Article 4), and Crimes under Sierra Leonean Law (Article 5). See generally the Statute of the SCSL.

81 This is a logical inference made from the wordings of the different international instruments that have recognised instigation as a mode of participation in international criminal law. These instruments are: the Rome Statute of the ICC, Article 25(3); the Statute of the SCSL, Article 6(1); the Statute of the ICTR, Article 6(1); the Statute of the ICTY, Article 7(1); the Draft Code of Crimes against the Peace and Security of Mankind, 1996, Article 2(3)(f); the Draft Code of Offences against the Peace and Security of Mankind, 1954, Article 2(13)(ii); the Charter of the IMTFE, Article 5; the Allied Control Council Law No. 10, Article II(2); and the Charter of the IMT, Nuremberg, Article 6(c).

In identifying and articulating the ingredients of instigation, I have built a list based on the jurisprudence of the ICTR. The essence of this is to illustrate how the Trial and Appeal Chambers have construed the word 'instigation' as it featured in its Statute. The two articles in which instigation features in the Statute of the ICTR have different requirements for the imposition of criminal responsibility. However, what constitutes instigation under both Articles is not so different. As discussed in Chapter Five, it is logical to argue that what would constitute instigation under Article 6(1) would not be different from instigation under Article 2(3)(c). However, such instigation must meet the statutory caveats for criminal responsibility to be imposed: it must be direct, public, and to commit the crime of genocide. On the other hand, under Article 6(1), such instigation must lead to any of the stages of any of the crimes over which the ICTR has jurisdiction.[82]

I put together all cases related to instigation, whether under Article 6(1) as a mode of participation, or Article 2(3)(c), which creates and punishes the inchoate crime of direct and public incitement to commit genocide. This structured analysis explains the key ingredients of instigation under the ICTR. The ICTR case-law does not structure its analysis of instigation this way. However, its case-law can be used in discussing these ingredients given the fact that these ingredients are all reflected in the judgments.

The Trial Chambers, in every given case, examined the nature of the accused's acts, the audience to which the accused spoke, the medium used, the context within which the speech was made and the resulting acts after the speech, to determine whether the accused, by such words, desired or intended to have the crimes committed. In developing the jurisprudence on instigation, the Trial Chambers have shown some degree of consistency. The judges have reasoned with the jurisprudence of the Nuremberg Tribunal, especially with regards to the *Julius Streicher Case*.[83] They have also stayed the line of logic reflected in the judgments of the various Trial Chambers at the ICTR in the different cases. While it is elusive to get a complete watertight definition in one case, it is easier to identify the common elements as articulated by the Trial and Appeal Chambers in the different cases in which it became an issue for adjudication.

---

82 As I discuss and argue in Chapter Four below, that is the strict and correct construction of Article 6(1) as opposed to what the Trial and Appeal Chambers have established that criminal responsibility would be imposed only if the accused's mode of participation substantially contributed to the commission of a crime over which the ICTR has jurisdiction.

83 For example, see the following cases: *Nahimana* et al (n. 5) (TC) para. 981; *Akayesu* (n. 3) para. 550.

There are four elements. Instigation as a mode of participation under the Statute of the ICTR (both under Articles 2(3)(c) and 6(1)) has been construed by both the Trial and Appeal Chambers to constitute four ingredients:

i. the accused made speeches, gestures or promises to some other person(s);
ii. that these speeches, gestures or promises had the effect of suggesting, encouraging, urging, prompting the commission of a crime;
iii. that the accused intended, or had knowledge that these crimes would be committed; and
iv. depending on whether criminal responsibility is being imposed under Article 6(1) or Article 2(3)(c), the Trial Chambers have added another requirement that such an instigation must substantially contribute to the commission of the crime if criminal responsibility is to be imposed under Article 6(1) of the Statute.

3.4.1 *Instigation Comprises Speeches, Words, Gestures*

Different cases tried at the Tribunal have given different definitions to, and ingredients of instigation. Instigation has been defined to include words, acts, speeches, gestures, which have the nature or effect of encouraging, persuading, prompting[84] or urging some other person to commit a crime.[85] This gamut of words is endless. The kinds of words or gestures that would amount to instigation vary. It may depend on the political context as well as cultural realities within every given community. So, where phrases such as 'go to work' or 'the job is not over' have been used in a country undergoing ethnic cleansing, they have been construed to qualify as instigation.

In *Akayesu*,[86] the Trial Chamber found that in the early hours of 19 April 1994, the accused joined a crowd of over a hundred people which had gathered around the body of a young member of *Interahamwe*[87] in Gishyeshe.[88] The accused took the opportunity to address the people, urged them to unite in order to eliminate the enemy.[89] During this meeting, the accused also received from the *Interahamwe* documents containing the names of

---

84 *Akayesu* (n. 3) para. 482.

85 *Akayesu* (n. 3) paras. 551–55. See also *Semanza* (n. 4) para. 381.

86 *Akayesu* (n. 3).

87 In Kinyarwanda, it means a group of persons who stand, fight or attack together. It was a Hutu paramilitary organisation during the Rwandan genocide.

88 *Akayesu* (n. 3) para. 673 (i).

89 *Akayesu* (n. 3) para. 673 (ii).

Rwandan Patriotic Front (RPF) accomplices, which he read out.[90] The Trial Chamber held that this amounted to instigation.

In *The Prosecutor v Georges Ruggiu*,[91] the accused, charged with, *inter alia*, direct and public incitement to commit genocide, admitted he made the following broadcasts over *RTLM*:

- he condemned the attitude of Agathe Uwilingiyimana, the Prime Minister, who was compromising the Rwandan political institutions and, further, demanded that she leave office;
- he congratulated the valiant combatants who were engaged in a battle against the 'Inyenzi' at Nyamirambo, including civilians, Interahamwe militiamen, members of political parties and military combatants;
- there would be a reward offered by the government for any one who killed or captured a white man fighting on the side of the RPF;
- they were having a 'good time' killing the Inyenzi and the population was determined to fight and chase the Inyenzi-Inkotanyi out of the country. He further called on the youth to 'work' with the Army;
- the population should be mobilised and the youth should 'work' throughout the country with the Army and the government to defend the country....[92]

The accused further admitted that his broadcasts over *RTLM* 'incited young Rwandans, *Interahamwe* militiamen and soldiers to engage in armed conflict against the "enemy" and its accomplices and to kill and inflict serious bodily and mental harm to Tutsis and moderate Hutus'.[93]

In the case of *Niyitegeka*,[94] the Trial Chamber found that on 13 May 1994, sometime between 7.00 am and 10.00 am, the accused 'was one of the leaders of a large-scale attack by thousands of armed attackers against Tutsi refugees at Muyira Hill.'[95] These attackers comprised *Interahamwe*, soldiers, policemen, and Hutu civilians. They chanted 'Tuba Tsemba Tsembe', which means 'Let's exterminate them', a reference to the Tutsis.[96] The Trial Chamber found that the accused, at this incident, was armed with a gun during the attack, in the course of which he shot at Tutsi refugees.[97] The attack resulted in the death of thousands of Tutsis. During this attack, the

---

90 *Akayesu* (n. 3) para. 673 (v).

91 Judgment, Case No.ICTR-97-32-I, T. Ch. I, 1 June 2000.

92 *Ruggiu* (n. 91) para. 44 (v). '*Inyenzi*' in Kinyarwanda means 'enemies', which referred to Tutsis.

93 Ibid.

94 *Niyitegeka* (n. 5).

95 Ibid para. 413.

96 Ibid.

97 Ibid.

accused instructed the attackers, showed them where to go and how to wage the attacks against the Tutsis.[98]

The Trial Chamber also found that the accused directly and publicly incited persons, including but not limited to local administrative officials, soldiers, civilian militias, communal police and local residents, 'to kill or cause serious bodily or mental harm to members of the Tutsi population with intent to destroy, in whole or in part, a racial or ethnic group'.[99] The charge of direct and public incitement to commit genocide was supported by evidence indicating that the accused held a meeting at Kucyapa after the large-scale attack on 13 May 1994 at Muyira Hill.[100] The purpose of this meeting was to decide the programme of killings for the next day, and to organise the killings of Tutsis in Bisesero.[101] The Trial Chamber found that the accused thanked the attackers for their participation in attacks.[102] He commended them for a 'good work', which was a reference to the killing of Tutsi civilians.[103] The accused told them 'to share the people's property and cattle, eat meat so that they would be strong to return the next day to continue the "work", that is, the killing.'[104] The following day, attacks were launched against the Tutsis in Bisesero throughout the day.[105] Having construed the meaning of the word 'work' used by the accused to mean the killing of Tutsis, the Trial Chamber found that the accused had the requisite intent to destroy, in whole or in part, the Tutsi ethnic group.[106] By 'urging attackers to work' and 'to eat meat so that they would be strong to return the next day to continue the "work"', the accused was held to be individually criminally responsible pursuant to Article 6(1) of the Statute of the ICTR.[107]

In the case of *Kajelijeli*,[108] the Trial Chamber found that on the morning of 7 April 1994, the accused instructed the *Interahamwe* at Byangabo Market and incited an assembled crowd there to 'kill and exterminate all those people in Rwankeri' and to 'exterminate the Tutsis'.[109] Furthermore, the accused ordered the *Interahamwe* to dress up and 'start to work'.[110]

98 Ibid.
99 Ibid para. 430.
100 Ibid para. 433.
101 Ibid.
102 Ibid.
103 Ibid.
104 Ibid.
105 Ibid.
106 Ibid para. 436.
107 Ibid para. 437.
108 *Kajelijeli* (n. 4).
109 Ibid para. 856.
110 Ibid.

On the basis of these statements made by the accused to the crowd, the Trial Chamber found it proved beyond reasonable doubt the accused was 'criminally responsible, pursuant to Article 6(1) of the Statute, for inciting directly and publicly the *Interahamwe* and the crowd to commit genocide by killing or causing serious bodily or mental harm to members of the Tutsi population in Rwankeri, Mukingo *Commune*.'[111]

In *Nahimana* et al,[112] the Trial Chamber found that the statements and publications of all three accused persons whipped up anti-Tutsi sentiment, and played a role in the atrocities perpetrated against the Tutsis and Hutu-moderates in Rwanda.[113]

In one of the publications carrying *The Ten Commandments* of the Bahutu people, its introduction warned its readers:

> The enemy is still there, among us, and is biding his time to try again, at a more propitious moment, to decimate us.
>
> Therefore, Hutu, wherever you may be, wake up! Be firm and vigilant. Take all necessary measures to deter the enemy from launching a fresh attack.[114]

The second part of the article was entitled 'The Tutsi ambition', in which Tutsis were described as 'bloodthirsty'. It referred to their continuing ideology of Tutsi domination over Hutus, and to the 'permanent dream of Tutsi' to restore Tutsi minority rule in the country. In another article, the Hutus were exhorted to wake up 'now or never' and be aware of a new Hutu

---

111 Ibid para. 860. It is noteworthy that these two paragraphs are just contradictory. Direct and public incitement to commit genocide is punishable under Article 2(3)(c) of the Statute. In cases where such an incitement, being direct and public, results in the commission of a crime, that same incitement would cause the instigator (accused person) to incur criminal responsibility under Article 6(1). It would have been legally correct for the Trial Chamber to establish that the accused incurs criminal responsibility under Article 6(1) of the Statute by virtue of the fact that his instigation, direct and public, resulted in the commission of genocide or crimes against humanity. It is incongruous with the wordings and jurisprudence of Article 6(1) and Article 2(3)(c) of the Statute to hold that 'the Accused is criminally responsible, pursuant to Article 6(1) of the Statute, for inciting directly and in public the *Interahamwe* and the crowd to commit genocide by killing or causing serious bodily or mental harm to members of the Tutsi population in Rwankeri, Mukingo *Commune*.' (para. 860). It would be correct for the Trial Chamber to say that the accused, by directly and publicly inciting the commission of genocide, incurs criminal responsibility under Article 2(3)(c) of the Statute. Furthermore, if such incitement resulted in the commission of genocide, the Trial Chamber ought to have stated that the accused's act of inciting the *Interahamwe* and crowd to commit genocidal acts, which were in fact committed, would incur criminal responsibility under Article 6(1) of the Statute.

112 *Nahimana* et al (n. 5) (TC).

113 See generally *Nahimana* et al (n. 5) (TC) paras. 949–1045.

114 *The Prosecutor v Ferdinand Nahimana, Jean Bosco Barayagwiza and Hassan Ngeze*, Judgment Summary, Case No. ICTR-99-52-T. T. Ch. I, 3 December 2003, Para. 12.

ideology. Hutu readers were urged to 'be prepared to defend themselves against this scourge', and to 'cease feeling pity for the Tutsi!'

The Trial Chamber found that *The Appeal to the Conscience of the Hutu* and *The Ten Commandments* of the Hutu included within it, published in *Kangura* No. 6 in December 1990, conveyed both contempt and hatred for the Tutsi ethnic group, and for Tutsi women in particular as enemy agents. The former publication conveyed Tutsi women as a 'ruthless enemy, determined to conquer the Hutu, and called on the Hutu to take all necessary measures to stop the enemy.'[115] The cover of *Kangura*, edition No. 26, promoted violence by conveying the message that the machete should be used to eliminate the Tutsis once and for all. It was a direct and public call for the destruction of the Tutsi ethnic group. Through hate propaganda and fear-mongering, *Kangura* paved the way for the preparation for, and perpetration of, genocide and other atrocities in Rwanda. It did this by 'whipping the Hutu population into a killing frenzy'.[116] The Trial Chamber also found that Hassan Ngeze manned and supervised roadblocks in Gisenyi in 1994 that identified targeted Tutsi civilians who were subsequently taken to and killed at the Commune Rouge. He often drove around with a megaphone in his vehicle, mobilising the population to come to CDR meetings and spreading the message that the *Inyenzi* would be exterminated, *Inyenzi* meaning, and understood to mean, the Tutsi ethnic minority. The Trial Chamber found that these words amounted to instigation to kill Tutsi civilians.[117]

Ferdinand Nahimana, in a Radio Rwanda broadcast on 25 April 1994, said he was happy *RTLM* had played an instrumental role in awakening the Hutu majority, and that the population had stood up with a view to halting the enemy.[118] He equated the enemy with the Tutsi ethnic group.[119] As the mastermind of *RTLM*, the Trial Chamber found that Ferdinand Nahimana 'set in motion the communications weaponry that fought the war of media, words, newspapers and radio stations' he described in his Radio Rwanda broadcast of 25 April as a complement to bullets.[120]

Jean-Bosco Barayagwiza said in public meetings 'let's exterminate them', with 'them' meaning the Tutsi population.[121] After separating the Tutsi

[115] *Nahimana* et al (n. 114) para. 16.
[116] *Nahimana* et al (n. 114) para. 17.
[117] *Nahimana* et al (n. 114) para. 64.
[118] *Nahimana* et al (n. 114) paras. 1–78.
[119] Ibid.
[120] Ibid.
[121] Ibid.

from the Hutu and humiliating the Tutsi by forcing them to perform the *Ikinyemera* (a traditional dance), at several public meetings, he threatened to kill them and said it would not be difficult. These statements, as the Trial Chamber ruled, amounted to direct and public incitement to genocide.[122]

In *The Prosecutor v Joseph Serugendo*,[123] the charges against the accused concerned 'the *Interahamwe* and the killing campaign, and RTLM re-installation and operation in July 1994. With regard to the first of these issues, Serugendo [the accused], as a member of the *Interahamwe*, is alleged to have planned with other leaders of the MRND between 1992 and 17 July 1994 political meetings and rallies in order to indoctrinate, sensitize, and incite members of the *Interahamwe* to kill or cause serious bodily or mental harm to members of the Tutsi population, with the aim of destroying the Tutsi ethnic group'.[124]

The accused acknowledged these allegations, stating that between early 1992 and 1994, he, as a member of *Inherahamwe*, 'planned with the leaders of the MRND, and the *Interahamwe* militias, political meetings and rallies aimed at inciting members of the *Interahamwe* to kill or cause serious harm to members of the Tutsi population with the goal of destroying the Tutsi ethnic group'.[125]

In *Bikindi*,[126] the accused broadcast over loudspeakers statements such as 'the majority' to 'rise up and look everywhere possible' and not to 'spare anybody' (referring to the Tutsis as the minority). The Trial Chamber held that this 'unequivocally constitutes a direct call to destroy the Tutsi ethnic group'.[127] The Trial Chamber found that the accused's address to the population while returning from Kayove, asking 'Have you killed the Tutsis here?' and whether they had killed the 'snakes' was a 'direct call to kill Tutsis, pejoratively referred to as snakes'.[128]

In *Kalimanzira*,[129] the Trial Chamber found that the accused attended a public meeting at the Nyabisagara football field 'where he thanked the audience for their efforts at getting rid of the enemy, but warned them not to grow complacent, to remain armed at all times, and exhorted the crowd to keep searching for enemies hidden in the bush or in other persons

122 *Nahimana* et al (n. 114) para. 102.
123 Judgment, Case No.ICTR-2005-84-I, T. Ch. I, 12 June 2006.
124 *Serugendo* (n. 123) para. 20. See also *The Prosecutor v Joseph Serugendo*, Corrigendum of Indictment, Case No. ICTR-2005-84-I, OTP, 21 July 2005, Para. 8.
125 *Serugendo* (n. 123) para. 21.
126 *Bikindi* (n. 5).
127 *Bikindi* (n. 5) para. 423.
128 Ibid.
129 *Kalimanzira* (n. 3).

homes, which they did'.[130] The Trial Chamber also found that the accused instructed them to destroy the homes of dead Tutsis and plant trees in their place. The Trial Chamber held that 'by instructing the people present to kill any surviving Tutsis, demolish their homes, and wipe out any traces of their existence, there is no reasonable doubt that the accused intended to incite the audience present to commit acts of genocide'.[131]

In *Muvunyi*,[132] the accused was charged with inciting the local population to perpetrate massacres against the Tutsis at the Butare prefecture.[133] The Trial Chamber found that during this meeting, the accused said that the Hutus had made a mistake in marrying the young Tutsi girls and hiding them. One witness mentioned that the accused said that such Hutus had to hand over the Tutsis. The accused used proverbs such as 'when a snake wraps itself around a calabash, you have to kill the snake and break the calabash'.[134]

From the above, it is evident that words, gestures and speeches comprise instigation. In the cases discussed above, the various Trial Chambers held that the words, gestures and speeches to the public, made orally or via printed media, amounted to instigation.

3.4.2 *Instigation Implies a Suggestion that the Crime must or Should be Committed*

The words, acts, speeches, promises, threats or gestures must have the effect of suggesting, encouraging, urging, or prompting another to commit a crime.[135] It is the impact of these on the mind of the person instigated that results in the crime. The person uttering these words has the desire to see the crime committed. However, the instigator influences the mind of another by encouraging, urging, prompting the person instigated to commit the crime. Given that there existed a plan to eliminate Tutsis and Hutu-moderates, a plan which was voluntarily subscribed to by the broader Hutu majority, all the statements and gestures made by the accused persons,

130 Ibid para. 613.
131 Ibid.
132 *Muvunyi* (n. 5).
133 Ibid para. 2.
134 *Muvunyi* (n. 5) para. 63.
135 *Alfred Musema v The Prosecutor*, Judgment, Case No. ICTR-96-13-A, Appeal Chamber, 16 November 2001, Para. 381. See also *Ntakirutimana and Ntakirutimana* (n. 4) para. 787; *Kayishema and Ruzindana* (n. 4) (AC) paras. 186, 198; *Bagilishema* (n. 4) paras. 30, 33; *Musema* (n. 4) para. 126; *Rutaganda* (n. 4) para. 34; *Kayishema and Ruzindana* (n. 4) (TC) paras. 199, 207; *Akayesu* (n. 3) para. 477.

from *Akayesu*[136] to *Kalimanzira*,[137] were made with the understanding that the crimes must or should be committed.

3.4.3 *Instigator must Intend or Have Knowledge that the Crime will be Committed*

The instigator's desire is to see a crime committed.[138] A person seeks to have this done through another person. The use of words, threats, making of promises and different kinds of gestures are intended to impact (influence) the mind of another so that he or she engages in this criminal activity and materialises it by committing the crime. The person instigated brings to completion the criminal desires of another person (the instigator).

These statements to the broader Hutu population were mostly made at the time a full-scale perpetration of atrocities had commenced. The political realities and cultural contexts suggested the existence of a state of intense animosity between these two ethnicities. These statements were made in the hope that they would cause Hutu civilians and other militia groups to kill the Tutsis. Every statement made by every accused person that qualified as instigation was made with the intention that the crimes instigated would be committed.

In *Ruggiu*,[139] the accused admitted that over *Radio Télévision Libre des Milles Colignes* (*RTLM*), he intermittently played songs with the intention to encourage the population to fight the enemy. One such song was 'Naanga Abakwtie', which means 'I do not like the Hutu'.[140] The accused acknowledged that 'RTLM broadcasts reflected the political ideology and plans of extremist Hutus, particularly members of MRND and the Coalition for the Defence of the Republic'.[141]

In *Niyitegeka*,[142] more important and relevant paragraphs of the Trial Chamber's judgment detail not just the accused's participation, but also the existence of a joint criminal enterprise: that is, 'persons acting with a

136 *Akayesu* (n. 3).
137 *Kalimanzira* (n. 3).
138 *Kayishema and Ruzindana* (n. 4) (AC) paras. 118–19. See also *Ntakirutimana and Ntakirutimana* (n. 4) para. 787; *Musema* (n. 126) para. 379; *Bagilishema* (n. 4) paras. 30, 33; *Musema* (n. 4) para. 126; *Rutaganda* (n. 4) para. 43; *Kayishema and Ruzindana* (n. 4) (TC) paras. 199, 207; *Akayesu* (n. 3) para. 477.
139 *Ruggiu* (n. 91).
140 Ibid para. 44 (x).
141 *Ruggiu* (n. 91) para. 44 (xi).
142 *Niyitegeka* (n. 5).

common purpose'.[143] The Trial Chamber stated the different roles played by the accused and concluded as follows:

> Based on the above [the different acts committed by the accused], together with the Accused's leadership role and personal participation in the attacks in Bisesero, where the Interahamwe were chanting 'Let's exterminate them', being in reference to the Tutsi; the Accused's association with officials and prominent figures at these attacks; his acts of shooting at Tutsi during these attacks; his act of killing the old man and young boy, both Tutsi, his transportation of weapons and procurement of gendarmes for an attack on Mubuga Church against the Tutsi hiding inside, the Chamber finds the Accused perpetrated these acts with the requisite intent to destroy, in whole or in part, the Tutsi ethnic group.[144]

As the cases of *Ruggiu* (*supra*) and *Niyitegeka* (*supra*) suggest, an instigator's intention can be established by looking at the purpose underlying the statements made. In *Ruggiu*,[145] though he played songs over *RTLM*, his intention was to encourage the population (Hutus) to fight the enemy (the Tutsis). In *Niyitegeka*,[146] the Trial Chamber established that the accused's intention to have the crimes committed could be discerned from his membership in a joint criminal enterprise in which different individuals had a common plan: to have the crimes committed.

3.4.4 *The Instigation must Substantially Contribute to the Commission of the Crime*

Although this is not required under Article 2(3)(c) which deals with the inchoate crime of direct and public incitement to commit genocide, it is required for the imposition of criminal responsibility under Article 6(1): the jurisprudence of the Tribunal points to the existence of a causal link between the instigation and the crime committed. The words, threats, promises and gestures must substantially contribute to the commission of the crime.[147] In other words, there must be proof of a causal link between the instigation and the resultant crime.[148] However, the Trial and Appeal Chambers have not defined what 'substantial contribution' is. Neither have they outlined any guidelines on how to make a determination as to whether

143 Ormerod (n. 2) 182; Heaton (n. 2) 386–91.
144 Ibid paras. 416, 419.
145 *Ruggiu* (n. 91).
146 *Niyitegeka* (n. 5).
147 *Musema* (n. 4) para. 120.
148 *Kayishema and Ruzindana* (n. 4) (TC) paras. 199, 207. See also *Akayesu* (n. 3) paras. 480–84.

an accused's mode of participation was substantial or not. Unfortunately, the judgments of both the Trial and Appeal Chambers do not discuss the meaning of 'substantial contribution'. This leaves any scholar in search of definitions and guidelines in uncertainty and triggers speculation. The key question here is whether 'substantial contribution' means having a significant role in the decision of the person instigated to commit the crime. Furthermore, looking at the broad and complex issues that surround causation in criminal law, another question comes up: must the instigation be the operative cause of the commission of the crime? In other words, to what extent must it impact the commission of the crime for the instigator to be held criminally responsible?

This requirement has been consistently made by the Trial and Appeal Chambers since its first judgment in *Akayesu*.[149] However, it is limited to cases where instigation would lead to the imposition of criminal responsibility under Article 6(1). In cases since *Akayesu*,[150] the Trial and Appeal Chambers have consistently repeated this requirement of a substantial contribution to the crime for there to be the imposition of criminal responsibility under Article 6(1).[151] As I argue, this requirement is the unfortunate outcome of the poor construction of Article 6(1).

In the previous paragraphs, I have examined the ingredients of instigation under both Articles 2(3)(c) (which deals with direct and public incitement to commit genocide) and 6(1) (which makes instigation a mode of participation in any crime over which the Tribunal has jurisdiction). These ingredients were never developed in any single case. Rather, the collection was obtained after a thorough examination of different cases on instigation (under both Articles 2(3)(c) and 6(1)). With an understanding of these ingredients, I now look at how they have been applied in the various cases in which instigation (under Article 2(3)(c), 6(1), or both) came up.

3.5 Applying the Ingredients of Instigation to ICTR Case-Law

To examine the jurisprudence of the ICTR on instigation, the first task is to identify two classes of cases: first, cases in which it came up for adjudication by the Trial Chambers as a mode of participation in any crime; and

149 *Akayesu* (n. 3).
150 Ibid.
151 *Hategekimana* (n. 4) para. 644; *Kalimanzira* (n. 3) para. 161; *Kajelijeli* (n. 4) para. 759; *Ntakirutimana and Ntakirutimana* (n. 4) para. 787; *Kayishema and Ruzindana* (n. 4) (AC) paras. 186, 198; *Bagilishema* (n. 4) paras. 30, 33; *Musema* (n. 4) para. 126; *Rutaganda* (n. 4) para. 34; *Kayishema and Ruzindana* (n. 4) (TC) paras. 199, 207; *Akayesu* (n. 3) para. 477.

second, in cases of direct and public incitement to commit genocide. In most of the cases, these two overlapped: instigation as a mode of participation was accompanied by a charge of direct and public incitement to commit genocide. However, in a few cases, a charge of direct and public incitement to commit genocide was the lone charge. As an inchoate offence punishable by the Tribunal, it was not accompanied by instigation as a mode of participation.

3.5.1 *The Trial Chambers' Jurisprudence on Instigation*

In the previous sections, I have examined instigation. First, I looked at it as an inchoate crime under common law. Second, I traced its legislative history in key international instruments. Third, featuring in the Statute of the ICTR, I examined the ingredients of instigation, into which I fitted the cases of the ICTR. It is important to note that both the Trial and Appeal Chambers of the ICTR, in cases related to instigation, neither developed nor approached it in this way. Rather, they discussed it on a case-to-case basis. However, they reflect some consistency in portraying these ingredients.

In putting together these ingredients, I looked at instigation more broadly. In other words, I made no distinction as to whether it is under Article 6(1) or Article 2(3)(c). As mentioned earlier, these two Articles are not mutually exclusive, for instigation may lead to the imposition of criminal responsibility under either or both of these Articles. In such cases, instigation must meet the different statutory requirements. Under Article 6(1), it is sufficient to prove that the words or gestures made by the instigator led to either the planning, preparation or execution of any of the crimes over which the Tribunal has jurisdiction. However, that same instigation would lead to the imposition of criminal responsibility under Article 2(3)(c) if it is proved that it was direct, public, and to commit the crime of genocide.

In the following paragraphs, I move from a general discussion of instigation as it appears broadly under the Statute of the ICTR to a more specific theme: its application under Article 6(1). Instigation is one of the modes of participation under Article 6(1) of the Statute of the ICTR. Given the different elements of instigation, it is necessary to examine the cases where it came up as a mode of imposing criminal responsibility. Furthermore, I must look at the way the Trial Chambers construed it as a mode of participation.

The essence of this exercise is to know how the Trial Chambers of the ICTR have approached instigation as a mode of participation under Article

6(1). This information will be pivotal in Chapter Five where I critique the Trial Chambers' construction of Article 6(1). More specifically, in making a well-reasoned argument on how the Trial and Appeal Chambers have erroneously construed Article 6(1), I am compelled to discuss the nature and state of jurisprudence as it exists now. This will form the basis upon which I give Article 6(1) a broad statutory construction, highlighting both its bifurcated and inchoate nature. Furthermore, in arguing that Article 6(1) and Article 2(3) are not mutually exclusive when it comes to instigation, these narratives and details are more than necessary because, first, they corroborate my arguments, and second, they give the reader the basic details of the work of the Trial and Appeal Chambers on this subject. I will take a chronological look at the cases where instigation featured as a mode of participation under Article 6(1).

Akayesu[152] was the first trial to be conducted and completed by the ICTR. The Trial Chamber faced numerous challenges such as finding definitions to the different modes of participation under Article 6(1) of the Statute of the ICTR,[153] the meaning of direct and public incitement to commit genocide and its inchoate character,[154] and the issue of cumulative convictions (instances where the same facts amount to different offences over which the Tribunal has jurisdiction).[155] *Akayesu*[156] has become the thrust of the jurisprudence on the procedural and substantive content of the Statute, often cited by the Trial Chambers.

In *Akayesu*,[157] one of the important issues for adjudication was the wording of Article 6(1).[158] Article 6(1) defines the various modes of participation (in the planning, preparation or execution of the crimes over which the ICTR has jurisdiction) through which a person would incur criminal responsibility. Under Article 6(1), a person who 'planned, instigated, ordered, committed or otherwise aided and abetted in the planning, preparation or execution of a crime' over which the Tribunal has jurisdiction shall be individually responsible for such a crime. The inference to make here is simple: in addition to incurring criminal responsibility as a principal actor, the accused would incur responsibility, if at any stage in the preparation or execution of the crime, he ordered, planned, instigated, aided and

152 *Akayesu* (n. 3).
153 Ibid paras. 472–85.
154 *Akayesu* (n. 3) paras. 481, 549–62.
155 *Akayesu* (n. 3) paras. 461–70.
156 *Akayesu* (n. 3).
157 Ibid.
158 Article 6(1) is the Statute's statement of primary and direct criminal responsibility.

abetted another person or persons to commit any of the crimes over which the Tribunal has jurisdiction.

Article 6(1) widened its umbrella to cover those who became involved at different stages of the criminal activity; from conception or planning to materialisation.[159] This is a requirement of causation. Article 6(1) carries a statutory caveat: criminal responsibility will only be imposed if the participation of such a person actually led to the commission of the crime.[160] In other words, where such ordering, planning, instigation or aiding and abetting[161] does not lead to the commission of the crime, there is no criminal responsibility.[162] The only exception to this is the inchoate offence of attempt to commit genocide, which, per the Statute, is punishable without the offence of genocide being committed.

Akayesu[163] posits a point of law: criminal responsibility can be imposed on an individual only when it is proved that his mode of participation (instigation) actually led to the commission of any crime over which the ICTR has jurisdiction.[164] By analogy, where the instigation does not lead to the commission of any these crimes, criminal responsibility cannot be imposed under Article 6(1). Criminal responsibility under Article 6(1) requires actual commission of the crime. Instigation without any resulting crime is not punishable as an inchoate crime under Article 6(1) of the Statute. The notion of inchoate crimes does not exist when the crime in question qualifies as crimes against humanity, war crimes or violations of the laws of war. There is no inchoate crime as conspiracy to commit crimes against humanity as well as war crimes. So, an accused person who planned, ordered, instigated or aided and abetted the commission of crimes against humanity or war crime is not criminally responsible if such a crime was never committed.

---

159 The Trial Chamber held that 'Article 6(1) covers various stages of the commission of a crime.' *Akayesu* (n. 3) para. 473. This line of reasoning was endorsed and continued by the Trial Chamber in its judgment in *Kayishema and Ruzindana* (n. 4) (TC) para. 196.

160 *Hategekimana* (n. 4) para. 644; *Kalimanzira* (n. 3) para. 161; *Kajelijeli* (n. 4) para. 759; *Ntakirutimana and Ntakirutimana* (n. 4) para. 787; *Kayishema and Ruzindana* (n. 4) (AC) paras. 186, 198; *Bagilishema* (n. 4) paras. 30, 33; *Musema* (n. 4) para. 126; *Rutaganda* (n. 4) para. 43; *Kayishema and Ruzindana* (n. 4) (TC) paras. 199, 207; *Akayesu* (n. 3) para. 477.

161 In *Akayesu*, the words 'aiding and abetting' were given a disjunctive construction by the Trial Chamber. See *Akayesu* (n. 3) para. 484. In *Kayishema and Ruzindana*, the Trial Chamber held that 'aiding and abetting' were not synonymous to the other forms of participation, and could give rise to individual responsibility. See *Kayishema and Ruzindana* (n. 4) (TC) para. 196.

162 *Akayesu* (n. 3) para. 473.

163 *Akayesu* (n. 3).

164 *Akayesu* (n. 3) para. 482.

The Trial Chamber approved this line of thinking as the Nuremberg Charter and Tribunal did in the cases before it. It construed Article 6(1) to be consistent with the judgments of Nuremberg, which held that persons who ordered, planned, instigated the commission of the crimes would be individually criminally responsible for them.[165] This reasoning was further affirmed by the wording of the Draft Code of Crimes against the Peace and Security of Mankind, which mentioned the five forms of participation and deemed criminal responsibility to be imposed only when the crime in question 'in fact occurs'.[166]

Recognising that instigation and incitement are synonymous with each other and can be used interchangeably,[167] the Trial Chamber established that these two concepts, instigation and incitement, have different meanings under some legal systems, especially Civil Law. The Trial Chamber remarked that even if it were to assume that the two concepts are synonymous with each other, the important question to be answered was whether instigation as a form of participation under Article 6(1) of the Statute required the 'direct and public' elements as it was included in the qualification of the type of incitement necessary for the crime of genocide. The Trial Chamber further held that instigation as a form of participation per Article 6(1) of the Statute involves 'prompting another to commit an offence'; but is different from incitement in that it is punishable only where the instigation actually leads to the commission of the offence desired by the instigator.[168]

In *Kayishema and Ruzindana*,[169] the prosecutor charged one of the accused persons for direct and public incitement to commit genocide. Though such a charge failed due to a lack of supporting evidence, the Trial Chamber engaged in a statutory construction of Article 6(1) of the Statute. Staying in line with the logic of the Trial Chamber in *Akayesu*,[170] the Trial Chamber found no reason to depart from the 'logical and well-founded expressions of international law', holding that 'if any of the modes of participation delineated in Article 6(1) can be shown, and the necessary *actus*

165 *Akayesu* (n. 3) paras. 473–74.

166 *Akayesu* (n. 3) para. 475. See also the ILC, Article 2(3).

167 *Akayesu* (n. 3) para. 481. See also *Kalimanzira* (n. 3) para. 511.

168 *Akayesu* (n. 3) para. 482. However, instigation was held to be synonymous with incitement and provocation in *Kalimanzira* (n. 3) para. 511. This in effect overturned the opinion of the Trial Chamber in *Akayesu* where it held that these words were not synonymous (*Akayesu* (n. 3) paras. 481–82 as in some legal systems).

169 *Kayishema and Ruzindana* (n. 4) (TC).

170 *Akayesu* (n. 3).

reus and *mens rea* are evidenced, then that would suffice to adduce criminal responsibility'[171] under Article 6(1). The Trial Chamber established a two-stage test which must be satisfied in order to establish criminal responsibility under Article 6(1). This test requires first, demonstration that the person participated. In other words, it must be proved that the person's conduct contributed to the commission of an illegal act (crime over which the Tribunal has jurisdiction). Second, that such a person acted with knowledge or intent, which comprises an awareness that he is participating in a crime.[172]

Elaborating on the first point, the Trial Chamber considered what amounted to the *actus reus* of participation. Acknowledging the jurisprudence of the Tribunal on this in *Akayesu*[173] and that of the ICTY in *The Prosecutor v Duško Tadić*,[174] it found it firmly established that for an accused person to be criminally responsible, it must be proved beyond every reasonable doubt that his conduct contributed to, or 'had an effect on' the commission of the crime. However, what constitutes the *actus reus* of participation and the requisite contribution of the accused 'inevitably varies with each mode of participation set out in Article 6(1).'[175]

Participation does not require physical presence of the accused at the place of the crime.[176] Furthermore, his or her contribution need not be a direct one.[177] Neither must his or her role be 'a tangible one.'[178] Each of the modes of participation may, independently, give rise to criminal responsibility.

Given the breadth of the scope of participation that may give rise to criminal responsibility under Article 6(1), the Trial Chamber required a 'clear awareness that this participation will lead to the commission of a crime.'[179]

---

171 *Kayishema and Ruzindana* (n. 4) (TC) para. 197.

172 *Kayishema and Ruzindana* (n. 4) (TC) para. 198.

173 *Akayesu* (n. 3) paras. 480–84.

174 Judgment, Case No. IT-94-1, T. Ch., 7 May 1997, Paras. 673–74, 688–92.

175 *Kayishema and Ruzindana* (n. 4) (TC) para. 199. See also *Akayesu* (n. 3) paras. 480–85.

176 *Kayishema and Ruzindana* (n. 4) (TC) para. 200.

177 Ibid.

178 Ibid.

179 *Kayishema and Ruzindana* (n. 4) (TC) para. 203, footnote 117, where the Trial Chamber held as follows: 'Crime' here refers to any of the crimes over which the Tribunal has jurisdiction (genocide, crimes against humanity and violations of Article 3 Common to the Geneva Conventions and Additional Protocols II). The actual commission of a crime will suffice. The only distinctions are those statutorily provided under the definition of genocide and the offences punishable, such as conspiracy to commit genocide, attempt to commit genocide and direct and public incitement to genocide (which are all inchoate offences, and are punishable irrespective of whether the crime of genocide is committed).

The prosecution has the onus of proving that through the accused's mode of participation, whether by acts or omissions, the accused contributed *substantially* to the commission of a crime, and that depending on the accused's mode of participation in question, he or she was at least aware that his or her conduct would contribute to the crime.[180]

In *Musema*,[181] the Trial Chamber followed the logic and conclusions reached by the Trial Chamber in *Akayesu*,[182] where its opinion on the principle of individual criminal responsibility under Article 6(1) of the Statute was stated. As the Trial Chamber affirmed, it reasoned its judgment as previous Trial Chambers in the cases of *Kayishema and Ruzindana*,[183] and *Rutaganda*[184] judgments. These judgments provided a compelling reason for the Trial Chamber to hold that the basic tenets underlying the imposition of criminal responsibility on the accused had been fulfilled.[185] As a consequence, the accused was found individually criminally responsible for the crimes for which he was charged.[186]

In one of its observations, the Trial Chamber stated that the wording of the principle of criminal responsibility under Article 6(1) implicitly requires that the planning or preparation actually leads to the commission of the crime.[187] However, a statutory exception to this observation is provided in Article 2(3) of the Statute, which makes direct and public incitement to commit genocide punishable. Criminal responsibility per this Article is not contingent upon the perpetration of the crime of genocide. The Genocide Convention, in creating, defining and punishing the crime of genocide, defined the specific acts that would qualify as genocidal and what acts would be punishable. A conspiracy to commit genocide (the common law notion of conspiracy consists of nothing more than an unequivocal agreement to perpetrate an unlawful act);[188] an attempt to commit genocide, complicity in the planning of genocide and direct and public incitement to commit genocide are all punishable per the ICTR Statute, as well as the Genocide Convention. As inchoate crimes, an attempt to commit genocide and conspiracy to commit genocide are crimes *per se*, and criminal liability for them is incurred once the elements of the inchoate crimes are proved.

180 *Kayishema and Ruzindana* (n. 4) (TC) para. 207.
181 *Musema* (n. 4).
182 Ibid para. 112.
183 *Kayishema and Ruzindana* (n. 4) (TC).
184 *Rutaganda* (n. 4).
185 *Musema* (n. 4) para. 113.
186 *Rutaganda* (n. 4).
187 *Musema* (n. 4) para. 115.
188 *Musema* (n. 4) paras. 190–91.

These inchoate crimes introduce a distinction as raised by the Trial and Appeal Chambers. Inchoate crimes such as conspiracy to commit genocide, direct and public incitement to commit genocide and an attempt to commit genocide are applicable only to the crime of genocide. In other words, there can be no attempt to commit crimes or conspiracy to commit crimes against humanity.[189] Given the nature of inchoate crimes, they are punishable irrespective of whether they lead to the actual commission of the main crime: this is so because the Statute of the ICTR makes them punishable as inchoate crimes.[190] Their definitions make them crimes in themselves, and a completed commission is irrelevant to criminal responsibility.[191]

In its analysis, the Trial Chamber defined the second form of participation, incitement to commit a crime, as involving 'instigating another, directly or publicly, to commit an offence.' Such instigation, it held, would be punishable only where it leads to the actual commission of the crime. The only exception to this, as aforementioned, is the case of genocide where Article 2(3)(c) of the Statute makes direct and public incitement to commit genocide punishable, irrespective of whether such direct and public incitement actually leads to the commission of the crime.[192]

The imposition of these strictures that the instigation be direct and public has so far not been followed by the Tribunal in any case since *Musema*.[193] Instigation as a mode of participation under Article 6(1) of the Statute of the ICTR must not be direct and public but must lead to the commission of any of the crimes over which the ICTR has jurisdiction.

In *Semanza*[194] the indictment alleges that between 1991 and 1994, the accused chaired numerous meetings during which he made threatening remarks against the Tutsis. During such meetings, he incited, planned, and organised massacres of Tutsi civilians,[195] for which he was charged for direct and public incitement to commit genocide.[196] The indictment

[189] The definition of criminal responsibility under Article 6(1) covers different modes of participation, and does not deal specifically with cases of inchoate crimes.

[190] Statute of the ICTR, Articles 2(3)(b)–(d). See also the Genocide Convention, Article 2(b)–(d); *Nahimana* et al (n. 114) para. 109 where the Trial Chamber adopted the definition of conspiracy as propounded earlier in the case of *Musema* (n. 4) as 'an agreement between two or more persons to commit the crime of genocide.'

[191] *Musema* (n. 4) para. 116.

[192] *Musema* (n. 4) para. 120.

[193] *Musema* (n. 4).

[194] *Semanza* (n. 4).

[195] *The Prosecutor v Laurent Semanza*, Indictment, Case No. ICTR-97-20, OTP, 13 February 1996, Paras. 3.7, 3.8.

[196] *Semanza* (n. 195) para. 11.

further states that between 7 April and 30 April, 1994, in Gikoro commune, the accused incited a group to rape Tutsi women before killing them. This actually resulted in the rape of two women and the death of one of them.[197] Therefore, the elements of *actus reus, mens rea,* and causation were all fulfilled in this instance. Counts 10, 11, 12, and 13 of the indictment charge the accused with rape, torture and murder as crimes against humanity respectively, and serious violations of Common Article 3 and Additional Protocol II (part of Count 13).[198] The indictment also alleges that on 8 April, 1994, Laurent Semanza instigated a group of *Interahamwe* in Bicumbi to kill members of a particular Tutsi family. This resulted in the death of four family members and two neighbours. These constitute the particulars of Count 14 of the indictment, charging him with murder as a crime against humanity.[199]

Citing Article 6(1) of the Statute of the ICTR, the Trial Chamber held that the principle of criminal responsibility is not limited to cases of individuals who physically commit a crime; but also to those who participate in, and contribute to a crime in other ways per the rules of accomplice liability.[200] Criminal liability under Article 6(1) can be imposed only when the crime within the Tribunal's jurisdiction must have been completed.[201] Inchoate crimes are not criminalised by Article 6(1) of the Statute.[202] However, they are punishable under the Statute for the crime of genocide.[203]

Additionally, to satisfy Article 6(1), the participation of the accused 'must have *substantially* contributed to, or have had a *substantial* effect on, the completion of a crime.'[204]

Instigation as a form of participation was construed to mean 'urging, encouraging, or prompting another person to commit a crime.'[205] An act qualifying as instigation must not be direct and public,[206] but requires

---

197 *Semanza* (n. 4) para. 12; *Semanza* (n. 195) para. 3.17.

198 *Semanza* (n. 4) para. 12.

199 *Semanza* (n. 4) para. 13; *Semanza* (n. 195) para. 3.19.

200 *Semanza* (n. 4) para. 376. See also *Kayishema and Ruzindana* (n. 4) (AC) para. 185; *Musema* (n. 4) para. 114; *Rutaganda* (n. 4) para. 33; *Kayishema and Ruzindana* (n. 4) (TC) paras. 196–97; *Akayesu* (n. 3) para. 473.

201 *Semanza* (n. 4) para. 375.

202 Ibid.

203 Statute of the ICTR, Article 2(3)(b), (c), and (d).

204 *Semanza* (n. 4) para. 379. See also *Ntakirutimana and Ntakirutimana* (n. 4) para. 787; *Kayishema and Ruzindana* (n. 4) (AC) paras. 186, 198; *Bagilishema* (n. 4) paras. 30, 33; *Musema* (n. 4) para. 126; *Rutaganda* (n. 4) para. 43; *Kayishema and Ruzindana* (n. 4) (TC) paras. 199, 207; *Akayesu* (n. 3) para. 477.

205 *Semanza* (n. 4) para. 381. See also *Bagilishema* (n. 4) para. 30;*Akayesu* (n. 3) para. 482.

206 *The Prosecutor v Jean-Paul Akayesu,* Judgment, Case No. ICTR-96-4-A, Appeal Chamber, 1 June 2001, Paras. 478–82.

proof of a causal connection between the act of instigation and the commission of the crime.[207]

In *Kajelijeli*,[208] the Trial Chambers recognised established jurisprudence to the effect that an accused person can incur criminal responsibility only if it is shown that his or her participation *substantially contributed to, or has had a substantial effect on, the completion of a crime under the Statute*.[209]

Defining instigation as a form of participation, the Trial Chamber described it as 'prompting another person to commit an offence',[210] adding that such an instigationneed not be direct or public.[211] It further held that both positive acts and omissions may qualify as instigation, but are punishable on proof of a causal relationship between the instigation and the commission of the crime.[212]

In *Kalimanzira*[213] one of the charges was direct and public incitement to commit genocide pursuant to Article 2(3)(c) of the Statute and individual criminal responsibility under Article 6(1).[214] In this case, the Trial Chamber was faced with the task of considering whether and when instigation will attract criminal responsibility under Article 6(1) and Article 2(3) of the Statute. Recognising the blurred distinction between instigation to commit genocide under Article 6(1) of the Statute and direct and public incitement to commit genocide under Article 2(3)(c) of the Statute, the Trial Chamber held that incitement is synonymous with instigation,[215] provocation and encouragement; all three words are capable of interchangeable usage when describing conduct underlying certain modes by which genocide may be committed. As has been established in previous cases, instigation under Article 6(1) is a mode of liability; and individual criminal responsibility would be incurred by an accused person only if the instigation in fact *substantially contributed to the commission of one of the crimes* over which the Tribunal has jurisdiction.[216] On the other hand, direct and public incitement to commit genocide is itself a crime, requiring no demonstration that

[207] *Bagilishema* (n. 4) para. 30.

[208] *Kajelijeli* (n. 4).

[209] *Kajelijeli* (n. 4) para. 759 (emphasis added). See also *Ntakirutimana and Ntakirutimana* (n. 4) para. 787; *Kayishema and Ruzindana* (n. 4) (AC) paras. 186, 198; *Bagilishema* (n. 4) paras. 30, 33; *Musema* (n. 4) para. 126; *Rutaganda* (n. 4) para. 43; *Kayishema and Ruzindana* (n. 4) (TC) paras. 199, 207; *Akayesu* (n. 3) para. 477.

[210] *Semanza* (n. 4) para. 381; *Bagilishema* (n. 4) para. 30.

[211] *Semanza* (n. 4) para. 381.

[212] *Semanza* (n. 4) para. 381; *Bagilishema* (n. 4) para. 30.

[213] *Kalimanzira* (n. 3).

[214] *Kalimanzira* (n. 3) para. 506.

[215] *Kalimanzira* (n. 3) para. 511.

[216] *Kalimanzira* (n. 3) para. 512.

the direct and public incitement in fact contributed in any way to the commission of genocidal acts.[217] Confronted with the arduous task of distinguishing the implications of instigation as a mode of participation under Article 6(1) and Article 2(3)(c) of the Statute, the Trial Chamber summarised the legal position as follows:

> – Incitement resulting in the commission of a genocidal act is punishable under the combination of Articles 2 (3) (a) and 6 (1) of the Statute as Genocide by way of Instigation;
> – Incitement resulting in the commission of a genocidal act and which may be described as 'direct' and 'public' is punishable under either Article 2 (3) (c) of the Statute as Direct and Public Incitement to Commit Genocide, or under the combination of Articles 2 (3) (a) and 6 (1) of the Statute as Genocide by way of Instigation;
> – Incitement not resulting in the commission of a genocidal act but which may be described as 'direct' and 'public' is only punishable under Article 2 (3) (c) of the Statute; and,
> – Incitement not resulting in the commission of a genocidal act, and which may not be described as 'direct' and 'public', is not punishable under the Statute.[218]

In *Hategekimana*[219] the Trial Chamber considered the jurisprudence of instigation as a mode of participation. Holding it to be synonymous with incitement, it defined instigation as prompting another person to commit a crime.[220] The *mens rea* comprises the intent to instigate another to commit a crime or, at a minimum, 'the awareness of the substantial likelihood that a crime will be committed in the execution of the acts or omissions instigated'.[221]

The above discussions expose the Trial Chambers' construction of, and approach to Article 6(1) of the Statute of the ICTR. These give the bases upon which I critically examine and appraise both the wording of Article 6(1) and the approach taken by the Trial Chambers in construing Article 6(1). That task, however, will be done in a subsequent part of this book (Chapter Four).

As recently as 2009, the recurrent confluence between Article 6(1) and Article 2(3)(c) of the Statute was addressed by the Trial Chamber in *Kalimanzira*.[222] It identified this intersection and developed the

217 *Kalimanzira* (n. 3).
218 *Kalimanzira* (n. 3).
219 *Hategekimana* (n. 4).
220 *Hategekimana* (n. 4) para. 644.
221 Ibid.
222 *Kalimanzira* (n. 3).

'Kalimanzira Principles' for them to be applied in cases where instigation appears under Article 6(1) and Article 2(3)(c) of the Statute. As I will argue in Chapter Four, these principles serve as guidelines, yet, remain seriously flawed because of their strict construction of, and limitation to the crime of genocide as a crime under Article 6(1) of the Statute.

In most of these cases dealing with direct and public incitement to commit genocide under Article 2(3)(c) of the Statute of the ICTR, a recurrent and defensive line of argument was predicated upon the right to free speech both as recognised in international law and a cornerstone of democracy.

3.6 The Free Speech Argument

A recurrent argument that was raised by the accused persons and deliberated upon by the Trial and Appeal Chambers of the ICTR deals with free speech as an established and recognised right in international law and a cornerstone of democracies. In *Akayesu*,[223] though not raised, the Trial Chamber looked at the Julius Streicher Case and the reasoning of the Nuremberg Tribunal in its judgment in analysing the role Julius Streicher played in the atrocities perpetrated by the Nazi Regime.[224] In *Nahimana* et al,[225] the Trial Chamber articulated that the 'case squarely addresses the role of the media in the genocide that took place in Rwanda in 1994'.[226] In *Bikindi*,[227] the Trial Chamber made an assessment of the historical, cultural and political context of Simon Bikindi's songs, and if they impacted the planning, preparation and commission of the atrocities in Rwanda.[228] In all these cases, the right to free speech has been discussed, and the jurisprudence of the Trial and Appeal Chambers establish clearly that though a right in international law and a cornerstone of democracies, there are limits to free speech. Furthermore, in assessing the impact of a speech that amounts to instigation, three key guidelines have to be looked at: first, the purpose of the speech; second, the context in which it was made; and third, if there was a causal link between the speech and the resulting crimes committed.[229]

223 *Akayesu* (n. 3).
224 Ibid para. 550.
225 *Nahimana* et al (n. 5) (TC).
226 Ibid para. 979.
227 *Bikindi* (n. 5).
228 Ibid paras. 378–97.
229 *Nahimana* et al (n. 5) (TC) paras. 1001–07. See discussion below on these guidelines.

3.6.1 *The Meaning and Evolution of the Right to Free Speech*

In law, the concept of free speech as a right means the freedom to speak freely without censorship. It is synonymous with freedom of expression, and it is not limited to the freedom of verbal speech but includes any act of seeking, receiving and imparting information or ideas in others irrespective of the medium used.

The right to free speech is three-dimensional: first, it covers the right to seek and obtain information and ideas; second, the right to receive information and ideas; and third, the right to impart information and ideas.[230] The medium through which freedom of speech is exercised can be orally, written, in print, through internet or even forms of arts.

The right to free speech can be traced as far back as early human rights documents,[231] whose gradual emergence dates as far back as the era of European Enlightenment. The English Bill of Rights of 1689 was restrictive in allocating this right. It was limited to, and only, in Parliament. About a century later, the Declaration of the Rights of Man and of the Citizen was adopted during the French Revolution. Affirming it as an inalienable right, the Declaration provided that the 'free communication of ideas and opinions is one of the most precious of the rights of man' and adds a caveat that every citizen has the right to speak, write and print with freedom 'but shall be responsible for such abuses of this freedom and shall be defined by law'.[232]

3.6.2 *The Right to Free Speech in International Law*

The right to free speech is recognised under the Universal Declaration of Human Rights which states that everyone has the 'right to freedom of opinion and expression', and this includes the 'freedom to hold opinions without interference and to seek, receive and impart information and ideas through any media and regardless of frontiers.'[233]

---

230 See generally Larry Alexander, *Is There a Right to Freedom of Expression?* (Cambridge Studies in Philosophy and Law 2006); Lee C. Bollinger and Geoffrey R. Stone, *Eternally Vigilant: Free Speech in the Modern Era* (University of Chicago Press 2003); Haig Bosmajian, *Freedom Not to Speak* (New York University Press 1999); Stefan Braun, *Democracy off Balance: Freedom of Expression and hate Propaganda Law in Canada* (University of Toronto Press 2004).

231 David Smith, 'Timeline: A History of Free Speech' *The Guardian* (London: 2006), <http://www.guardian.co.uk/media/2006/feb/05/religion.news>>. Retrieved on 2 May 2010.

232 Declaration of the Rights of Man and of the Citizen, Article 11.

233 Universal Declaration of Human Rights, United Nations General Assembly Resolution 217A, U.N.G.A. 3rd Session, U.N. Doc. A/RES/3/217A (1948) of 10 December 1948, Article 19.

The International Covenant on Civil and Political Rights (hereinafter referred to as the ICCPR) recognises the right to free speech as it stipulates that everyone 'shall have the right to hold opinions without interference' and the 'right to freedom of expression' which shall include 'the freedom to seek, receive and impart information and ideas of all kinds, regardless of frontiers, either orally, in writing or in print, in the form of art, or through any other media of his choice' subject to the restrictions stipulated in Article 19(3).[234]

Regional human rights organisations also recognise the right to freedom of speech. The various regional human rights instruments expressly articulate the right to free speech. The European Convention for the Protection of Human Rights and Fundamental Freedoms states that everyone has the 'right to freedom of expression', which includes the 'freedom to hold opinions and to receive and impart information and ideas without interference by public authority regardless of frontiers.'[235] Captioned 'Freedom of Thought and Expression', the Inter-American Convention on Human Rights also recognises the right to freedom of expression which includes the 'freedom to seek, receive, and impart information and ideas of all kinds, regardless of frontiers, either orally, in writing, in print, in the form of art, or through any other medium of one's choice'.[236] The African Charter on Human and Peoples Rights affirms the right to free speech in the following words:

> 1. Every individual shall have the right to receive information.
> 2. Every individual shall have the right to express and disseminate his opinions within the law.[237]

Though not binding, the Universal Declaration of Human Rights is considered evidence of customary international law.

[234] The ICCPR, 16 December 1966, 999 U.N.T.S. 171, Article 19. See also the International Convention on the Elimination of All Forms of Racial Discrimination, United Nations General Assembly Resolution 2106A (XX), U.N. GAOR, 20th Session, 1406th Plenary Meeting, U.N. Doc. A/RES/20/2016 of 20 December 1965; 660 U.N.T.S. 195, Article 5; United Nations Declaration on the Elimination of All Forms of Racial Discrimination, United Nations General Assembly Resolution 1904 (XVIII), U. N. GAOR, 1261st Plenary Meeting, U.N. Doc. A/RES/18/1904 (XVIII) of 20 November 1963, Article 9.

[235] European Convention for the Protection of Human Rights and Fundamental Freedoms, 4 November 1950, 213 U.N.T.S. 222, 312 ETS 5, as amended by Protocol No. 11 of 11 May 1994, Article 10(1).

[236] Inter-American Convention on Human Rights, 22 November 1969, 1144 U.N.T.S. 123, Article 13.

[237] African Charter on Human and Peoples' Rights, 27 June 1981, OAU Doc. CAB/LEG/67/3 rev. 5; 1520 U.N.T.S. 217, Article 9.

3.6.3 *The Limits to Free Speech in International Law*

The very international instruments recognising the right to free speech spell out limitations. Under the ICCPR, 'any propaganda for war' and 'advocacy of national, racial or religious hatred that constitutes incitement to discrimination, hostility or violence; shall be prohibited by law.[238] Regional human rights instruments also contain limitations to the right to free speech. The European Convention on Human Rights clearly defines the limits to free speech under the Convention:

> The exercise of these freedoms, since it carries with it duties and responsibilities, may be subject to such formalities, conditions, restrictions or penalties as are prescribed by law and are necessary in a democratic society, in the interests of national security, territorial integrity or public safety, for the prevention of disorder or crime, for the protection of health or morals, for the protection of the reputation or the rights of others, for preventing the disclosure of information received in confidence, or for maintaining the authority and impartiality of the judiciary.[239]

The Inter-American Convention on Human Rights stipulates as follows prohibits and criminalises any 'propaganda for war and any advocacy of national, racial, or religious hatred' constituting 'incitements to lawless violence or to any other similar action against any person or group of persons on any grounds including those of race, color, religion, language, or national origin'.[240] The African Charter simply says the exercise of freedom of speech must be 'within the law',[241] insinuating that national legislation regulates its exercise thereof.

3.6.4 *The Trial and Appeal Chambers' Guidelines*

Given these provisions contained in international instruments, the Trial and Appeal Chambers adjudicated the right to free speech in international law and its limits as contained in the same international instruments. In Rwanda, instigators used different media portals: they ranged from musical compositions that were played over the radio, articles published in newspapers, speeches made over the radio, use of vehicles equipped with a public address system to statements made in political rallies and other gatherings of Hutus in places like schools and stadia.

---

238 ICCPR, Article 20.

239 European Convention on Human Rights, Article 10(2).

240 Inter-American Convention on Human Rights, Article 13(4) and (5).

241 African Charter on Human and Peoples' Rights, Article 9(2). See alsoArticles 27(2), 28.

The Trial and Appeal Chambers examined the totality of these statements, songs and publications made by the various individuals charged. They examined the jurisprudence of regional human rights adjudicatory bodies related to free speech, and articulated three guidelines that must be used in order to determine whether the said statement, article or song transcended the limits of free speech. In *Nahimana* et al, the Trial Chamber stated them as follows: the purpose of the speech, article or song; the context (cultural, political or social) in which it was made; and the existence of a causal link (whether it resulted in the commission of atrocities).[242]

It is therefore settled in international law that though the right to free speech is recognised, there are established limits to it. Individuals are free to articulate their opinions as they wish, but when it results in the commission of atrocities, such opinions will be assessed based on the purpose(s) underlying their dissemination; the context within which they were made, and finally, if there exists any causal link between such opinions and the crimes committed.

3.7 Conclusion

In the discussions above, I have examined instigation as a mode of participation in common law in order to depict its inchoate character as a crime, and as a mode of participation. This mode of participation was given baptism by the Charter of the IMT, Nuremberg, as it imposed criminal responsibility on those who instigated any of the crimes over which the Nuremberg Tribunal had jurisdiction.[243] Since then, subsequent international instruments have recognised instigation as a mode of participation.[244] The Statute of the ICTR is not different.

As discussed earlier, instigation features under Article 6(1) as a mode of participation that would lead to the imposition of criminal responsibility for any of the crimes over which the ICTR has jurisdiction. It also appears under Article 2(3)(c), which deals with direct and public incitement to commit genocide.

---

242 *Nahimana* et al (n. 5) (TC) paras. 1001–07.

243 Charter of the IMT, Nuremberg, Article 6(c).

244 Examples include: the Rome Statute of the ICC, Article 25(3); the Statute of the SCSL, Article 6(1); the Statute of the ICTY, Article 7(1); the Draft Code of Crimes against the Peace and Security of Mankind, 1996, Article 2(3)(f); the Draft Code of Offences against the Peace and Security of Mankind, 1954, Article 2(13)(ii); the Charter of the IMTFE, Tokyo, Article 5; the Allied Control Council Law No. 10, Article II(2).

These two Articles, as discussed above (and below in Chapter Four), have different scopes of application. Under Article 2(3)(c), incitement must be direct, public, and to the crime of genocide. Therefore, for criminal responsibility to be imposed under Article 2(3)(c), it must be proved that the accused's instigation meets the criteria of 'direct' and 'public'; and that it was to commit the crime of genocide. As has been mentioned above, direct and public incitement to commit genocide is an inchoate crime: criminal responsibility will be imposed irrespective of whether such incitement successfully leads to the commission of genocide or not.[245]

On the other hand, instigation as a mode of participation under Article 6(1) must lead to any of the stages of any of the crimes over which the ICTR has jurisdiction. These stages are planning, preparation or execution. The crimes over which the ICTR has jurisdiction are genocide,[246] crimes against humanity,[247] and violations of Article 3 common to the Geneva Conventions and of Additional Protocol II.[248] Having discussed ingredients of instigation, and the free speech argument as raised in some of the trials, the next Chapter examines one of the crimes over which the ICTR has jurisdiction: crimes against humanity.

245 *Muvunyi* (n. 5) paras. 24–25; *Kalimanzira* (n. 3) para. 510; *Bikindi* (n. 5) para. 419; *Nahimana* et al (n. 5) (AC), paras. 678–79; *Nahimana* et al (n. 5) (TC) paras. 678, 720; *Kajelijeli* (n. 4) para. 855; *Niyitegeka* (n. 5) para. 431; *Musema* (n. 4) para. 120; *Rutaganda* (n. 4) para. 38; *Akayesu* (n. 3) para. 562.

246 Statute of the ICTR, Article 2.

247 Statute of the ICTR, Article 3.

248 Statute of the ICTR, Article 4.

CHAPTER FOUR

THE CONSTITUENT ELEMENTS OF CRIMES AGAINST HUMANITY UNDER THE STATUTE OF THE ICTR

4.1 Introduction

In the previous Chapter, I examined instigation as a mode of participation under both Article 6(1) and 2(3)(c) of the Statute of the International Criminal Tribunal for Rwanda (hereinafter referred to as the ICTR). Article 6(1) defines the imposition of criminal responsibility: it states the different modes of participation, which must lead to any of the stages of any of the crimes over which the ICTR has jurisdiction. These crimes are genocide,[1] crimes against humanity,[2] and Violations of Article 3 Common to the Geneva Conventions and of Additional Protocol II.[3] As discussed in the previous chapters, instigation is one of the modes of participation which, if it leads to the planning, preparation or execution of any of the crimes over which the ICTR has jurisdiction, criminal responsibility will be imposed.[4]

In this Chapter, I select one of the crimes over which the ICTR has jurisdiction, and is well articulated in Article 6(1): crimes against humanity.[5] I chose crimes against humanity for several reasons. First, amongst the other crimes, it is the oldest.[6] Second, even though the oldest, and as I show

---

1 United Nations Security Council Resolution 955, U. N. SCOR, 3453rd meeting, U.N. Doc. S/RES/955 (1994), to which was annexed the Statute of the ICTR. The crime of genocide is defined in the Statute of the ICTR, Article 2.

2 Statute of the ICTR, Article 3.

3 Statute of the ICTR, Article 4.

4 Statute of the ICTR, Article 6(1). This is the logical construction of the wording of Article 6(1) which defines the imposition of criminal responsibility under the Statute of the ICTR.

5 Statute of the ICTR, Article 3.

6 The word 'genocide' came into existence only after 1945 after it was coined by Ralph Lemkin. See generally Lemkin R, 'Genocide as a Crime under International Law' (1947) 41 *American Journal of International Law* 145. It became an international crime in 1948 when the Convention on the Prevention and Punishment of the Crime of Genocide (or the Genocide Convention) was passed by the United Nations General Assembly on 9 December 1948. See the *Convention on the Prevention and Punishment of the Crime of Genocide*, United Nations General Assembly Resolution 260(III), U.N. GAOR, 3rd Session, 179th meeting, U.N. Doc. A/RES/260A (1948) of 9 December 1948. Violations of Article 3 Common to the Geneva

in the subsections below, since it became a crime in international law, it has received different formulations by different institutions at different times.[7] Third, as argued below, the Statute of the ICTR introduced novel elements in its definition of crimes against humanity which, hitherto, had never featured in any international instrument.[8] These novel definitional elements portray the uniqueness of crimes against humanity, which, as I discuss in the next chapter, require the existence of a joint criminal enterprise for its planning, preparation or execution. Fourth, in the next chapter, I argue that the crime of crimes against humanity and the crime of genocide, though legally characterised differently, their *actus reus* share much resemblance. An act of killing may qualify as a genocidal act if it was perpetrated with the intent to destroy a people, in part or in whole. The same act of killing would qualify as a crime against humanity if it was committed as part of a widespread or systematic attack directed against any civilian population on any of the discriminatory grounds. The similarities shared by these two crimes have to be articulated because, as I argue in the succeeding chapter, the approach of the prosecutors and the jurisprudence of both the Trial and Appeal Chambers suggest that crimes against humanity and genocide are mutually exclusive. Therefore, factual allegations leading to a charge of instigation to genocide (whether under Article 6(1) or Article 2(3)(c)) have been limited to genocide only, and cannot be used to impose criminal responsibility under Article 6(1), which makes instigation a mode of participation in the planning, preparation or execution of crimes against humanity (as one of the crimes over which the ICTR has jurisdiction).

This illogical approach and incorrect position is shown in the indictments of several accused persons charged with direct and public incitement

Conventions and of Additional Protocol II, though constituting crimes contained in the Geneva Conventions, had not been phrased as such in any international instrument prior to the Statute of the ICTR.

[7] For the different formulations on crimes against humanity, see the Rome Statute of the ICC, U. N. Doc. A/CONF.183/9 (1998), reprinted in 37 I.L.M. 999 (1998), Article 7(1); the Statute of the Special Court for Sierra Leone, annexed to the Agreement between the United Nations and the Government of Sierra Leone on the Establishment of a Special Court for Sierra Leone pursuant to United Nations Security Council Resolution 1315, U.N. SCOR, 4186th meeting, U.N. Doc. S/RES/1315 (2000), Article 2; the Statute of the ICTR, Article 3; the Statute of the ICTY, annexed to United Nations Security Council Resolution 827, U.N. SCOR, 3217th meeting, U.N. Doc. S/RES/827 (1993), Article 5; the Charter of the IMTFE, Tokyo, Article 5(c); Allied Control Council Law No. 10, Article II, and the Charter of the IMT, Nuremberg, Article 6(c).

[8] As discussed in the subsections below, these definitional elements are 'a widespread or systematic attack', 'directed against' 'any civilian population' on 'national, political, ethnic or religious grounds'. See Statute of the ICTR, Article 3.

to genocide.[9] For some of these accused individuals, the same factual allegations leading to a charge of direct and public incitement to commit genocide were used to impose criminal responsibility for instigation to genocide under Article 6(1).[10] Though not precisely stated as 'instigation to genocide', the prosecutors elected to use the broader phraseology of Article 6(1), stating all the modes of participation and how they led to genocide[11] or crimes against humanity.[12] This practice by the prosecutors does not help illuminate the understanding of instigation as a mode of participation under Article 6(1) in general, and in particular, in the commission of crimes against humanity. This position is untenable and unjustifiable. As I argue in Chapter Five, factual allegations used to found a charge of direct and public incitement to commit genocide ought to be used to impose criminal responsibility for instigation under Article 6(1).

---

9 *The Prosecutor v Callixte Kalimanzira*, Amended Indictment, Case No. ICTR-2005-88-I, OTP, 21 July 2005, Count 3, Paras. 18–27; *The Prosecutor v Joseph Serugendo*, Corrigendum of Indictment, Case No. ICTR-2005-84-I, OTP, 21 July 2005, Count 4, Paras. 51–73; *The Prosecutor v Simon Bikindi*, Amended Indictment, Case No. ICTR-2001-72-I, OTP, 15 June 2005, Count 4, Paras. 31–41; *The Prosecutor v Tharcisse Muvunyi*, Amended Indictment, Case No. ICTR-2000-55A-T, OTP, 23 December 2003 (a retrial on the lone charge of direct and public incitement to genocide); *The Prosecutor v Eliézer Niyitegeka*, Amended Indictment, Case No. ICTR-96-14-T, OTP, 25 November 2002, Count 4, Paras. 5.1–6.71; *The Prosecutor v Juvénal Kajelijeli*, Amended Indictment, Case No. ICTR-98-44A-I, OTP, 25 January 2001, Count 4, Paras. 2.1–4.18; *The Prosecutor v Jean-Bosco Barayagwiza*, Amended Indictment, Case No. ICTR-97-19, OTP, 14 April 2000, Count 4, Paras. 5.1–7.13; *The Prosecutor v Ferdinand Nahimana*, Amended Indictment, Case No. ICTR-96-11, OTP, 15 November 1999, Count 3, Paras. 4.1–6.27; *The Prosecutor v Hassan Ngeze*, Amended Indictment, Case No. ICTR-97-27, OTP, 10 November 1999, Count 4, Paras. 5.1–7.15; *The Prosecutor v Georges Henri Yvon Joseph Ruggiu*, Amended Indictment, Case No. ICTR-97-32-I, OTP, 10 December 1998, Count 2, Paras. 3.1–5.12; and, *The Prosecutor v Jean-Paul Akayesu*, Amended Indictment, Case No. ICTR-96-4-I, OTP, June 1997, Count 4, Paras. 14–15.

10 An example is Callixte Kalimanzira, charged with three crimes, amongst which is the inchoate crime of direct and public incitement to genocide. To further explain the charge, the Office of the Prosecutor stated the imposition of criminal responsibility as follows: 'Callixte Kalimanzira is individually responsible, pursuant to Article 6(1) of the Statute, for the crime of direct and public incitement to commit genocide in that he planned, instigated, ordered to commit or otherwise aided and abetted in the planning, preparation or commission of crimes. The particulars of the crimes for which he incurs individual criminal responsibility are set out in paragraphs....' *Kalimanzira* (n. 9) para. 18. This is the confusing statement of the law, in which Articles 6(1) and 2(3)(c) have been blended and confusingly interpreted.

11 *The Prosecutor v Ferdinand Nahimana*, Amended Indictment, Case No. ICTR-96-11, OTP, 15 November 1999, Count 3, Paras. 4.1–6.27.

12 *The Prosecutor v Joseph Serugendo*, Corrigendum of Indictment, Case No. ICTR-2005-84-I, OTP, 21 July 2005, Counts 2, 4–5, Paras. 25–96; *The Prosecutor v Simon Bikindi*, Amended Indictment, Case No. ICTR-2001-72-I, OTP, 15 June 2005, Counts 2, 4–6, Paras. 18–48; *The Prosecutor v Juvénal Kajelijeli*, Amended Indictment, Case No. ICTR-98-44A-I, Counts 2, 4–9, Paras. 3–9.

More puzzling is the fact that even in such situations, instigation is limited to genocide. Instigation under Article 6(1) covers every crime over which the ICTR has jurisdiction.[13] Though crimes against humanity have been prosecuted at the ICTR, the approach of the prosecutors and the jurisprudence of both the Trial and Appeal Chambers suggest that instigation to crimes against humanity under Article 6(1) is at best a legal abstract concept. In my opinion, this is the outcome of an incorrect construction and application of Article 6(1), and is unreflective of the letter of Article 6(1).

In this Chapter, I examine crimes against humanity under the Statute of the ICTR. I focus on the key definitional elements which reveal the unique nature of this crime: crimes against humanity require a joint criminal enterprise for their planning, preparation or execution. The jurisprudence of both the Trial and Appeal Chambers of the ICTR establishes that criminal responsibility under Article 6(1) can be imposed only when it is proved that the accused's mode of participation substantially contributed to the commission of any of the crimes over which the ICTR has jurisdiction.[14] Part of my argument raised in the next chapter critiques this substantial contribution requirement based on the fact that the definition of crimes against humanity under the Statute of the ICTR requires some collective participation or the existence of a joint criminal enterprise. A joint criminal enterprise exists when several persons act with a common purpose.[15] In such cases, and in line with the rules of imposing criminal responsibility on persons in a joint criminal enterprise, every individual bears responsibility for every act he or she agreed to have committed.[16] Requiring a substantial contribution in cases of joint criminal enterprise is not only an arduous

---

[13] Statute of the ICTR, Article 6(1).

[14] *The Prosecutor v Idelphonse Hategekimana*, Judgment, Case No. ICTR-00-55, T. Ch. II, 6 December 2010, Para. 644; *The Prosecutor v Callixte Kalimanzira*, Judgment, Case No. ICTR-05-88-T, T. Ch. III, 22 June 2009, Para. 512; *The Prosecutor v Juvénal Kajelijeli*, Judgment, Case No. ICTR-96-44-T, T. Ch. II, 1 December 2003, Para. 759; *The Prosecution v Laurent Semanza*, Judgment, Case No. ICTR-97-20, T. Ch. II, 15 May 2003, Para. 379; *The Prosecutor v Elizaphan Ntakirutimana and Gérard Ntakirutimana*, Judgement, Case No. ICTR-96-17-T, T. Ch. I, 21 February 2003, Para. 787; *Clément Kayishema and Obed Ruzindana v The Prosecutor*, Judgement, Case No. ICTR-95-1A, Appeal Chamber, 1 June 2001, Paras. 186; *The Prosecutor v Ignace Bagilishema*, Judgement, Case No.ICTR-95-1-A, T. Ch. I, 7 June 2001, Paras. 30, 33; *The Prosecutor v Alfred Musema*, Judgment, Case No. ICTR-96-13-T, T. Ch. I, 27 January 2003, Para. 115; *The Prosecutor v Georges Rutaganda*, Judgment, Case No. ICTR-96-3-T, T. Ch. I, 6 December 1999, Para. 43; *The Prosecutor v Clément Kayishema and Obed Ruzindana*, Judgment, Case No. ICTR-95-1-T, T. Ch. I, 21 May 1999, Paras. 199–207; *The Prosecutor v Jean-Paul Akayesu*, Judgment, Case No. ICTR-96-4, T. Ch. I, 2 September 1998, Para. 477.

[15] David Ormerod, *Smith and Hogan Criminal Law* (12th edn., Oxford University Press 2008) 182; Russell Heaton, *Criminal Law Textbook* (Oxford University Press 2004) 386–91.

[16] Ibid.

task, but it also does not square with the rules of criminal responsibility for such cases.[17] Furthermore, it becomes a futile and an uncustomary venture in determining with precision what role every member of such a joint criminal enterprise played. As one legal scholar put it eloquently, 'it is a feature of criminal responsibility that it can be distributed without being divided.'[18]

Before I look into definitional elements of crimes against humanity under the Statute of the ICTR, it is important to begin with a synoptic examination of the evolution of crimes against humanity. The essence of this is to show that before the Statute of the ICTR, crimes against humanity existed as a crime in international law. Furthermore, it also unearths the different formulations that were made by different institutions at different times as they tried to define crimes against humanity and its constituent elements.

4.2 An Outline of the Evolution of Crimes Against Humanity

The evolution of crimes against humanity under international law can be divided into five main phases: first, the pre-1945 era when it existed in the realm of international law as a 'term of art'; second, the Charters of the International Military Tribunals (first, Nuremberg, which first defined crimes against humanity in international criminal law; and second, Tokyo, which simply repeated the words of the Charter of the Nuremberg Tribunal on crimes against humanity); third, the work of the United Nations War Crimes Commissions (hereinafter referred to as UNWCC) and the International Law Commission (hereinafter referred to as the ILC); fourth, the Statutes of the United Nations Security Council's *ad hoc* Tribunals, and last, the Rome Statute of the International Criminal Court (hereinafter referred to as the ICC). As will be seen in the following discussion, the formulations were fundamentally different prior to the Statute of the ICTR. However, international instruments after the Statute of the ICTR such as the Rome Statute of the ICC and Statute of the Special Court for Sierra Leone (hereinafter referred to as the SCSL) have, to some extent, incorporated most of the definitional elements of crimes against humanity as introduced by the Statute of the ICTR.

17 Ibid.

18 Michael Walzer, *Just and Unjust Wars* (3rd edn., Basic Books 2000) 309.

4.2.1 *The Concept of Crimes Against Humanity before World War Two*

In the words of a Swiss jurist, crimes against humanity are as old as humanity itself.[19] Following the massacre of Armenians by Turkey, Great Britain, France and Russia, in describing the massacres in a declaration on 28 May 1915, gave 'crimes against humanity' the very first international usage.[20] Its usage was not as a crime under international law, but as a 'term of art'.[21] The events in Turkey were described as 'crimes against humanity and civilisation for which all members of the Turkish Government would be held responsible together with its agents implicated in the massacres'.[22] In drafting this declaration, Great Britain, France and Russia had in mind at least three perspectives based on the context in which they were operating: first, the notion of crimes against humanity and civilisation included the killings of ethnic minority groups. This, usually, was done by the group in power. Secondly, despite the fact that the complaining states (Great Britain, France and Russia) lacked the ability to deliver on their promise, they had a clear understanding of the principles of individual criminal responsibility. Third, the crimes committed were very distinct from war crimes: they occurred within Turkish territory, and the killings were not linked to the worldwide conflict in which Turkey was involved.[23]

The distinction between crimes against humanity and war crimes, as made by Great Britain, France and Russia, though appearing in 1915, was sieved from the laws of war. Their distinction was the offspring of the language of the Martens Clause of the Fourth Hague Convention Concerning the Laws and Customs of War on Land. The Martens Clause provided that, to the extent not dealt in the Convention, 'the inhabitants and the belligerents shall remain under the protection of and subject to the principles of the law of nations, as established by and prevailing among civilised nations, by the laws of humanity, and the demands of public conscience'.[24]

A notion akin to that of crimes against humanity appeared at the end of the First World War. This was contained in a report dated 29 March 1919.

---

19 Jean Graven, 'Les Crimes Contre l'Humanité' (1950–I) 76 *RECEUIL DES COURS* 427, 433.

20 Roger S. Clark, 'Crimes against Humanity' in George Ginsburgs and V.N. Kudriavtsev (eds), *The Nuremberg Trial and International Law* (Martinus Nijhoff Publishers 1990) 177–212, 177.

21 Ibid.

22 Quoted in Egon Schwelb, 'Crimes Against Humanity' (1946) 23 *Brit. Y. B. Int'l L.*181.

23 Clark (n. 20) 178.

24 See the Martens Clause of the Fourth Hague Convention of 1907 Concerning the Laws and Customs of War on Land, reprinted in 2 *Am. J. Int'l. L.* 90 (Supp. 1908), quoted by Clark (n. 20) 178.

It was by a majority of the so-called Commission of Fifteen Members of the Preliminary Peace Conference. This Commission considered prosecution of persons 'guilty of offenses against the laws and customs of war or the laws of humanity.'[25] The phraseology itself posed some interpretive problems: 'Guilty of offenses against the laws and customs of war or the laws of humanity' appeared as a crime that lacked sufficient precision as it did not spell out which crimes would fit into what category ('laws and customs of war' or 'the laws of humanity'). Furthermore, it did not disclose whether the insertion of the word *or* was to provide an alternative: either an act was classified as a violation of the laws and customs of war, or the laws of humanity. Though the Commission considered the possibility of prosecution of persons 'guilty of offences against the laws and customs of war or the laws of humanity', their efforts were weakened by the dissenting opinions of two members of the Commission, Robert Lansing and James S. Brown, both from the United States. They were of the opinion that the cooperation of the United States in such an enterprise

> was frustrated by the insistence on the part of the majority that criminal liability should, in excess of the mandate of the Conference, attach to the laws and principles of humanity, in addition to the laws and customs of war, and that the jurisdiction of the high court should be specifically extended to 'heads of state'.[26]

They dismissed the concept of crimes against humanity as 'not the object of punishment by a court of justice', but rather one of 'moral law' that lacked any 'fixed and universal standard'.[27] This handicapped the work of the Commission, making it impossible for its recommendation for the prosecution of persons 'guilty of offences against the laws and customs of war or the laws of humanity' to be considered in the final peace treaty. Consequently, the Treaty of Versailles made no move towards any trials for crimes against humanity.[28]

---

[25] Commission on the Responsibility of the Authors of the War and on Enforcement of Penalties, *Report Presented to the Preliminary Peace Conference,* 29 March 1919, reprinted in (1920) 14 *AJIL* 95, 144. See also Lord Wright 'War Crimes Under International Law' (1946) 62 *LAW Q. REV.* 40, 48–49; Graven (n. 19) 446–51.

[26] See Memorandum of Reservations Presented by the Representatives of the United States to the Report of the Commission on Responsibilities, quoted by Clark (n. 20) 179 (footnote 7).

[27] Commission on the Responsibility of the Authors of the War and on Enforcement of Penalties (n. 25). See also Wright (n. 25) 40, 48–49; Graven (n. 19) 446–51.

[28] The Treaty of Versailles contained limited provisions for the trial of the former German Kaiser and other German military persons who allegedly, were guilty of war crimes, but were never translated into action. See Remigus Bierzanek, 'War Crimes: History and Definition' in M. Cherif Bassiouni (ed), III *International Criminal Law* (Dobbs Ferry 1987); Clark (n. 20) 179.

At the end of the First World War, efforts to develop crimes against humanity as a crime in international law yielded no positive results. Despite the fact that it was mentioned at the Preliminary Conference, it did not go beyond a 'term of art' and a label that recognised it as debased moral but non-criminal conduct justiciable before a court of law.

4.2.2 *The Allied Powers' Formulations on Crimes against Humanity*

Beyond 1919, the concept of crimes against humanity resided only in shadows of international discourse. There was little or no effort towards its codification until in the early 1940s when it resurfaced.[29] This time, it was the United Nations War Crimes Commission (UNWCC);[30] and subsequently, at the London Conference, where discussions on what would amount to war crimes, and the drafting of the Charter of the IMT took place.[31] Suggestions arose to the effect that 'some machinery should be established for dealing with atrocities committed on racial, political or religious grounds in enemy territory'.[32] This was a major development that yielded positive results in 1945 with crimes against humanity being included in the Charter of the IMT.

On 8 May 1945, Germany unconditionally surrendered to the Allied Powers.[33] On 8 August 1945, the Allied Powers ratified the London Agreement.[34] As an annexure to the London Agreement, the Charter of the

[29] Clark (n. 20) 179.

[30] The United Nations War Crimes Commission was set up by a decision of a diplomatic conference on 20 October 1943 The UNWCC was created on 20 October 1943 by representatives of the seventeen Allied nations. It was the only international framework that dealt with the issue of war crimes and war criminals during the Second World War, and it continued to operate until 31 March 1948. In the course of its existence, it had created a total of 8,178 files (representing 36,810 individuals and groups). Most important notions elaborated by the UNWCC found their way into the Nuremberg Charter. See generally Michael S. Blayney, 'Herbert C. Pell, War Crimes and the Jews' (1976) 65 *American Jewish Historical Quarterly* 335–52; Donald Bloxham, *Genocide on Trial: War Crimes Trials and the Formation of Holocaust History and Memory* (Oxford University Press 2001); Arieh J. Kochavi, *Prelude to Nuremberg: Allied War Crimes Policy and the Question of Punishment* (University of North Carolina Press 1998); Bradley F. Smith, *The Road to Nuremberg* (Basic Books 1981); Clark (n. 20).

[31] Clark (n. 20) 179–80.

[32] See, e.g., Despatch from the British Ambassador (Halifax) to the United States' Secretary of State, 19 August 1944, in *Foreign Relations of the United States,* Diplomatic Papers 1944, Vol. I, General, 1351, 1352.

[33] Clark (n. 20) 180.

[34] Nineteen states subsequently acceded to the Agreement. Annexed to this Agreement was the Charter of the IMT. See Agreement for the Prosecution and Punishment of the Major War Criminals of the European Axis, 8 August 1945, 59 Stat. 1544, 82 UNTS 279; M. Cherif Bassiouni, *Crimes against Humanity in International Criminal Law* (Kluwer Law International 1999) 1.

IMT for the Trial of the Major War Criminals expressly mentioned its purposes: first, to establish a military tribunal (which became known as the Nuremberg Tribunal) to try 'major war criminals';[35] second, to specify the crimes it would have jurisdiction to try;[36] and third, to stipulate principles of criminal responsibility.[37] Defining the crimes over which it had jurisdiction, the Nuremberg Charter was empowered to try and punish the major war criminals for, *inter alia*, crimes against humanity.[38] The Nuremberg Charter defined crimes against humanity as

> murder, extermination, enslavement, deportations, and other inhumane acts committed against any civilian population, before or during the war; or persecutions on political, racial or religious grounds in execution of or in connection with any crime within the jurisdiction of the Tribunal, whether or not in violation of the domestic law of the country where perpetrated.[39]

The wording of Article 6(c) required that the acts must be committed against a civilian population before or during the war. It statutorily established a nexus between the crimes and the war in order for them to qualify as crimes against humanity.[40]

Beyond the Nuremberg Charter, two other historic pieces of legislation containing definitions of crimes against humanity were enacted. The first was the Allied Control Council Law No. 10, enacted in 1945 by the Allied

---

35 Charter of IMT, Nuremberg, Article 1. Under the 1943 Moscow Declaration by the Allies, the trial and judgment of minor war criminals would take place in the countries where they committed their crimes.

36 Charter of the IMT, Nuremberg, Article 6(c).

37 See the Charter of the IMT, Nuremberg, Part II (Articles 6–11). See also the Declaration of German Atrocities, 1 November 1943, 1943, reprinted in (1944) 38 *AJIL* (Supp.) 3, 7–8. The imposition of criminal responsibility was articulated under Article 6(c) of the Charter of the IMT, Nuremberg.

38 Crimes against peace (Article 6(a)) and war crimes (Article 6(b)) were the other crimes over which the Nuremberg Tribunal had jurisdiction. As mentioned earlier, the concept of genocide was still new in international discourse, and only became an international crime on 9 December 1948 following the adoption of the Genocide Convention.

39 Charter of IMT, Nuremberg, Article 6(c).

40 However, vagueness, ambiguities and uncertainties in the wording of Article 6(c) resulted in intense debates by international law scholars. Conflicting interpretations of the various versions of the text defining crimes against humanity arose, which led to the Berlin Protocol of 6 October 1945. It eliminated the semicolon and replaced it with a comma. This new phrasing of the Berlin Protocol buried every doubt and made clear that 'in execution of or in connection with any crime within the jurisdiction of the Tribunal' would be construed to apply to the entire context of the paragraph. It would also constitute an important restriction on the scope of the concept of crimes against humanity. See Bassiouni (n. 34) 227–32; Clark (n. 20) 177–92.

Powers.[41] Allied Control Council Law No. 10 defined crimes against humanity as

> [A]trocities and offences, including but not limited to murder, extermination, enslavement, deportation, imprisonment, torture, rape, or other inhumane acts committed against any civilian population, or persecutions on political, racial or religious grounds, whether or not in violation of the domestic laws of the country where perpetrated.[42]

The definition contained in Article II(c) of Allied Control Council Law No. 10 had some similarities and differences that pertained to the definition in Article 6(c) of the Charter of the Nuremberg Tribunal.[43]

The third piece of legislation to define crimes against humanity was the Charter of the International Military Tribunal for the Far East (hereinafter referred to as the IMTFE), Tokyo. It established the Tokyo Tribunal 'for the just and prompt trial and punishment of major war criminals in the Far East',[44] and simply repeated *mutatis mutandis* the wording of Article 6(c) of the Nuremberg Charter. Entitled 'Jurisdiction over Persons and Offenses', the Tokyo Charter created and defined crimes against humanity to mean

> murder, extermination, enslavement, deportation, and other inhumane acts against any civilian population, before or during the war, or persecutions on

---

[41] This was a piece of municipal legislation enacted by the Allied Powers following the unconditional surrender of Germany on 8 May 1945. Having supreme legislative authority over Germany, the Control Council Law No. 10 was not intended to be an international instrument, but a piece of national legislation providing the Allied Powers the legal basis for subsequent criminal prosecutions in Germany. Its applicability was to the various zones of occupation by the Allied Powers. Bassiouni (n. 34) 3–6.

[42] Allied Control Council Law No. 10, Article II (c).

[43] First, in its wording, the Allied Powers stated that Control Council Law No. 10 was enacted for the 'prosecution of war criminals and other similar offenders other than those dealt with by the International Military Tribunal' In the wording of crimes against humanity, an enlistment of the crimes was preceded by the words 'Atrocities and offences' (Article II(1)(c)), whereas the Charter of the IMT, Nuremberg, defined crimes against humanity without such annotation. The Allied Control Council Law No. 10 also made use of broad phraseology in the definition of crimes against humanity, injecting the words 'included but not limited to' (Article II(1)(c)). New crimes like rape and imprisonment were added despite the possibility of sub-classifying them under the umbrella of 'other inhumane acts' like the Charter of the IMT, Nuremberg, did (see Article 6(c)). Article 6(c) of the Charter of the IMT, Nuremberg, required that the acts amounting to crimes against humanity be committed 'in execution of, or in connection with any crime [crimes against peace, war crimes and crimes against humanity] within the jurisdiction of the Tribunal, whether or not in violation of the domestic law of the country where perpetrated.' By inserting the clause 'whether or not in violation of the domestic laws of the country where perpetrated' (Article II(1)(c)), the nexus requirement was made redundant in the formulation articulated by Allied Control Council Law No. 10 (Article II(1)(c)).

[44] Charter of the IMTFE, Tokyo, Article 1.

> political or racial grounds in execution of or in connection with any crime within the jurisdiction of the Tribunal, whether or not in violation of the domestic law of the country where perpetrated.[45]

Like the Charter of the Nuremberg Tribunal, it stated that the category of persons who would be subject to the jurisdiction of the IMTFE, Tokyo, included 'leaders, organizers, instigators and accomplices participating in the formulation or execution of a common plan or conspiracy to commit any of the foregoing crimes….'[46] It also mentioned that the commission of these crimes would be 'before or during the war,' and 'in execution of or in connection with any crime within the jurisdiction of the Tribunal'.[47] However, a noticeable variation existed in the definitions stipulated in these two Charters. Article 5(c) of the Charter of the IMTFE, Tokyo, did not make 'persecution' subject to 'religious' grounds. It confined it to 'political or racial grounds'.[48] This variation, though slight, seemed to be triggered by a significant difference in the events leading to them: Nazi atrocities in Europe, especially the extermination of millions of Jews and treatment of citizens in occupied countries, had no exact equivalent in the Asian region or conflict.[49]

Beyond these three different formulations by the Allied Powers, the UNWCC[50] and the ILC[51] engaged in protracted works attempting to propound a definition of crimes against humanity.

---

45 Ibid Article 5(c). Though crimes against humanity were subject to the jurisdiction of the IMTFE, Tokyo, no individual was indicted and charged for crimes against humanity. The Tokyo Tribunal indicted individuals for murder; making it a distinct novelty. At Nuremberg, the crime of murder was not considered a specific crime, except where it was committed as a means of perpetrating war crimes or crimes against humanity. The prosecution's argument was based on the theory that killings in an unlawful war would constitute murder by virtue of the illegal nature of the war. With no legal precedents, the murder charges became the subject of much controversy, and have since then, never been repeated in international law. Neil Boister & Robert Cryer, *The Tokyo International Military Tribunal: A Reappraisal* (Oxford University Press 2008) 154.

46 Charter of the IMT, Nuremberg, Article 6(c); and Charter of the IMTFE, Tokyo, Article 5(c).

47 Charter of the IMTFE, Tokyo, Article 5(c).

48 Ibid.

49 None of the indicted individuals was charged for crimes against humanity. However, they were tried for the offence of murder, which appeared unprecedented and controversial, and has never been repeated in any international criminal tribunal. See Boister & Cryer (n. 45).

50 See footnote 30 above.

51 The International Law Commission was created for the purpose of promoting 'the progressive development of international law and its codification'. See the United Nations General Assembly Resolution 174(II), U.N. GAOR, 2nd Session, 123rd meeting, U.N. Doc. A/RES/174(II) of 21 November 1947. The United Nations General Assembly Resolution 177(II)

Prior to 1945, crimes against humanity existed as a jurisprudential phantom, lacking any fixed definition in international law. Despite the recognition of the importance of such a concept to cover atrocities perpetrated by belligerents in times of war, the concept took no positive development until 1945 when Nuremberg became its baptismal locus following its inclusion in the Charter of the IMT, Nuremberg. The development of the concept of crimes against humanity, and its inclusion as a serious crime in international law since Nuremberg, both address recognisable and indisputable levels of state-organised and perpetrated cruelty against humanity which the international community cannot ignore because they are perpetrated in different territories. As one scholar puts it, 'only those crimes which either by their magnitude and savagery or by their large number or by the fact that a similar pattern was applied at different times and places, endangered the international community or shocked the conscience of mankind, warranted intervention by States other than that on whose territory the crimes had been committed, or whose subjects had become their victims.'[52]

4.2.3 *The Work of the United Nations War Crimes Commission and International Law Commission*

Having examined these three texts, the UNWCC was able to extrapolate and postulate some basic guidelines in understanding the meaning of crimes against humanity. First, it propounded that there were two categories of crimes against humanity: the 'murder' type, which covered crimes such as murder, extermination, enslavement, deportation; and the 'persecution' type, which covered crimes committed based on racial, religious or political grounds. Second, it established that crimes against humanity of the 'murder' and 'persecution' type needed to be perpetrated against a civilian population. This meant they would obviously fall out of its scope if they were inflicted upon military personnel. It added a caveat related to the pattern in which the crimes are committed: they needed to be systematic or widespread in pattern. By this requirement, isolated incidents of crimes would not qualify as crimes against humanity. This requirement that the

mandated the International Law Commission to formulate 'the principles of international law recognised' in the Charter of the IMT, Nuremberg, and 'in the judgment of the Tribunal.' See the United Nations General Assembly Resolution 177(II), U.N. GAOR, 2nd Session, 123rd meeting, U.N. Doc. A/RES/177(II) of 21 November 1947; Bassiouni (n. 34) 179.

52 Bassiouni (n. 34) 37.

crimes be committed as part of a widespread or systematic attack was aimed at altering the nature of the crimes and elevate them from ordinary crimes prohibited and punishable by municipal penal laws to serious crimes under international law.

Another conclusion reached at by the UNWCC was that it was irrelevant if the crimes were committed before, during, or after a war. So too were the nationalities of the victims. It was immaterial whether the crimes committed were in violation of the laws of the place (*lex loci*) where they were committed. Lastly, it held that the classification of responsible persons would be widened to cover not just the ringleaders, but also the actual perpetrators of the crimes. It posited that crimes against humanity may be committed by simply enacting a piece of legislation that encourages, orders or permits the commission of any of the crimes, such as unjustified killings, racial discrimination, mass deportations, torture and rape.[53]

In post-Nuremberg, the international community directed its efforts towards the drafting of a Code of Offences Against the Peace and Security of Mankind.[54] The ILC, barely over a year after its creation, had its first session in 1949. This session was characterised by deliberations, and in 1950, the ILC presented a report in which crimes against humanity were defined as

> Murder, extermination, enslavement, deportation and other inhuman acts done against any civilian population, or persecutions on political, racial or religious grounds, when such acts are done or such persecutions are carried on in execution of or in connexion with any crime against peace or any war crime.[55]

After 1950, four decades elapsed without any formal adoption of a definition of what constituted crimes against humanity. In 1991, the International Law Commission made another formulation.[56] However, three years later

53 Ibid.

54 It was an effort that was begun on 21 November 1947, which resulted in the Draft Code of Crimes against Peace and Security of Mankind. It has not been adopted by the United Nations General Assembly. By 1987, it had become the Code of Crimes against the Peace and Security of Mankind. See Bassiouni (n. 34) 179.

55 Principle VI(c) of *Principles of International Law Recognized by the Charter of the Nuremberg Tribunal and the Judgment of the Tribunal.* See also Bassiouni (n. 34) 180.

56 'An individual who commits or orders the combination of any of the following violations of human rights:

- Murder
- Torture
- Establishing or maintaining over persons a status of slavery, servitude or forced labour
- Persecution on social, political, racial, religious or cultural grounds in a systematic manner or on a mass scale; or

(in 1994), the ILC would depart significantly from its own earlier definition when it produced a Draft Statute for an ICC.[57] Two years after this extensive formulation, the ILC reconsidered its definition of crimes against humanity and propounded a more abridged version. It defined crimes against humanity to mean

> ...any of the following acts, when committed in a systematic manner or on a large scale and instigated or directed by a Government or by any organization or group:
> a. murder;
> b. extermination;
> c. torture;
> d. enslavement;
> e. persecution on political, racial, religious or ethnic grounds;

– Deportation or forcible transfer of population....' (Article 21 of the 1991 Draft Code of Crimes).

57 'A person commits crimes against humanity, whether in time or peace or war, when:
a. he is in a position of authority and orders, commands, or fails to prevent the systematic commission of the acts described below, against a given segment of the civilian population;
b. he is in a position of authority and participates in the making of a policy or program designed to systematically carry out the acts described below against a given segment of the civilian population;
c. he is in a senior military or political position and knowingly carries out or orders others to carry out systematically the acts described below against a segment of the civilian population;
d. he knowingly commits the acts described below with the intent to further a policy of systematic persecution against a segment of the civilian population without having a moral choice to do otherwise.
1. The acts constituting 'crimes against humanity' when committed systematically against a segment of the civilian population are:
a. extermination;
b. murder, including killings done by creating conditions likely to cause death;
c. enslavement, including slave-related practices;
d. discriminatory and arbitrary deportation;
e. imprisonment, in violation of international norms on the prohibition of arbitrary arrest and detention;
f. torture;
g. rape and other serious assaults of a sexual nature;
h. persecution, whether based on laws or practices targeting select groups or their members in ways that seriously and adversely affect their ethnic, cultural or religious life, their collective well-being, and welfare, or their ability to group identity;
i. other inhumane acts, including but not limited to serious attacks upon physical integrity, personal safety, and individual dignity, such as physical mutilation, forced impregnation or forced carrying to term foetuses that are the product of forced impregnation, and unlawful human experimentation.'

f. institutionalized discrimination on racial, ethnic or religious grounds involving the violation of fundamental human rights and freedoms and resulting in seriously disadvantaging a part of the population;
g. arbitrary deportation of forcible transfer of population;
h. arbitrary imprisonment;
i. forced disappearance of persons;
j. rape, enforced prostitution and other forms of sexual abuse;
k. other inhumane acts which severely damage physical or mental integrity, health or human dignity, such as mutilation and severe bodily harm.[58]

4.2.4 *The Statutes of the United Nations'* Ad Hoc *Tribunals*

Approximately four decades after the Charter of the IMT, Nuremberg, events in the territory of the former Yugoslavia created a fecund ground upon which another formulation of crimes against humanity would be made. Evidence of war crimes and other gruesome human rights violations that occurred in the territory of the former Yugoslavia attracted the attention of the international community. The United Nations Security Council expressed concern over violations of international law in the territory, and affirmed the concept of individual criminal responsibility for such violations.[59]

On 6 October 1992, the United Nations Security Council created a Commission of Experts to examine the violations of international law that had taken place in the region.[60] In its interim report, the Commission concluded that serious violations of international law were taking place. It recommended the creation of an *ad hoc* international criminal tribunal.[61]

58 The Draft Code of Crimes Against the Peace and Security of Mankind, 1996, Article 18.

59 For example, United Nations Security Council Resolution 713, U.N. SCOR, 3009th meeting, U.N. Doc. S/RES/713 (1991), 25 September 1991.

60 United Nations Security Council Resolution 780, U. N. SCOR, 3119th meeting, U.N. Doc. S/RES/713 (1992). The Commission of Experts' mandate was not just to reach legal conclusions, but also to obtain evidence that would be used for prosecution; and also establish a database of information. See Letter of 9 February 1993, from the Secretary-General, addressed to the President of the Security Council, 10 February 1993, U.N. Doc. S/25274, at 7–11 (hereinafter referred to as Yugoslavia Commission First Interim Report).

61 Yugoslavia Commission First Interim Report (n. 60). A second interim report was produced by the Commission in October 1993, and then a final report in May 1994. See Letter dated 5 October 1993, from the Secretary-General to the President of the Security Council, 6 October 1993, U.N. Doc. 2/26545; Letter dated 24 May 1994, from the Secretary-General to the President of the Security Council, 27 May 1994, U.N. Doc. S/1994/674. The Commission on Human Rights also appointed a Special Rapporteur whose activities were coordinated with those of the Commission of Experts. See The Situation of Human Rights in the Territory of the Former Yugoslavia, 3 September 1992, U.N. Doc. A/47/418-S/24516; The Situation of Human Rights in the Territory of the Former Yugoslavia, 6 November 1992, U.N. Doc. A/47/635-S/24766.

Following the Commission's report, on 11 February 1993, the United Nations Security Council declared that the violations of international humanitarian law in the former Yugoslavia amounted to, and constituted a grave threat to international peace and security. The United Nations Security Council created an international tribunal to address them; and requested the Secretary-General of the United Nations to prepare a report implementing this decision.[62] The Secretary-General's Report contained a draft statute for an *ad hoc* international criminal tribunal. It also took the view that such an *ad hoc* international criminal tribunal be established by resolution rather than treaty.[63]

The United Nations Security Council, pursuant to Chapter VII of the United Nations' Charter, unanimously passed Resolution 827 on 25 May 1993. This created the ICTY. It was the first time an *ad hoc* international criminal tribunal was created in international law. Resolution 827 adopted the draft Statute of the ICTY as expressed in the Secretary-General's report.

The Statute of the ICTY gave the ICTY jurisdiction over crimes against humanity which it defined as

> ...the following crimes when committed in armed conflict, whether international or internal in character, and directed against any civilian population:
> a. murder;
> b. extermination;
> c. enslavement;
> d. deportation;
> e. imprisonment;
> f. torture;
> g. rape;
> h. persecutions on political, racial and religious grounds;
> i. other inhumane acts.[64]

---

[62] United Nations Security Council Resolution 808, U.N. SCOR, 3175th meeting, U.N. Doc. S/RES/808 (1993), 22 February 1993.

[63] Report of the Secretary-General pursuant to paragraph 2 of the United Nations Security Council Resolution 808, 3 May 1993, U.N. Doc. S/25704 (hereinafter referred to as the Secretary-General's Yugoslavia Report). The consideration to have the Statute adopted by a United Nations Security Council Resolution under pursuant to Chapter VII of the United Nations' Charter was influenced by a number of factors: first, a treaty would be a laborious exercise, whereas a Security Council Resolution would be much quicker and easier. Second, such a Security Council Resolution would bind all states, whereas a treaty would bind only those states that are parties to it. Third, it would be more difficult to secure active participation and cooperation of some member states.

[64] Statute of the ICTY, Article 5.

Except for the addition of rape and imprisonment and some other slight differences,[65] the wording was akin to that of Article 6(c) of the Nuremberg Charter. Article 5 of the Statute took a major departure from the UNWCC's conclusions on crimes against humanity, which required that the crimes committed be systematic or widespread. In departing from this requirement, it articulates that the crimes be 'committed in armed conflict'.[66] However, it specifically defines the crime of persecution as based on political, racial and religious grounds. Like some other formulations,[67] it adds the words 'other inhumane acts',[68] with no specificity as to what may amount to an inhumane act.

On 8 November 1994, the United Nations Security Council established the second *ad hoc* tribunal, the ICTR.[69] Like the first, the United Nations Security Council acted pursuant to Chapter VII of the United Nations' Charter.[70] The Statute of the ICTR articulated the crimes over which it has jurisdiction.[71] It has jurisdiction over crimes against humanity, and defines it to mean

> ...the following crimes when committed as part of a widespread or systematic attack against any civilian population on national, political, ethnic, racial or religious grounds:

65 The Statute made redundant the Nuremberg requirement that the commission of crimes against humanity be connected to the other crimes (crimes against peace and war crimes). See generally the Charter of the IMT, Nuremberg, Article 6(c).

66 Ibid.

67 See the Charter of the IMT, Nuremberg, Article 6(c); Charter of the IMTFE, Tokyo, Article 5(c); the Statute of the ICTY, Article 5(i). See also, other (recent) international developments leading to the definition of crimes against humanity. For example, the Rome Statute of the ICC, Article 7(k); the Statute of the SCSL, Article 2(i).

68 Statute of the ICTY, Article 5(i).

69 United Nations Security Council Resolution 955, U. N. SCOR, 3453rd meeting, U.N. Doc. S/RES/955 (1994) to which was annexed the Statute of the International Criminal Tribunal for Rwanda. See also Report of the Secretary-General Pursuant to Paragraph 5 of Security Council Resolution 955 (1994), 13 February 1995, UN Doc. S/1995/134, at 2 (reasons for establishing the ICTR under Chapter VII).

70 The organisation and functioning of the ICTR were similar to those of the ICTY in numerous aspects. First, they were all created pursuant to Chapter VII of the United Nations' Charter. Second, they are all subsidiary, though independent, organs of the Security Council. Third, their organisational structures are identical, with separate prosecutorial, adjudicative and administrative organs. The adjudicative organs comprise of three Trial Chambers and an Appeals Chamber, having similar rules of organisation and procedures. Furthermore, they share a common Appellate Chamber, a common prosecutor and some common prosecutorial staff. See the Statute of the ICTR, Articles 10, 11, 12 (2), 15(3), and 16(3). However, unlike the ICTY, the ICTR carries its operations in different locations. The Office of the Prosecutor and Appeals Chambers are located in The Hague; the investigatory and prosecutorial units operate in Rwanda, and the Trial Chambers sit in Arusha, United Republic of Tanzania.

71 Statute of the ICTR, Articles 2, 3, and 4.

a. murder;
b. extermination;
c. enslavement;
d. deportation;
e. imprisonment;
f. torture;
g. rape;
h. persecutions on political, racial and religious grounds;
i. other inhumane acts.[72]

In defining crimes against humanity, the Statute of the ICTR reiterates one of the conclusions of the UNWCC: that the attack on civilian population constituting these enumerated crimes be 'systematic or widespread'.[73] It deviates from the definition offered by the preceding Statute of the ICTY, which articulates that crimes against humanity be 'committed in armed conflict',[74] while the Statute of the ICTR defined them to be 'crimes committed as part of a widespread or systematic attack against any civilian population....'[75] As will be seen later, this requirement and its accompanying characteristics of an attack now make up the core elements of the definition of crimes against humanity. In other words, an accused would be convicted of crimes against humanity only when it is proved that he did not only commit any of the enlisted crimes, but that such enlisted crime was committed within the framework of an attack, which was widespread or systematic in pattern, directed against a civilian population, and such an attack was based on 'national, political, ethnic, racial or religious grounds.'[76]

4.2.5 *The Rome Statute of the ICC*

Despite the differences in these two *ad hoc* Statutes, the Statute of the ICTR served as a blueprint used in formulating a definition of crimes against humanity in the Rome Statute of the ICC. It provided the conceptual framework from which the definitional elements of crimes against humanity would be borrowed.[77] Established to 'exercise its jurisdiction over persons for the most serious crimes of international concern',[78] its definition of

[72] Statute of the ICTR, Article 3.
[73] Ibid.
[74] Statute of the ICTY, Article 5.
[75] Statute of the ICTR, Article 3.
[76] Ibid. See the discussion below for a thorough analysis of the meaning of these words which jointly constitute the definitional requirements of crimes against humanity.
[77] The formulation stipulated in Article 3 of the Statute of the ICTR provided much of the framework upon which subsequent formulations were made, except for the slight deviations. See the Rome Statute of the ICC, Article 7(1); the Statute of the SCSL, Article 2.
[78] Rome Statute of the ICC, Article 1.

crimes against humanity was akin to the formulation of the Statute of the ICTR.[79] It defines crimes against humanity as

> ...any of the following acts when committed as part of a widespread or systematic attack directed against any civilian population, with knowledge of the attack:
> a. Murder;
> b. Extermination;
> c. Enslavement;
> d. Deportation or forcible transfer of population;
> e. Imprisonment or other severe deprivation of physical liberty in violation of fundamental rules of international law;
> f. Torture;
> g. Rape, sexual slavery, enforced prostitution, forced pregnancy, enforced sterilization, or any other form of sexual violence of comparable gravity;
> h. Persecution against any identifiable group or collectivity on political, racial, national, ethnic, cultural, religious, gender as defined in paragraph 3, or other grounds that are universally recognized as impermissible under international law, in connection with any act referred to in this paragraph or any crime within the jurisdiction of the Court;
> i. Enforced disappearance of persons;
> j. The crime of apartheid;
> k. Other inhumane acts of a similar character intentionally causing great suffering, or serious injury to body or to mental or physical health.[80]

Fifty three years after the Charter of the Nuremberg Tribunal, the definition of crimes against humanity had undergone a tremendous evolution,[81] resulting in the formal adoption of the distinct definitional requirements of crimes against humanity. It departed significantly from previous definitions of crimes against humanity preceding the Statute of the ICTR, and incorporated, with slight changes, the definition contained in the Statute of the ICTR. It discarded the stipulation of the Statute of the ICTY that the crimes be committed when 'in armed conflict'.[82] The stipulated discriminatory grounds ('national, political, ethnic, racial or religious')[83] did not appear in the Rome Statute of the ICC.[84] To a greater extent, the definition

[79] Statute of the ICTR, Article 3. See also the Statute of the ICTY, Article 5.

[80] Rome Statute of the ICC, Article 7(1). While the jurisprudence of the ICC is still being developed, for a general understanding of the core elements of these crimes see the following: Otto Triffterer, *Commentary on the Rome Statute of the International Criminal Court: Observers' Notes, Article by Article* (2nd edn., Hart Publishing 2008); Antonio Cassese, Paola Gaeta and John R.W.D. Jones, *The Rome Statute of the International Criminal Court: A Commentary* (Oxford University Press 2002).

[81] Bassiouni (n. 34).

[82] Statute of the ICTY, Article 5.

[83] Statute of the ICTR, Article 3.

[84] See generally the wording of Rome Statute of the ICC, Article 7(1).

of crimes against humanity under the Rome Statute of the ICC is similar to that of the Statute of the ICTR. Like the Statute of the ICTR, the Rome Statute of the ICC articulates definitional elements: these crimes must be committed as part of an attack that is widespread or systematic in pattern, and, directed against any civilian population.[85] Furthermore, it imports and expands the constituent crimes, with definitions as to their meanings.[86]

The Rome Statute of the ICC is a significant development in international criminal law. Unlike most of the preceding formulations, it is not an *ex post facto* treaty with a retroactive effect.[87] It offers a working definition with the consensus of the global community, not just on its definition and constituent crimes, but even its classification as a serious crime under international law.[88] An issue that comes up is whether this formulation of crimes against humanity per the Rome Statute of the ICC closes every hitherto existing gap, and serves as an acceptable paradigm to other developments in international law. Events that have unfolded beyond the Rome Statute leading to the formulation of crimes against humanity help answer this question.[89]

From the above discussion, it is settled in international law that the definition of crimes against humanity requires that the act of the accused be committed as part of a widespread or systematic attack that is directed against a civilian population, with knowledge of the attack.[90] The requirement of 'knowledge of the attack' was introduced by the Rome Statute of the ICC.[91] Under the Statute of the ICTR, that requirement is absent. Rather, it requires that such an attack be discriminatory: that is, it must be perpetrated on racial, ethnic, religious, national or political grounds.[92] In the following discussion, I examine this element of discriminatory grounds and the other elements contained in the definition of crimes against humanity under the Statute of the ICTR. This analysis is important because, as will be seen in Chapter Five below, it highlights the uniqueness of crimes against humanity as group crimes which require the existence of a joint criminal enterprise for their planning, preparation and execution.

---

85 The Rome Statute of the ICC, Article 7(1), which makes express mention that these crimes be committed as part of an attack, and '...with knowledge of the attack'.

86 Rome Statute of the ICC, Article 7(1).

87 Rome Statute of the ICC, Article 11(1).

88 Rome Statute of the ICC, Article 7(1).

89 Statute of the SCSL.

90 Rome Statute of the ICC, Article 7(1); Statute of the SCSL, Article 2.

91 Rome Statute of the ICC, Article 7(1).

92 Statute of the ICTR, Article 3.

4.3 The Definitional Elements of Crimes Against Humanity Under the Statute of the ICTR

Traditionally, in criminal law, a crime comprises two elements: first, the *actus reus* (the material elements), and second, the *mens rea* (the requisite mental element) of that crime.[93] The definition of an *actus reus* includes acts, omissions and even circumstances.[94] For example, in the crime of driving under the influence, driving is the conduct. The circumstance is 'being under influence'. In the crime of being in possession of stolen property, being in possession is the conduct element of the crime, and the stolen nature of the property is the circumstance that must accompany such prescribed and prohibited conduct.[95]

This analysis of the constituent elements of a crime is different in the case of crimes against humanity under the Statute of the ICTR.[96] Its definition articulates a set of circumstances within which the prescribed conduct must be committed.[97] This set of circumstances is referred to as the definitional (or essential) elements of crimes against humanity. The Statute of the ICTR requires that any of the crimes must be committed as part of a widespread or systematic attack, directed against any civilian population, and on any of the discriminatory grounds.[98] Therefore, the fact that an accused committed murder is insufficient to found a charge of crimes against humanity. It must be proved that such an act of murder meets the prescribed circumstances: that such an act of murder was committed within, a part or in furtherance of a widespread or systematic attack,

---

[93] Ormerod (n. 15) 42–177; Joshua Dressler, *Understanding Criminal Law* (5th edn., LexisNexis 2009) 85–143; Michael J. Allen and Simon Cooper, *Elliott & Wood's Cases and Materials on Criminal Law* (9th edn., Sweet & Maxwell 2006) 25–145; Heaton (n. 15) 13–76; Philip Asterley Jones and Richard Card, *Cross and Jones' Introduction to Criminal Law* (8th edn., Butterworths 1976) 25–30.

[94] Ormerod (n. 15) 42–93; Dressler (n. 93) 85–115; Heaton (n. 15) 13–40.

[95] Ibid.

[96] The Statute of the ICTR provides not only the conduct elements, but also a specific set of circumstances which must accompany the various conduct elements. These specific set of circumstances are referred to as the definitional (or essential) elements of crimes against humanity, and it highlights the uniqueness of crimes against humanity as it distinguishes it from other ordinary crimes.

[97] A good example is the crime of murder as a crime against humanity. Murder consists of intentionally killing another. To kill another intentionally is a prohibited conduct. For such a killing to qualify as a crime against humanity, it must be proved that it was perpetrated within the specified circumstances: within, as a part or in furtherance of a widespread or systematic attack directed against any civilian population on any of the discriminatory grounds.

[98] Statute of the ICTR, Article 3.

directed against any civilian population and committed on any of the discriminatory grounds.

As discussed earlier, the wording of Article 3 of the Statute of the ICTR which defines crimes against humanity further reveals a unique feature of crimes against humanity: they are group crimes, or require the involvement of several persons in their planning, preparation or execution. These three different stages of criminal activity are emphasised because the imposition of criminal responsibility under Article 6(1) covers any of the modes of participation that leads to any of these stages of any of the crimes. If the definition of crimes against humanity under Article 3 requires the involvement of several persons, then, it is logical to argue that these persons would be imposed criminal responsibility if through any of the modes under Article 6(1) they cause the planning, preparation or execution of crimes against humanity (as well as the other crimes over which the ICTR has jurisdiction).

It is therefore important to examine these definitional elements because in the next chapter, I argue that the very definitional elements envisage the existence of a joint criminal enterprise. Within this joint criminal enterprise, different individuals played different roles at different times. However, they had a common purpose: the commission of crimes. As is customary in cases of joint criminal enterprise, every member thereof bears the same degree of responsibility for the crimes committed.[99] If this approach and logical analysis were adopted by the prosecutors and Trial and Appeal Chambers of the ICTR, then, instigation would not be limited to incitement to genocide; and the substantial contribution to commission as a prerequisite to the imposition of criminal responsibility under Article 6(1) would not be made.

The Statute of the ICTR defines crimes against humanity as '...the following crimes when committed as part of a widespread or systematic attack against any civilian population on national, political, ethnic, racial or religious grounds...' Per this definition under the Statute of the ICTR, for there to be crimes against humanity, it must be proved that any of the enlisted crimes was committed as part of a 'widespread or systematic attack against a civilian population'.[100] Such an attack must be perpetrated on discriminatory grounds (racial, ethnic, national, religious or political). The accused

---

[99] Ormerod (n. 15) 182; Heaton (n. 15) 386–91.

[100] *Semanza* (n. 13) para. 326; *The Prosecutor v Jean-Paul Akayesu*, Judgment, Case No. ICTR-96-4, Appeal Chamber, 1 June 2001, Paras. 460–69; *Musema* (n. 13) paras. 199–211; *Rutaganda* (n. 13) paras. 65–71; *Kayishema and Ruzindana* (n. 13) (TC) paras. 119–34.

must commit any of the enlisted crimes with knowledge that there is a widespread or systematic attack.[101] These definitional elements can be summarised as follows:

i. there must be an attack;
ii. the attack is widespread or systematic;
iii. the crime committed by the accused must be within, part or in furtherance of, the widespread or systematic attack;
iv. the widespread or systematic attack is directed against a civilian population;
v. the widespread or systematic attack is discriminatory in nature: that is, it is perpetrated on racial, ethnic, religious, national or political grounds;
vi. and the perpetrator acted with knowledge of the attack (the *mens rea* or mental element).

The Trial and Appeal Chambers have shown remarkable consistency in recognising these definitional elements as constituting an integral part of the definition of crimes against humanity. As their jurisprudence establish, these definitional elements serve as distinguishing features that highlight the unique character of crimes against humanity.

Though fundamentally different from the definition of crimes against humanity under the Statute of the ICTY, the Trial and Appeal Chambers of the ICTY have also recognised that these definitional elements represent the current and correct definition of crimes against humanity. The Statute of the ICTY has undergone numerous amendments, and the initial definition of crimes against humanity has not been amended. However, the Trial and Appeal Chambers of both the ICTR and ICTY recognise these definitional elements. In discussing these elements therefore, I use the jurisprudence of both Tribunals. Given the fact that the Trial and Appeal Chambers of the ICTR have used the jurisprudence of the ICTY, I will make intermittent references to cases from the ICTY.

4.3.1 *The Attack*

The requirement of an attack as part of the definitional elements of crimes against humanity denotes 'a course of conduct involving the commission of acts of violence.'[102] The requirement of an attack is not limited to the

---

101 Rome Statute of the ICC, Article 7(1).

102 Guénaël Mettraux, *International Crimes and the ad hoc Tribunals* (Oxford University Press 2005) 156. See the following cases: *Kayishema and Ruzindana* (n. 13) (TC) para. 122

conduct of hostilities. An attack may occur without the presence of hostilities. The requirement of an attack covers the maltreatment of persons who take no active part in hostilities.[103] Furthermore, there is no requirement that the attack be directed against the enemy.[104] The attack may be directed against any civilian population, including any part of the state's population.

An attack in itself does not constitute a crime against humanity. It merely serves as the 'vehicle for the commission of crimes against humanity.'[105] It is the framework or foundation, within and upon which the enlisted crimes are perpetrated.[106]

The definitional requirement of an attack connotes an enterprise that is being executed as part of a policy or plan. It is the framework within which a common purpose is established and materialised; and the acts of the accused persons are in furtherance of that common purpose. It uncovers the existence of a joint criminal enterprise. Within this joint criminal enterprise, there are different actors who may be at different places and times, play different roles, but acting individually or collectively to perpetrate the acts within the framework of the attack. The perpetration of these acts constitutes the materialisation and consummation of the attack contained in the policy of the joint criminal enterprise. As Mettraux puts it,

> ...the attack requirement appears to be a descriptive device that captures in one word a pattern of criminal activity, in the context of which the acts of the

---

where the Trial Chamber described the *attack* as 'the event in which the enumerated crimes must form part'. In *Akayesu* (n. 13), the Trial Chamber gave a slightly different definition of the meaning of 'attack': 'The concept of "attack" may be defined as an unlawful act of the kind enumerated in Article 3(a) to (i) under the Statute, like murder, extermination, enslavement, etc.' (para. 581); *Kajelijeli* (n. 13) para. 867; *Musema* (n. 13) para. 205; *Rutaganda* (n. 13) para. 70; and the Rome Statute of the ICC, 17 July 1998, Article 7, Para. 2, UN Doc. A/CONF.183/9 (1998), which defined an attack in the following words: '"Attack directed against any civilian population" means a course of conduct involving the multiple commission of acts referred to in paragraph 1 against any civilian population, pursuant to or in furtherance of a state of organisational policy to commit such attack.'

103 The Appeal Chamber held that 'the attack in the context of a crime against humanity is not limited to the use of armed force; it encompasses any mistreatment of the civilian population....' See *Dargoljub Kunarac, Radomir Kovač & Zoran Vuković v The Prosecutor*, Judgment, Case No. IT-96-23 & 23/1-T, Appeal Chamber, 12 June 2002, Para. 86; *The Prosecutor v Dargoljub Kunarac, Radomir Kovač & Zoran Vuković*, Judgment, Case No. IT-96-23 & 23/1-T, T. Ch., 22 February 2001, Para. 416.

104 Pursuant to the definition of crimes against humanity, 'civilian population' is the phraseology used, which can be construed to be opposite to 'armed population'. See the subsection on 'civilian population' below.

105 Mettraux (n. 102) 157.

106 Ibid.

accused must have taken place to be regarded as crimes against humanity. To the extent that the acts of the accused can be sufficiently linked to that attack, they acquire a greater criminal dimension which sets them apart from purely domestic crimes and differentiates them from ordinary war crimes.[107]

4.3.2 *There must be a Widespread or Systematic Attack*

The words 'widespread or systematic' as part of the qualifier of the attack disclose the scale (widespread) or the organised nature (systematic) of the attack.[108] Either or both of these two definitional requirements will suffice to translate a crime to crimes against humanity. The adjectives alternate, and have a disjunctive rather than conjunctive effect: proof that the attacks were either widespread or systematic is sufficient to amount to crimes against humanity.[109]

The word 'widespread' has been used to mean the large-scale nature of the attack, measured by the number of victims involved.[110] An attack may

---

107 Ibid 161.

108 In *The Prosecutor v Fatmir Limaj, Haradin Baa and Isak Muslui*, Judgment, Case No. IT-03-66-T, T. Ch. II, 30 November 2005, it was held that the requirements of widespread or systematic are 'disjunctive rather than cumulative', holding that the word 'widespread' refers to 'the large scale nature of the attack and the number of victims,' while 'systematic' means 'the organized nature of the acts of violence and the improbability of their random occurrence.' The inclusion of the words 'widespread or systematic' distinguishes 'non-accidental repetition of similar conduct on a regular basis,' which reveals the systematic nature of the attacks. See also *Tihomir Blaškić v The Prosecutor*, Judgment, Case No. IT-95-14, Appeal Chamber, 29 July 2004, Para. 101 (citing *Kunarac* et al (n. 103) (AC) para. 94). In *Kunarac* et al (n. 103), the Appeal Chamber stated its view that 'the assessment of what constitutes a "widespread" or "systematic" attack is essentially a relative exercise in that it depends upon the civilian population which, allegedly, was being attacked. A Trial Chamber must therefore "first identify the population which is the object of the attack and, in light of the means, methods, resources and result of the attack upon the population, ascertain whether the attack was indeed widespread or systematic". The consequences of the attack upon the targeted population, the number of victims, the nature of the acts, the possible participation of officials or authorities or any identifiable patterns of crimes, could be taken into account to determine whether the attack satisfies either or both requirements of a "widespread" or "systematic" attack vis-à-vis this civilian population.' Para. 95.

109 *Kunarac* et al (n. 103) (AC) para. 93 (and the references cited therein); *Blaškić* (n. 108) para. 101. In the Report of the Secretary-General (ICTY), the Statute of the ICC and the work of the ILC, the conditions of scale and 'systematicity' are not necessarily cumulative. In other words, any of the acts, even inhumane acts, can be characterised as crimes against humanity if any of the two conditions is met. See *The Prosecutor v Tihomir Blaškić*, Judgment, Case No. IT-95-14. T. Ch., 3 March 2000, Para. 207; *Kunarac* et al (n. 103) (TC) para. 427; *The Prosecutor v Jean de Dieu Kamuhanda*, Judgment, Case No.ICTR-95-54A-T, T. Ch. II, 22 January 2004, Para. 664; *Kajelijeli* (n. 13) paras. 869–70; *Rutaganda* (n. 13) paras. 67–68; *Akayesu* (n. 13) para. 579. See also the ILC, 1991 ILC Report and 1996 ILC Report.

110 See *Akayesu* (n. 13) para. 580; Mettraux (n. 102) 170–72; William A. Schabas, *The UN International Criminal Tribunals: The Former Yugoslavia, Rwanda and Sierra Leone* (Cambridge University Press 2006) 191–96.

be widespread as a result of the cumulative effect of a series of acts. It may also be widespread based on the effect of a single act of extraordinary magnitude.[111] 'Systematic' refers to the organised nature of the attack, including the improbability of their random occurrence. The systematic pattern of an attack is revealed by the non-accidental repetition of similar acts or conduct on a regular basis.[112]

In practice, these two adjectives describing the nature of the attacks do overlap. An attack that is widespread may also be systematic.[113] A widespread attack targeting a civilian population requires some level of planning or organisation. So too is an attack that is systematic in pattern, as it has the purpose, potential, frequency and effect of reaching and affecting many people, thereby satisfying the widespread requirement. The history of the situation may be examined in its entirety to determine whether there was a widespread or systematic attack. Mettraux has outlined some factors to be considered by a Trial Chamber in determining whether there was a widespread or systematic attack: the number of criminal acts, the number of victims, the existence of criminal patterns, the existence of a policy or plan targeting specific group(s) of individuals, the inescapability of the attack, the involvement of military or political authorities, the logistics and financial resources involved, the existence of public statements or political views underpinning the events, the means and methods used in the attacks and the adoption of discriminatory measures.[114]

In determining whether an attack was widespread or systematic in pattern, the Trial Chamber examines the totality of the circumstances pertaining to the situation or events. The Trial Chamber must identify the population which has been targeted and determine whether there was an attack against this population. As to the pattern of the attack, the Trial Chamber considers the means, methods and resources used, and the outcome(s) of the attack to determine if the attack in question was widespread or systematic.[115]

---

111 The Trial Chamber in *Rutaganda* defined widespread to mean 'massive, frequent, large-scale action, carried out collectively with considerable seriousness and directed against a multiplicity of victims'. See *Rutaganda* (n. 13) para. 68.

112 *Rutaganda* (n. 13) para. 68. See also the Trial Chamber's definition of systematic which it held to be a 'thoroughly organized action, following a regular pattern on the basis of a common policy and involving substantial public or private resources.'

113 Numerous Chambers (Trial) in the *ad hoc* tribunals have found that the attacks waged against the population were both widespread and systematic. See *The Prosecutor v Duško Tadić*, Judgment, Case No. IT-94-1, T. Ch., 7 May 1997, Para. 660; *Rutaganda* (n. 13) para. 67; *Kayishema and Ruzindana* (n. 13) (TC) para. 576; *Akayesu* (n. 13) para. 652.

114 Mettraux (n. 102) 171.

115 *Kunarac* et al (n. 103) (TC) para. 430. On appeal, it was held that in determining whether an attack satisfies either or both requirements of 'widespread' or 'systematic' attack against

Under the definitional requirements of crimes against humanity, only the attack must be widespread or systematic in pattern.[116] It is not necessary that the accused's specific act is 'widespread' or 'systematic'. Unless it was isolated, a single act would qualify as a crime against humanity if it was perpetrated within the framework of an attack.[117] In the Rwandan experience, a good example would be the single killing of a Tutsi. If such a killing was perpetrated against a Tutsi as part of a widespread or systematic attack directed against the Tutsis (a civilian population), then, that single act qualifies as murder as a crime against humanity. As long as the crime committed by the accused is part of an attack and this attack is widespread or systematic, then, the numerical value (in terms of impact) of the accused's crime becomes irrelevant.

4.3.3 *The Crime Committed by the Accused must be within, Part or in Furtherance of the Widespread or Systematic Attack*

Not every crime committed during an attack constitutes crimes against humanity. For an act to count as a crime against humanity, it must be proved that such a crime was committed within, part or in furtherance of the widespread or systematic attack.[118] There is a link between the crime committed by the accused and the widespread or systematic attack. As the Appeal Chamber of the ICTY held the correct legal position is that the act of the accused must be 'part of' a pattern of widespread and systematic crimes directed against a civilian population.[119] Therefore, the fact that an accused killed someone is not sufficient to amount to crimes against humanity: it must be shown further that the killing was done as part or in furtherance of a widespread or systematic attack.

---

a civilian population, it would take into account factors such as the nature of the acts, the consequences of such acts upon the targeted population, the number of victims, the participation of officials and other authorities, civilian or military, and any identifiable pattern in the commission of crimes. *Kunarac* et al (n. 103) (AC) para. 95.

116 *Kunarac* et al (n. 103) (AC) para. 96; *Kunarac* et al (n. 103) (TC) para. 430; *Blaškić* (n. 108) para. 101.

117 *Kunarac* et al (n. 103) (AC) para. 96; *The Prosecutor v Zoran Kupreškić, Drago Josipović, Vladimir Šantić, Mirjan Kupreškić, Vlatko Kupreškić, Dragan Papić*, Judgment, Case No. IT-95-16-T, T. Ch., 14 January 2000, Para. 550, where the Trial Chamber held: 'For example, the act of denouncing a Jewish neighbour to the Nazi authorities – if committed against a background of widespread persecution – has been regarded as amounting to a crime against humanity. An isolated act, however – i.e. an atrocity which did not occur within such a context – cannot.'

118 *Kayishema and Ruzindana* (n. 13) (TC) para. 135.

119 *Tadić* (n. 113) paras. 248, 255; *Kunarac* et al (n. 103) (AC) para. 99, where it was held that the 'acts of the accused must constitute part of the attack'.

In order to establish a nexus between the attack and act of the accused, the Trial Chambers of the ICTY have formulated two rules.[120] First, the perpetrator must commit an act or participate in a way affecting the furtherance of the attack. The application of this rule is based on an objective appreciation of the nature and consequences of the act of the perpetrator. The accused person's act therefore, must not be looked at as an isolated incident,[121] but within the framework it was committed.[122] The perpetrator does not have to commit a series of acts in order to fulfil the nexus requirement. In principle, a single act of the perpetrator will suffice to establish the nexus requirement.[123] The important point is that the accused intentionally perpetrates his act in order to further the widespread or systematic attack directed against the civilian group in question. The second rule deals with the knowledge on the part of the perpetrator. The perpetrator must be aware that there is an on-going attack against any civilian population; and his act constitutes part of the attack.[124] This requirement may appear difficult to prove without compelling evidence. However, inference of this knowledge can be made from the circumstances preceding, during and after the perpetration of the act or waging of the attack. Attendance at meetings where the attack was conceived or discussed in detail, and subsequent participation (such as planning, ordering, aiding and abetting, and even failing to prevent) in the perpetration of the acts envisaged in the

---

[120] See *Tadić* (n. 113) paras. 248, 255; *Kunarac* et al (n. 103) (AC) para. 99; *The Prosecutor v Mitar Vasiljević*, Judgment, Case No. IT-98-32-T, T. Ch. II, 29 November 2002, Para. 32; *Limaj* et al (n. 108) para. 162.

[121] An isolated incident will not qualify as a crime against humanity. The rationale behind this position is the detachment of the crime from the core of the attack for it to be considered to be part thereof. See *Kunarac* et al (n. 103) (AC) para. 100, where it was established that if the crime 'is so far removed from that attack, having considered the context and circumstances in which it was committed, it cannot reasonably be said to have been part of the attack.'

[122] See *Kunarac* et al (n. 103) (TC) para. 592, where it was held that there did exist a nexus between the acts of the accused (consisting of various forms of sexual violence, acts of torture and enslavement perpetrated against Muslim women and girls) and the attack against the Muslim civilian population of the Foca region. It was established that the accused did not only know of the attacks but also perpetrated the attacks by taking exploiting the situation that created it.

[123] *Tadić* (n. 113) para. 649, where it was held that 'a single act by a perpetrator taken within the context of a widespread or systematic attack against a civilian population entails individual criminal responsibility and an individual perpetrator need not commit numerous offenses to be liable. Although it is correct that isolated, random acts should not be included in the definition of crimes against humanity, that is the purpose of requiring that the acts be directed against a civilian population....' See also *Blaškić* (n. 108) para. 101.

[124] *Kunarac* et al (n. 103) (TC) para. 418. See also Mettraux (n. 102) 156–63; Schabas (n. 110) 191–96.

attack are of a high evidentiary value in determining if the perpetrator knew of the attack.[125] Participation here involves (but is not limited to) planning, ordering, instigating, aiding and abetting. Furthermore, in cases where prevention is viable, a failure to prevent the commission of the crimes would be considered in determining whether the accused knew of the attack.[126]

There is no legal rule as to the timeliness of the perpetration of the act. It must not be committed in the heart of the attack for it to be connected with the attack. In *Kunarac* et al, the Appeals Chambers established that the

> acts of the accused must be part of the 'attack' against the civilian population, but they need not be committed in the midst of that attack. A crime which is committed before or after the main attack against the civilian population or away from it could still, if sufficiently connected, be part of that attack.[127]

Time and place play no significant role as long as there is a nexus between the act perpetrated and the attack. The act may be perpetrated before, during, or after the attack.[128] Its occurrence may span a period of months after the main bulk of atrocities have been committed. As long as there is some nexus between the act and the attack, it will amount to crimes against humanity. A criminal act perpetrated in a neighbouring or distant village will amount to a crime against humanity if it can be proved that the criminal act was connected to the attack. As mentioned earlier, the nexus requirement between the perpetrator's act and the attack can be inferred from the circumstances surrounding the perpetrator's act, and also, the 'characteristics, aims, nature, and consequence' of the perpetrator's acts.[129]

4.3.4 *The Attack is Directed Against any Civilian Population*

The definitional requirements of crimes against humanity stipulate that the attack, widespread or systematic in pattern, must be directed against any civilian population.[130] The phrase 'directed against any civilian population'

---

125 *Kunarac* et al (n. 103) (TC) para. 418.

126 For an understanding of the historical evolution of criminal responsibility in international criminal law, see the Charter of the IMT, Nuremberg, Article 6(c); the Charter of the IMTFE, Tokyo, Article 5(c); the Statute of the ICTY, Article 7(1); the Statute of the ICTR, Article 6(1); the Rome Statute of the ICC, Article 25; and the Statute of the SCSL, Article 6(1).

127 *Kunarac* et al (n. 103) (AC) para. 100.

128 Ibid.

129 *Kajelijeli* (n. 13) para. 866; *Semanza* (n. 13) para. 326.

130 Statute of the ICTR, Article 3. See also the Rome Statute of the ICC, Article 7(1).

contains three distinct elements worthy of discussion: 'directed against', 'any', and 'civilian population'.

The phrase 'directed against' means that a civilian population must be the primary target of the attack. The attack must be aimed at a civilian population and not just an incidental victim of it. It is not the act of the accused that must target a civilian population but the attack as a whole.[131] Jurisprudence from the Tribunals shows a valid recognition that it is the attack, and not the act of the accused, that must be directed against any civilian population.[132] In determining whether such an attack is primarily directed against any civilian population, the courts will, including other things, look at

> the means and method used in the course of the attack, the status of the victims, their number, the discriminatory nature of the attack, the nature of the crimes committed in its course, the resistance to the assailants at the time and the extent to which the attacking force may be said to have complied or attempted to comply with the precautionary requirements of the laws of war. To the extent that the alleged crimes against humanity were committed in the course of an armed conflict, the laws of war provide a benchmark against which the Chamber may assess the nature of the attack and the legality of the acts committed in its midst.[133]

The perpetrator of an act only needs to have intended to inflict injury upon his or her victim with knowledge of the overall context within which his act was perpetrated. This therefore, makes it unnecessary for him to have intended to inflict injury against a broader population.

The word 'any' signifies that crimes against humanity can be committed against any (part of a) civilian population. Distinguishing features such as nationality, race, ethnicity, gender, age, or any other, are irrelevant. It eliminates any further classification of humanity: a civilian population is the only requirement. Stateless persons can be victims of crimes against humanity. This caveat makes it possible for any civilian population to be the primary aim of the attack; and can be committed by anyone against any civilian population. Geographical limitations or the presence of hostilities do not make it impossible to perpetrate acts against a civilian population that will amount to crimes against humanity.[134]

---

[131] Statute of the ICTR, Article 3; and the Rome Statute of the ICC, Article 7.

[132] *The Prosecutor v Duško Tadić*, Judgment, Case No. IT-94-1, Appeal Chamber, 15 July 1999, Para. 248; *Rutaganda* (n. 13) para. 71; *Akayesu* (n. 13) para. 582.

[133] *Kunarac* et al (n. 103) (AC) para. 91. See also *The Prosecutor v Miladen Naletilić and Vinko Martinović*, Judgment, Case No. IT-98-34, Appeal Chamber, 3 May 2006, Para. 235.

[134] *Vasiljević* (n. 120) para. 33; *Kunarac* et al (n. 131) (TC) para. 423; *Tadić* (n. 113) para. 635. In *Sivakumar v Canada (Minister of Employment and Immigration)* [1994] FC 433, it was

The phrase 'civilian population' eliminates isolated or random acts from amounting to crimes against humanity. The word 'population' cannot be construed to mean the entire population of a circumscribed geographical location against which the attack is directed. However, it will qualify as an attack directed against a 'civilian population' if it can be established that the scale, methods, and resources involved in waging the attack targeted a civilian population generally or indiscriminately rather than selected members of that population.[135] Citing the Trial Chamber judgment in *Kunarac* et al,[136] Mettraux advances the following to be a definition of population for the purpose of crimes against humanity:

> ...a sizeable group of people who possess some distinctive features that mark them as targets of the attack. The 'population' must form a somewhat self-contained group of individuals, either geographically or as a result of other common features. A group of individuals randomly or fortuitously assembled – such as a crowd at a football game – could not be regarded as a 'population' under this definition.[137]

The phrase 'civilian population' serves as an indicator in determining which group or groups of people may in fact be the target of an attack. It is therefore necessary to consider the size of the population within the context of the attack. Where there is a small numerical value of individuals such as detainees in a penal institution, that would not qualify as a population unless it is proven that the crimes committed against them is part of a wider criminal campaign or enterprise. In *Limaj* et al,[138] the Trial Chamber stated held that it must be shown that enough 'individuals were targeted in the course of the attack', or that they were 'targeted in such a way' that the Trial Chamber is satisfied that the attack was 'in fact directed against a civilian 'population' and not against 'a limited and randomly selected number of individuals'.[139] The widespread or systematic pattern of the attack is determined by looking at the population against which such an attack is directed. Cosmopolitan societies in which different individuals with distinct characteristics live together may be considered a civilian population, as well as each of the distinct groups living therein. It is unnecessary to

acknowledged that crimes against humanity can be committed against enemy populations as well as against a country's citizens. The current definition of crimes against humanity makes it unnecessary and irrelevant to demonstrate that the victims of the crimes have a nexus to any particular side of a conflict. See *Kunarac* et al (n. 103) (TC) para. 423.

135 *Kunarac* et al (n. 103) (AC) para. 90.

136 *Kunarac* et al (n. 103) (TC).

137 Mettraux (n. 102) 166.

138 *Limaj* et al (n. 108).

139 Ibid para. 160. See also *Kunarac* et al (n. 103) (AC) para. 90.

establish that a particular individual belongs to a particular group. The prosecution only needs to establish that the individual in question is a civilian, and that he or she was targeted as part of an attack against a civilian population. In *Akayesu*,[140] the Trial Chamber held that cases of inhumane acts that are committed against persons who do not fall within any of the discriminatory categories could still constitute crimes against humanity if the intention of the perpetrator was to further his attack against a group discriminated against. The focal point here, as revealed by the language of the Trial Chamber, is the perpetrator's requisite intent to commit crimes against humanity.[141]

In *Limaj* et al,[142] the Trial Chamber, recalling the 'absolute prohibition against targeting civilians in customary international law',[143] articulated these guidelines on what would amount to a civilian population. It held that a

> ...civilian population must be interpreted broadly and refers to a population that is predominantly civilian in nature. A population may qualify as 'civilian' even if non-civilians are among it, as long as it is predominantly civilian.... The presence within a population of members of resistance armed groups, or former combatants who have laid down their arms, does not as such alter its civilian nature.... As a result, the definition of a 'civilian' is expansive and includes individuals who at one time performed acts of resistance, as well as persons who were *hors de combat* when the crime was committed.... Relevant to the determination whether the presence of soldiers within a civilian population deprives the population of its civilian character are the number of soldiers as well as whether they are on leave.... There is no requirement that the victims are linked to any particular side of the conflict....[144]

To meet the requirement of a 'civilian population' as part of the definition of crimes against humanity, the population must be predominantly civilian.[145] The presence of non-civilians among the population may not alter the civilian character of a population; as they may not be regular units in large numbers. The presence of a huge number of soldiers or combatants within a population may alter the character of the population and deprive it of its civilian character or status.[146] 'Civilian population' includes all

140 *Akayesu* (n. 13).

141 Ibid para. 584.

142 *Limaj* et al (n. 108).

143 Ibid para. 156.

144 Ibid (footnotes omitted).

145 *Rutaganda* (n. 13) para. 71; *Akayesu* (n. 13) para. 582.

146 *Blaškić* (n. 108) para. 115, where the Appeal Chamber held that the number of soldiers, and whether they were on duty leave would be factors to be considered in determining whether a population was civilian.

persons with the exception of those whose duty is to maintain public order and do have the lawful means to exercise force, such as the police. In times of armed conflict, the 'civilian population' covers all individuals who are neither members of the armed forces nor legitimate combatants. This notion of civilians is not very different from the same notion under the laws of war.[147]

The requirement that the attack must be directed against a civilian population traditionally excludes soldiers and combatants as possible victims of crimes against humanity. In *Blaškić*,[148] the Appeal Chamber pointed out that the specific circumstances of the victim at the time of the acts are not conclusive in the determination of his civilian or non-civilian status. The fact that a combatant or soldier was unarmed or not engaged in combat at the time of the attack does not necessarily or conclusively entitle him to the status of a civilian. Attacks against military personnel or combatants do not amount to crimes against humanity. However, they will amount to crimes against humanity if the attacks on military personnel or combatants are a consequence, direct or indirect, of targeting the civilian population. The presence (permanent or temporary) of few soldiers to safeguard a village or city would not alter the character of the population if attacks are launched against the population of the geographical entity.

4.3.5 *The Attack must be Discriminatory in Nature*

The attack waged against a civilian population must be discriminatory in nature. The Statute of the ICTR stipulates that the discriminatory nature of the attack can be racial, ethnic, religious, political or national.[149] Discrimination on any of these grounds suffices.[150]

4.3.6 *The* Mens Rea *of Crimes Against Humanity*

Given the fact these definitional elements help portray the requirement of a joint criminal enterprise within which these crimes can be committed, it is necessary to examine briefly the requisite mental element (*mens rea*) of crimes against humanity. The perpetrator must be aware that there is a

147 *Musema* (n. 13) para. 282; *Rutaganda* (n. 13) para. 71; *Akayesu* (n. 13), para. 582.

148 *Blaškić* (n. 108).

149 Statute of the ICTR, Article 3. See also *Semanza* (n. 13) para. 331; *Rutaganda* (n. 13) para. 72; *Akayesu* (n. 13) para. 582.

150 *Rutaganda* (n. 13) para. 72.

widespread or systematic attack that is directed against a civilian population, and his acts are perpetrated as part of, within or in furtherance of the widespread or systematic attack. Knowledge of the specifications of the attack is not necessary. Neither does the accused need to know that such an attack is being directed against a civilian population. As said in *Kunarac* et al, it 'is the attack, not the acts of the accused, which must be directed against the target population and the accused person only needs to know that his acts are part thereof.'[151] The *mens rea* can be inferred from the accused's actions; such as wilfully accepting a particular function which obliged him to perpetrate the acts. The military position or civilian leadership of the accused, the *de jure* and *de facto* powers assigned to, and exercised by the accused, his voluntary assumption of important roles in a criminal organisation, his participation in perpetrating acts of violence, his physical presence at the scenes of these crimes as well as in meetings in which they were planned and instigated, the perpetration of detention, rape and other violent sexual acts, brutalisation, murder and extermination of civilians, including 'his utterances and references to the superiority of his group over the enemy group; the extent to which the crimes were reported in the media; the scale of the acts of violence, and the general historical and political environment in which the acts occurred; and the consistency and predictability of his criminal acts' are factors that can be used to determine the perpetrator's *mens rea*.[152]

4.4 Conclusion

The above discussion illustrates first, the legislative evolution of crimes against humanity, from when it resided in international discourse as a 'term of art',[153] to when it finally got crystallised as a positive and serious crime in international law;[154] and second, the definitional elements of crimes against humanity under the Statute of the ICTR.

---

151 *Kunarac* et al (n. 103) (AC) para. 103.

152 Mettraux (n. 102) 173. See also *Tadić* (n. 113), where it was emphasised that 'while knowledge is thus required, it is examined on an objective level and factually can be implied from the circumstances' (para. 657). In *Blaškić* (n. 108), it was held that 'knowledge on the part of the accused depends on the facts of a particular case; as a result, the manner in which this legal element may be proved may vary from case to case' (para. 126). See also *Kayishema and Ruzindana* (n. 13) (AC) paras. 133–34.

153 Clark (n. 20).

154 See the Charter of the IMT, Nuremberg, Article 6(c), the Charter of the IMTFE, Article 5 (c), the Statute of the ICTY, Article 5, the Statute of the ICTR, Article 3, the Rome Statute of

The above discussion does not merely highlight the evolution of crimes against humanity as a serious crime in international law. Neither does it only consider the definitional requirements of crimes against humanity. The discussion portrays the uniqueness of crimes against humanity, and in stipulating these chapeau elements, I bring out the necessity of group involvement for the planning, preparation and execution of crimes against humanity as implied by the definitional elements of crimes against humanity under the Statute of the ICTR. As Mettraux outlined what factors can be looked at in determining whether an attack was widespread or systematic,[155] it is impossible to have an attack that meets this threshold without the involvement of different individuals who play different roles at different times. The involvement of numerous individuals who partook in different ways in the atrocities in Rwanda helped in the formulation of both the definition of crimes against humanity (containing numerous and fundamental differences from the Statute of the ICTY) and the imposition of criminal responsibility. By stipulating the various modes of participation, which must lead to any of the stages of any of the crimes (planning, preparation or execution), the drafters clearly knew that a joint criminal enterprise must have been in place for atrocities of such a scale and magnitude to be executed. It is within this conceptual framework of the existence of a joint criminal enterprise that I critique the approach of the ICTR in construing instigation under Article 6(1) as a mode of participation that would incur criminal responsibility.

the ICC, Article 7(1), the Statute of the SCSL, Article 2 (at least, these are formulations which highlight not just the recognition of crimes against humanity as a serious crime, but (with the exclusion of the ICC) had individuals tried and convicted of crimes against humanity).

155 Mettraux (n. 102).

CHAPTER FIVE

CRITIQUING THE TRIAL AND APPEAL CHAMBERS' CONSTRUCTION OF INSTIGATION TO CRIMES AGAINST HUMANITY UNDER ARTICLE 6(1) OF THE STATUTE OF THE ICTR

5.1 Introduction

In the previous Chapters, I have examined instigation as a mode of participation under Article 6(1) of the Statute of the ICTR and one of the crimes over which the ICTR has jurisdiction: crimes against humanity. In this chapter, I critique the approach to, and jurisprudence of, both the Office of the Prosecutors and the Chambers (Trial and Appeal Chambers) of the ICTR on instigation as a mode of participation in the planning, preparation or execution of crimes against humanity.

The Statute of the ICTR defines the imposition of criminal responsibility in the following words:

> A person who planned, instigated, ordered, committed or otherwise aided and abetted in the planning, preparation or execution of a crime referred to in articles 2 to 4 [genocide, crimes against humanity and violations of Article 3 common to the Geneva Conventions and of Additional Protocol II] of the present Statute, shall be individually responsible for the crime.[1]

The jurisprudence of the Trial and Appeal Chambers establishes that criminal responsibility under Article 6(1) can be imposed only where his participation substantially contributes to the commission of the crimes under the jurisdiction of the ICTR.[2] This requirement is untenable. I argue that this

---

[1] Statute of the ICTR, annexed to United Nations Security Council Resolution 955, U.N. SCOR, 3453rd meeting, U.N. Doc. S/RES/955 (1994), Article 6(1).

[2] *The Prosecutor v Idelphonse Hategekimana*, Judgment, Case No. ICTR-00-55, T. Ch. II, 6 December 2010, Para 644; *The Prosecutor v Callixte Kalimanzira*, Judgment, Case No. ICTR-05-88-T, T. Ch. III, 22 June 2009, Para. 512; *The Prosecutor v Juvénal Kajelijeli*, Judgment, Case No. ICTR-96-44-T, T. Ch. II, 1 December 2003, Para. 759; *The Prosecution v Laurent Semanza*, Judgment, Case No. ICTR-97-20, T. Ch. II, 15 May 2003, Para. 379; *The Prosecutor v Gérard Ntakirutimana and Elizaphan Ntakirutimana*, Judgement, Case No. ICTR-96-17-T, T. Ch. I, 21 February 2003, Para. 787; *Clément Kayishema and Obed Ruzindana v The Prosecutor*, Judgement, Case No. ICTR-95-1A, Appeal Chamber, 1 June 2001, Paras. 186; *The Prosecutor v Ignace Bagilishema*, Judgement, Case No. ICTR-95-1-A, T. Ch. I, 7 June 2001, Paras. 30, 33; *The*

approach is the outcome of a myopic understanding and an erroneous construction of Article 6(1). I elucidate my criticisms by making the following arguments.

The first argument is that Article 6(1) has a bifurcated character. The imposition of criminal responsibility as spelt out in Article 6(1) requires the fulfilment of a two-stage process: first, an individual must have participated through any of the enlisted modes such as instigation. Second, this mode of participation (instigation as well as the other enlisted modes) must lead to any of the stipulated stages of any of the crimes, namely planning, preparation or execution.

The bifurcated character of Article 6(1) reveals its inchoateness. Inchoate crimes are crimes which are at their initial or preparatory stages, falling short of the commission of the complete crime.[3] In other words, materialisation of the whole crime is incomplete. A mode of participation (such as instigation) should not necessarily result in the commission of any of the crimes. By enlisting the different stages of participation, the Statute of the ICTR envisaged the contributory role of different individuals towards the different stages of the crimes. If any of the modes such as instigation led to any of the stages (planning, preparation or execution) of any of the crimes over which the ICTR has jurisdiction, then, criminal responsibility should be imposed. The Statute's use of a disjunction ('or') rather than a conjunction ('and') corroborates the view that proof that any of the modes led to any of the stages suffices for the imposition of criminal responsibility under Article 6(1). There is no statutory requirement that the contribution be 'substantial'.

As discussed below, instigation features under the Statute of the ICTR as a mode of participation that would lead to the imposition of criminal responsibility under Article 6(1), and also as an inchoate crime under Article 2(3)(c) which punishes direct and public incitement to commit genocide. The Trial and Appeal Chambers have established that instigation is synonymous with incitement, which makes it permissible for both words

---

Prosecutor v Alfred Musema, Judgment, Case No. ICTR-96-13-T, T. Ch. I, 27 January 2003, Para 115; *The Prosecutor v Georges Rutaganda*, Judgment, Case No. ICTR-96-3-T, T. Ch. I, 6 December 1999, Para 43; *The Prosecutor v Clément Kayishema and Obed Ruzindana*, Judgment, Case No. ICTR-95-1-T, T. Ch. I, 21 May 1999, Paras 199–207; *The Prosecutor v Jean-Paul Akayesu*, Judgment, Case No. ICTR-96-4, T. Ch. I, 2 September 1998, Para 477.

[3] David Ormerod, *Smith and Hogan Criminal Law* (12th edn., Oxford University Press 2008) 379; Joshua Dressler, *Understanding Criminal Law* (5th edn., LexisNexis 2009) 379–465; Michael J. Allen and Simon Cooper, *Elliott & Wood's Cases and Materials on Criminal Law* (9th edn., Sweet & Maxwell 2006) 438–99; Russell Heaton, *Criminal Law Textbook* (Oxford University Press 2004) 401–39.

to be used interchangeably.[4] The Trial and Appeal Chambers of the ICTR have developed the jurisprudence of instigation under these two Articles. However, no individual was ever indicted for instigation to crimes against humanity under Article 6(1) notwithstanding that the Statute allows this form of criminal liability.

The phrasing of this charge reflects a misunderstanding of the applicability of instigation to any of the crimes over which the ICTR has jurisdiction leading to the imposition of criminal responsibility under Article 6(1) and the strict limitation of direct and public incitement to commit genocide under Article 2(3)(c). Given the fact that there is a possibility of a confluence between Article 2(3)(c) and Article 6(1), I argue that the Trial and Appeal Chambers' limitation of instigation to, first, the inchoate crime of direct and public incitement to commit genocide under Article 2(3)(c), and secondly, to genocide under Article 6(1), is a result of an incorrect understanding of both the imposition of criminal responsibility under Article 6(1) and the nature of inchoate crimes. The practice of both the Trial and Appeal Chambers has ignored the fact that under Article 6(1), instigation is included as a mode of participation to crimes against humanity. The Trial and Appeal Chambers of the ICTR have conflated these two Articles, limiting instigation to direct and public incitement to commit genocide under Article 2(3)(c), and in few cases, extending it (though not clearly stated) to 'participation' in genocide. They have ignored instigation as a mode of participation in crimes against humanity under Article 6(1) which is one of the crimes brought under the purview of Article 6(1) in the imposition of criminal responsibility.

As discussed below, 'direct and public incitement to commit genocide' under Article 2(3)(c) may as well qualify as 'instigation' to genocide under Article 6(1). That same instigation may also qualify as a mode of participation in crimes against humanity under Article 6(1) given the fact that genocide and crimes against humanity, though legally characterised differently, with different definitional elements, share similar core elements of conduct.

From the above paragraph, it is evident that there is the possibility of instigation featuring under both Articles 6(1) and 2(3)(c). In fact, a confluence between Article 2(3)(c) and Article 6(1) occurred in many of the cases that have appeared before both the Trial and Appeal Chambers. This confluence was unnoticed until in the case of *Kalimanzira*[5] where the Trial

---

4 *Kalimanzira* (n. 2) para 511; *Akayesu* (n. 2) para 555.

5 *Kalimanzira* (n. 2).

Chamber articulated a set of guidelines on how to resolve this issue in future cases. I examine the 'Kalimanzira Principles', and further argue that though they constitute a significant step in this direction, they remain fundamentally flawed.

The jurisprudence of the Trial and Appeal Chambers of the ICTR establishes direct and public incitement to commit genocide as an inchoate crime. Criminal responsibility is imposed on any individual who directly and publicly incites the commission of the crime of genocide. As an inchoate crime, it is irrelevant to prove that such incitement successfully led to the commission of genocide. Given the nature of inchoate crimes, the question that arises is whether within the Rwandan context in which the atrocities were actually committed, the inchoateness of Article 2(3)(c) was lost? In other words, was it correct to indict, try and convict individuals of the inchoate crime of direct and public incitement to commit genocide when genocide was actually committed in Rwanda? I argue that it would have been correct to charge such individuals with instigation to genocide (at least) under Article 6(1) given the fact that factual allegations used to found a charge of direct and public incitement to commit genocide should have been used to found a charge of instigation to genocide (and even crimes against humanity) under Article 6(1).

I also argue that the crimes of genocide and crimes against humanity, as defined by the Statute of the ICTR, have very different definitional elements, especially the framework and intent within which each is committed. Article 2(2) of the Statute of the ICTR requires that for there to be genocide, the enlisted acts must be committed 'with intent to destroy, in whole or in part, a national, ethnical, racial or religious group....'[6] On the other hand, the definition of crimes against humanity requires that the accused perpetrates any of the crimes as part or in furtherance of a widespread or systematic attack that is directed against any civilian population and on any of the enlisted discriminatory grounds.[7] However, the various conducts that are included in the definitions of these two crimes are not very different. As I explain in the discussions below, conduct that qualifies as a genocidal act may also qualify as a crime against humanity if such conduct meets the definitional elements of both crimes and was perpetrated with the specific intent of the crimes. Therefore, though legally

---

[6] See also the *Convention on the Prevention and Punishment of the Crime of Genocide*, United Nations General Assembly Resolution 260(III), U.N. GAOR, 3rd Session, 179th meeting, U.N. Doc. A/RES/260A (1948), 9 December 1948, Article 2(2).

[7] Statute of the ICTR, Article 3.

characterised differently, genocide and crimes against humanity are not mutually exclusive because conduct that gives rise to a charge of genocide may also give rise to a charge of crime against humanity if it meets the definitional elements of the different crimes.

Therefore, instigation to commit genocide may well be treated as instigation to commit crimes against humanity. Such instigation should lead to the imposition of criminal responsibility under Article 6(1) for genocide and crimes against humanity if it led to either the planning, preparation or execution of any of these crimes.

Further, similar facts can give rise to multiple charges. An act constituting direct and public incitement to commit genocide may also qualify as instigation to genocide and instigation to crimes against humanity. Though this may trigger a fear of violating the procedural principle of cumulative convictions,[8] I argue that the jurisprudence of the Trial and Appeal Chambers has settled this issue: there are situations where same facts can be used for multiple charges.[9]

As discussed earlier, the Trial and Appeal Chambers of the ICTR have required that for criminal responsibility to be imposed under Article 6(1), it must be proved that the accused's mode of participation substantially contributed to the commission of the crime.[10] I refute this 'substantial contribution' requirement by looking at the definitional elements of crimes against humanity per the Statute of the ICTR, and squaring them with the Rwandan situation. Prior to the Statute of the ICTR, the crime of crimes against humanity had been defined differently by different international instruments.[11] However, the Statute of the ICTR defined crimes against humanity in an unprecedented way, introducing novel concepts such as

---

[8] The issue of cumulative convictions and the jurisprudence of the *Ad Hoc* Tribunals on it are discussed in detail below.

[9] *Alfred Musema v The Prosecutor*, Judgment, Case No. ICTR-96-13-A, Appeal Chamber, 16 November 2001, Paras. 346–70; *Akayesu* (n. 2) paras. 461–70. See also the discussions below relating to cumulative convictions.

[10] *Hategekimana* (n. 2) para. 644; *Kalimanzira* (n. 2) para. 512; *Kajelijeli* (n. 2) para. 759; *Semanza* (n. 2) para. 379; *Ntakirutimana* (n. 2) para. 787; *Kayishema and Ruzindana* (n. 2) (AC) para. 186; *Bagilishema* (n. 2) paras. 30, 33; *Musema* (n. 2) para. 115; *Rutaganda* (n. 2) para. 43; *Kayishema and Ruzindana* (TC) (n. 2) paras. 199–207; *Akayesu* (n. 2) para. 477.

[11] The different formulations on crimes against humanity have been expressed in international instruments such as the Rome Statute of the ICC, U.N. Doc. A/CONF.183/9 (1998), reprinted in 37 I.L.M. 999 (1998), Article 7(1); the Statute of the Special Court for Sierra Leone, annexed to the Agreement between the United Nations and the Government of Sierra Leone on the Establishment of a Special Court for Sierra Leone pursuant to United Nations Security Council Resolution 1315, U. N. SCOR, 4186th meeting, U.N. Doc. S/RES/1315 (2000), Article 2; the Statute of the ICTY, annexed to United Nations Security Council Resolution 827, U.N. SCOR, 3217th meeting, U.N. Doc. S/RES/827 (1993), Article 5; the Charter

the perpetration of the acts as part or in furtherance of an attack that is widespread or systematic, directed against any civilian population and on any of the discriminatory grounds.[12] The definitional elements highlight crimes against humanity as group crimes. As group crimes, they require some level of planning and coordination. They insinuate the existence of an agreement made by persons to perpetrate them. This agreement amounts to a conspiracy. In the conspiracy to wage an attack against the Tutsis, many individuals took part, and played different roles. This made it a joint criminal enterprise. As a joint criminal enterprise, criminal responsibility ought to be imposed on every member for every crime committed. The fact that the atrocities were committed in Rwanda is evidence that the participation of every member in that joint criminal enterprise was contributory, and not merely substantial, to the different stages of the crime. Contributory acts range from conception, design, planning, preparation, and finally, to execution. Therefore, to require that criminal responsibility under Article 6(1) can be imposed only where the participation of an individual 'substantially' contributed to the commission of a crime is an incorrect understanding of Article 6(1) and the notion of a joint criminal enterprise, wherein a plan was devised to perpetrate the crimes. The trend of events in Rwanda were not so different from that of Nazi Germany, and had the prosecutors identified the existence of a joint criminal enterprise in Rwanda within which these atrocities were formulated, prepared and finally executed, then, this substantial contribution requirement would be unnecessary. Furthermore, the role of instigators as individuals participating in the planning, preparation and execution of mass scale atrocities does not need to be overemphasised. Since the seminal judgment of the Nuremberg Tribunal in the *Julius Streicher Case*,[13] instigation as a mode of participation has been clearly recognised. Even though they (instigators) do not perpetrate the material elements of the crimes, they are as responsible as those who do because the purpose of their instigation is to bring about these crimes, and the crimes are perpetrated partly as a result of their instigation.

---

of the IMTFE, Tokyo, Article 5(c); Allied Control Council Law No. 10, Article II, and the Charter of the IMT, Nuremberg, Article 6(c).

12 Statute of the ICTR, Article 3.

13 Donna E. Arzt, 'Nuremberg, Denazification and Democracy: The Hate Speech Problem at the International Military Tribunal' (1995) Vol. XII 3 *N. Y. L. Sch. J. Hum. Rts.*, 689, 689–758. See generally D.A. Sprecher, *Inside the Nuremberg Trial: A Prosecutor's Comprehensive Account* (University Press of America 1999); Richard Breitman, *The Architect of Genocide: Himmler and the Final Solution* (The Bodley Head 1991).

The unfortunate result of this misunderstanding of the purport of Article 6(1) is that the jurisprudence on instigation as a mode of participation in the commission of crimes against humanity remains undeveloped, and instigation itself as a mode of participation has been confusingly limited to the crime of genocide.

In order to critique the jurisprudence of the Trial and Appeal Chambers on instigation to commit crimes against humanity under Article 6(1), I must first restate both the letter of the law and the jurisprudence of the Trial Chambers of the ICTR. Therefore, I commence this Chapter by looking at the imposition of criminal responsibility under Article 6(1) under the Statute of the ICTR. This is followed by an examination of instigation under the Statute of the ICTR (both under Article 6(1) and Article 2(3)(c)). I briefly state the Trial and Appeal Chambers' jurisprudence on instigation as a mode of participation under Article 6(1). The second part of this Chapter is a critical review of the jurisprudence. I start by giving a statutory construction of Article 6(1). The essence of this is to highlight its bifurcated and inchoate character. I then look at the confluence between Articles 6(1) and 2(3)(c). Developed by the Trial Chamber in the case of *Kalimanzira*,[14] I lay emphasis on the 'Kalimanzira Principles',[15] which, as I illustrate, became a major step in resolving this puzzle, yet, remain fundamentally flawed. I examine the definitional elements of crimes of genocide and crimes against humanity and demonstrate that, though the constituent crimes in their definitions are legally characterised differently, they are essentially similar. Therefore, an act may qualify as a crime against humanity and as genocide also if such an act is perpetrated in manners that reflect the definitional elements of these two crimes. I then look at the joint criminal enterprise approach, which, as I argue, would have been much better and effective in situating instigators within the context of instigating any or all of the crimes over which the Tribunal has jurisdiction.[16] The definitional elements of crimes against humanity, as elaborated in the previous Chapter, play a significant role here. Standing out as crimes which can only be committed by a group (in order to meet the definitional elements of an 'attack' that is 'widespread or systematic'),[17] it requires at least the three stipulated stages contained in Article 6(1) of the Statute of the ICTR. In my discussion,

---

14 *Kalimanzira* (n. 2).

15 *Kalimanzira* (n. 2) para. 516.

16 These crimes are genocide, crimes against humanity and Violations of Article 3 Common to the Geneva Conventions and of Additional Protocol II (see Articles 2–4 of the Statute of the ICTR).

17 Statute of the ICTR, Article 3.

I illustrate that, for there to be a widespread or systematic attack, there must be a joint criminal enterprise (criminal conspiracy). This joint criminal enterprise is made up of different persons who subscribe to, and participate in different ways and times, towards the fulfilment of the criminal purpose. If this holds true, then, it makes it unnecessary to require a substantial contribution before criminal responsibility can be imposed given the fact that instigators fit within the framework of a joint criminal enterprise, and cause the planning, preparation or execution of the crimes they agree to commit.

5.2 Construction of Article 6(1)

Under the Statute of the ICTR, an individual incurs criminal responsibility if that individual 'planned, instigated, ordered, committed or otherwise aided and abetted in the planning, preparation or execution' of a crime over which the Tribunal has jurisdiction.[18] This is the primary statement on the imposition of criminal responsibility. It covers the different modes of participation in the different stages (namely, planning, preparation or execution) of the crimes over which the Tribunal has jurisdiction (these crimes are genocide, crimes against humanity and violations of Article 3 common to the Geneva Conventions and of Additional Protocol II).

5.2.1 *Instigation Under the Statute of the ICTR*

In critiquing the jurisprudence of the Trial Chambers on instigation as a mode of participation in crimes against humanity, it is first of all necessary to identify a persistent problem that has confronted both the Trial and Appeal Chambers. The double appearance of instigation under the Statute of the ICTR, though covering specifically different situations, became a legal conundrum to both the Trial and Appeal Chambers of the ICTR especially in cases where there is an intersection between the two crimes.

Article 2(3)(c) and Article 6(1) provide as follows:

> Article 2(3)
> The following acts shall be punishable:
> c. Direct and public incitement to commit genocide....

---

[18] Statute of the ICTR, Article 6(1).

> Article 6(1)
> A person who planned, instigated, ordered, committed or otherwise aided and abetted in the planning, preparation or execution of a crime referred to in articles 2 to 4 [genocide, crimes against humanity and violations of Article 3 common to the Geneva Conventions and of Additional Protocol II] of the present Statute, shall be individually responsible for the crime.

The Trial Chambers have construed instigation to be synonymous with incitement, and have used it interchangeably to mean the same thing.[19] Instigation features in both Articles. In the former, it is the inchoate crime of direct and public incitement to commit genocide. In the latter, it is a mode of participation that leads to the imposition of criminal responsibility.

Article 6(1) deals with the imposition of criminal responsibility where an individual participated through, *inter alia*, instigation, in the planning, preparation or execution of any of the crimes over which the ICTR has jurisdiction. On the other hand, Article 2(3)(c) of the Statute punishes the inchoate crime of direct and public incitement to commit genocide. As discussed earlier, inchoate crimes are crimes which are still in their initial or preparatory stages: the crime is in the process of being committed, and its materialisation has not been completed.[20]

Under Article 2(3)(c), criminal responsibility is limited to the crime of genocide. However, the crime of genocide still appears under Article 6(1) as one of the crimes under the jurisdiction of the ICTR. Instigation features as a mode of participation under Article 6(1). There are some cases where an individual has been indicted for the crime of genocide under Article 6(1) and for direct and public incitement to commit genocide under Article 2(3)(c).[21]

---

19 *Kalimanzira* (n. 2) para 511; *Akayesu* (n. 2) para 481.

20 Ormerod (n. 3) 379; Dressler (n. 3) 379–465; Allen and Cooper (n. 3) 438–99; Heaton (n. 3) 401–39.

21 For an understanding of this prosecutorial practice, see the (Amended) Indictments of the following accused individuals: *The Prosecutor v Callixte Kalimanzira*, Amended Indictment, Case No. ICTR-2005-88-I, OTP, 21 July 2005, Count 3, Paras. 18–27; *The Prosecutor v Joseph Serugendo*, Corrigendum of Indictment, Case No. ICTR-2005-84-I, OTP, 21 July 2005, Count 4, Paras. 51–73; *The Prosecutor v Simon Bikindi*, Amended Indictment, Case No. ICTR-2001-72-I, OTP, 15 June 2005, Count 4, Paras. 31–41; *The Prosecutor v Tharcisse Muvunyi*, Amended Indictment, Case No. ICTR-2000-55A-T, OTP, 23 December 2003 (a retrial on the lone charge of direct and public incitement to genocide); *The Prosecutor v Eliézer Niyitegeka*, Amended Indictment, Case No. ICTR-96-14-T, OTP, 25 November 2002, Count 4, Paras. 5.1–6.71; *The Prosecutor v Juvénal Kajelijeli*, Amended Indictment, Case No. ICTR-98-44A-I, OTP, 25 January 2001, Count 4, Paras. 2.1–4.18; *The Prosecutor v Jean-Bosco Barayagwiza*, Amended Indictment, Case No. ICTR-97-19, OTP, 14 April 2000, Count 4, Paras. 5.1–7.13; *The Prosecutor*

Article 6(1) mentions instigation as a mode of participation in the planning, preparation or execution of any of the crimes over which the Tribunal has jurisdiction.[22] These crimes are genocide,[23] crimes against humanity,[24] and violations of Article 3 common to the Geneva Conventions and of Additional Protocol II.[25] Article 2(3)(c) punishes direct and public incitement to commit genocide. Such an incitement is limited to the crime of genocide. As an inchoate crime, the crime of genocide must not necessarily be committed for an accused person to be punishable per Article 2(3)(c).[26]

Though incitement and instigation are synonymous with each other,[27] there are some fine statutory and jurisprudential distinctions that have to be highlighted. First, under Article 6(1), instigation must lead to any of the crimes over which the Tribunal has jurisdiction.[28] Therefore, the provision covers an accused person who instigates genocide, crimes against humanity and violations of Article 3 common to the Geneva Conventions and of Additional Protocols II. The second distinction is that instigation under Article 2(3)(c) is limited only to the crime of genocide. For there to be criminal liability under this Article, such instigation must be both direct and public.[29] As a corollary, where such direct and public incitement is to commit any crime other than genocide, then, no criminal responsibility can be

v Ferdinand Nahimana, Amended Indictment, Case No. ICTR-96-11, OTP, 15 November 1999, Count 3, Paras 4.1–6.27; *The Prosecutor v Hassan Ngeze*, Amended Indictment, Case No. ICTR-97-27, OTP, 10 November 1999, Count 4, Paras 5.1–7.15; *The Prosecutor v Georges Henri Yvon Joseph Ruggiu*, Amended Indictment, Case No. ICTR-97-32-I, OTP, 10 December 1998, Count 2, Paras 3.1–5.12; and, *The Prosecutor v Jean-Paul Akayesu*, Amended Indictment, Case No. ICTR-96-4-I, OTP, June 1997, Count 4, Paras 14–15.

22 Planning, ordering, committing or otherwise aiding and abetting are the other modes of participation stipulated in Article 6(1) of the Statute of the ICTR.

23 Statute of the ICTR, Article 2.

24 Ibid Article 3.

25 Ibid Article 4.

26 *The Prosecutor v Tharcisse Muvunyi*, Judgment, Case No. ICTR-00-55A-T, T. Ch. III, 11 February 2010, Paras. 24–25; *Kalimanzira* (n. 2) para. 510; *The Prosecutor v Simon Bikindi*, Judgment, Case No. ICTR-01-72, T. Ch. III, 2 December 2008, Para. 419; *Ferdinand Nahimana, Jean-Bosco Barayagwiza and Hassan Ngeze v The Prosecutor*, Judgment, Case No. ICTR-99-52-A, Appeal Chamber, 28 November 2007, Paras. 678–79; *The Prosecutor v Ferdinand Nahimana, Jean-Bosco Barayagwiza and Hassan* Ngeze, Judgment, Case No. ICTR-99-52-T, T. Ch. I, 3 December 2003, Paras. 678, 720; *Kajelijeli* (n. 2) para. 855; *The Prosecutor v Eliézer Niyitegeka*, Judgment, Case No.ICTR-96-14-T, T. Ch. I, 16 May 2003, Para. 431; *Musema* (n. 2) para. 120; *Rutaganda* (n. 2) para. 38; *Akayesu* (n. 2) para. 562.

27 *Kalimanzira* (n. 2) para. 511; *Akayesu* (n. 2) para. 481.

28 *Kalimanzira* (n. 2) para. 161; *Kajelijeli* (n. 2) para. 759; *Ntakirutimana and Ntakirutimana* (n. 2) para. 787; *Kayishema and Ruzindana* (n. 2) (AC) paras. 186, 198; *Bagilishema* (n. 2) paras. 30, 33; *Musema* (n. 2) paras. 126, 379; *Rutaganda* (n. 2) para. 43; *Kayishema and Ruzindana* (n. 2) (TC) paras. 199, 207; *Akayesu* (n. 2) paras. 473, 477.

29 *Kalimanzira* (n. 2) paras. 515–16; *Akayesu* (n. 2) paras. 555–59.

incurred under Article 2(3)(c) by virtue of the fact that it is specifically limited to genocide.[30] Third, the jurisprudence of the Trial and Appeal Chambers requires that for criminal responsibility to be imposed under Article 6(1), it must be proved that the accused's mode of participation substantially contributed to the commission of a crime.[31] On the other hand, direct and public incitement to commit genocide is an inchoate crime: criminal responsibility is incurred irrespective of whether such direct and public incitement to commit genocide successfully leads to the commission of the crime of genocide.[32]

5.2.2 *The Trial and Appeal Chambers' Jurisprudence on Instigation Under Article 6(1)*

In the previous subsection, I have looked at instigation under the Statute of the ICTR. As mentioned above, Article 6(1) contains the different modes of participation in the crimes over which the ICTR has jurisdiction. Its application is therefore not restricted to any particular crime unlike Article 2(3)(c) which requires such instigation to be direct, public, and to the commission of the crime of genocide only.

In this subsection, I briefly state the Trial and Appeal Chambers' jurisprudence on instigation. I do this in order to portray the consistency the Trial and Appeal Chambers have shown in construing Article 6(1). It is in these cases that the 'substantial contribution' requirement has been emphasised. Critiquing this requirement is the crux of this Chapter. It is therefore necessary to consider briefly how the Trial Chambers have construed instigation as a mode of participation under Article 6(1).

In *Akayesu*,[33] the Trial Chamber examined the entire wording of Article 6(1),[34] which stipulates the different modes of participating in the

---

30 This is a logical construction of Article 2(3)(c) which makes direct and public incitement to commit genocide punishable. Imported from Genocide Convention, the rationale was to penalise those who directly and publicly incite the crime of genocide (considering that they played a great role in the planning and perpetration of the crime of genocide). See the Genocide Convention, Article 2(c). See also *Bikindi* (n. 26) para 388; *The Prosecutor v Georges Ruggiu*, Judgment, Case No. ICTR-97-32, T. Ch. I, 1 June 2000, Para 15; *Akayesu* (n. 2) para 551.

31 *Hategekimana* (n. 2) para. 644; *Kalimanzira* (n. 2) para. 161; *Kajelijeli* (n. 2) para. 759; *Ntakirutimana and Ntakirutimana* (n. 2) para. 787; *Kayishema and Ruzindana* (n. 2) (AC) paras. 186, 198; *Bagilishema* (n. 2) paras. 30, 33; *Musema* (n. 2) para. 126; *Rutaganda* (n. 2) para. 43; *Kayishema and Ruzindana* (n. 2) (TC) paras. 199, 207; *Akayesu* (n. 2) para. 477.

32 *Kalimanzira* (n. 2) para. 516; *Muvunyi* (n. 23) para. 24; *Bikindi* (n. 23) para. 419.

33 *Akayesu* (n. 2).

34 Article 6(1) stipulates the different forms of participation that would lead to the imposition if criminal responsibility.

planning, preparation or commission of any of the crimes over which the Tribunal has jurisdiction. It held that Article 6(1) covers the different stages of a criminal activity, from planning, through preparation to execution; and further established that the application of Article 6(1) required proof that participation (through any of the modes) actually led to the commission of any of the crimes.[35] The implication of this requirement is that where participation does not lead to the commission of the crime, no criminal responsibility can be imposed.[36] An exception to this, however, is Article 2(3)(c) which makes punishable the inchoate crime of direct and public incitement to commit genocide.

The Trial Chamber held incitement and instigation to be synonymous with each other and could be used interchangeably. As a mode of criminal participation under Article 6(1), it involves 'prompting another to commit an offence', and as distinguished from incitement under Article 2(3)(c), it is punishable only where such instigation actually leads to the commission of the crime desired by the instigator.[37]

In *Kayishema and Ruzindana*,[38] the Trial Chamber held that the imposition of criminal responsibility under Article 6(1) required first, demonstration that the person participated. In other words, it must be proved that the person's conduct contributed to the commission of a crime over which the Tribunal has jurisdiction. Secondly, it must be proved that such a person acted with knowledge or intent, which comprises an awareness that he is participating in a crime.[39] It held that for an accused person to be criminally responsible, it must be proved that his or her conduct contributed to, or 'had an effect on' the commission of the crime.'[40] Participation was considered not to require physical presence of the accused at the place of the crime.[41] The accused's contribution does not need to be direct.[42] Neither must the accused's role be 'a tangible one'.[43] Given the breadth of the scope

---

[35] *Hategekimana* (n. 2) para 644; *Kalimanzira* (n. 2) para 161; *Kajelijeli* (n. 2) para 759; *Ntakirutimana and Ntakirutimana* (n. 2) para 787; *Kayishema and Ruzindana* (n. 2) (AC) paras 186, 198; *Bagilishema* (n. 2) paras 30, 33; *Musema* (n. 2) para 126; *Rutaganda* (n. 2) para 43; *Kayishema and Ruzindana* (n. 2) (TC) paras 199, 207; *Akayesu* (n. 2) para 477.

[36] *Akayesu* (n. 2) paras. 473, 477.

[37] Ibid para. 482. As discussed below, since *Akayesu* (n. 2), instigation has been construed to be synonymous with incitement and provocation. See *Kalimanzira* (n. 2) para. 511.

[38] *Kayishema and Ruzindana* (n. 2) (TC).

[39] Ibid para. 198.

[40] *Kayishema and Ruzindana* (n. 2) (TC) para. 199. See also *Akayesu* (n. 2) paras. 480–85.

[41] *Kayishema and Ruzindana* (n. 2) (TC) para. 200.

[42] Ibid.

[43] Ibid. The Trial Chamber cited the ICTY case of *The Prosecutor v Anto Furundžija*, Judgment, Case No. IT-95-17/1, T. Ch. II, 10 December 1998, Paras. 207, 235.

of participation that may give rise to criminal responsibility under Article 6(1), the Trial Chamber required a clear awareness on the part of the accused that his participation would lead to the commission of a crime.[44] The Prosecution has the onus to prove that the accused's mode of participation, whether by acts or omissions, contributed *substantially* to the commission of a crime; and that depending on his mode of participation in question, he was at least aware that his conduct would contribute to the crime.[45]

In *Musema*,[46] the Trial Chamber stated that the wording of Article 6(1) implicitly requires that the planning or preparation actually leads to the commission of the crime.[47] It defined the second form of participation, incitement to commit a crime to involve 'instigating another, directly or publicly, to commit an offence.' Instigation, as it held, would be punishable only where it leads to the actual commission of the crime.

In *Semanza*,[48] the Trial Chamber held that the principle of criminal responsibility is not limited to cases of individuals who physically commit a crime, but also to those who participate in, and contribute to a crime in other ways per the rules of accomplice liability.[49] Under Article 6(1), criminal responsibility will be imposed only where a crime under the ICTR's jurisdiction has been completed.[50] Inchoate crimes are not criminalised by Article 6(1) of the Statute.[51] The Trial Chamber held that to satisfy Article 6(1), the participation of the accused 'must have *substantially* contributed to, or have had a *substantial* effect on, the completion of a crime.'[52] It construed instigation under Article 6(1) to mean 'urging, encouraging, or

44 *Kayishema and Ruzindana* (n. 2) (TC): 'Crime' here refers to any of the crimes over which the Tribunal has jurisdiction (genocide, crimes against humanity and violations of Article 3 Common to the Geneva Conventions and Additional Protocols II). The actual commission of a crime will suffice. The only distinctions are those statutorily provided under the definition of genocide and the offences punishable, such as conspiracy to commit genocide, attempt to commit genocide and direct and public incitement to commit genocide (which are all inchoate offences, and are punishable irrespective of whether the crime of genocide is committed) – Para 203, footnote 117.

45 *Kayishema and Ruzindana* (n. 2) (TC) para. 207.

46 *Musema* (n. 2).

47 *Musema* (n. 2) para. 115.

48 *Semanza* (n. 2).

49 Ibid para. 376.

50 *Semanza* (n. 2) para. 375.

51 Ibid.

52 Ibid para. 379 (emphasis added). See also *Ntakirutimana and Ntakirutimana* (n. 2) para. 787; *Kayishema and Ruzindana* (n. 2) (AC) paras. 186, 198; *Bagilishema* (n. 2) paras. 30, 33; *Musema* (n. 2) para. 126; *Rutaganda* (n. 2) para. 43; *Kayishema and Ruzindana* (n. 2) (TC) paras. 199, 207; *Akayesu* (n. 2) para. 477.

prompting another person to commit a crime.'[53] An act qualifying as instigation need not be direct and public.[54] However, it is required that such an act must be proved to have (had) a causal connection between the act of instigation and the commission of the crime.[55]

In *Kajelijeli*,[56] the Trial Chamber simply recognised established jurisprudence to the effect that an accused person can incur criminal responsibility under Article 6(1) only if it is shown that his or her participation *substantially contributed to, or has had a substantial effect on, the completion of a crime under the Statute*.[57] Examining instigation as a form of participation, the Trial Chamber described it to mean 'prompting another person to commit an offence';[58] adding that it does not have to be direct or public.[59] It further held that both positive acts and omissions may qualify as instigation,[60] but is punishable on proof of a causal relationship between the instigation and the commission of the crime.[61]

In *Kalimanzira*,[62] the Trial Chamber established that as in previous cases, instigation under Article 6(1) is a mode of liability; and that individual criminal responsibility would be incurred by an accused person only if the instigation in fact *substantially contributed to the commission of one of the crimes* over which the ICTR has jurisdiction.[63]

In *Hategekimana*,[64] the Trial Chamber considered the jurisprudence of instigation as a mode of participation. Holding it to be synonymous with incitement, it defined it as prompting another person to commit a crime.[65] The *mens rea* comprises the intent to instigate another to commit

---

[53] *Semanza* (n. 2) para 381. See also *Bagilishema* (n. 2) para 30; *Akayesu* (n. 2) para 482.

[54] *The Prosecutor v Jean-Paul Akayesu*, Judgment, Case No. ICTR-96-4-A, Appeal Chamber, 1 June 201, Paras. 487–82.

[55] *Bagilishema* (n. 2) para. 30.

[56] *Kajelijeli* (n. 2).

[57] Ibid para. 759 (emphasis added). See also *Kayishema and Ruzindana* (n. 2) (AC) paras. 186, 198; *Ntakirutimana and Ntakirutimana* (n. 2) para. 787; *Bagilishema* (n. 2) paras. 30, 33; *Musema* (n. 2) para. 126; *Rutaganda* (n. 2) para. 43; *Kayishema and Ruzindana* (n. 2) (TC) paras. 199, 207; *Akayesu* (n. 2) para. 477.

[58] *Semanza* (n. 2) para. 381; *Bagilishema* (n. 2) para. 30; *Akayesu* (n. 2) para. 39.

[59] *Semanza* (n. 2) para. 381; *Akayesu* (n. 2) para. 39.

[60] *The Prosecutor v Dario Kordić and Mario Čerkez*, Judgment, Case No. IT-95-14/2, T. Ch. III, 26 February 2001, Para. 387.

[61] *Semanza* (n. 2) para. 381; *Bagilishema* (n. 2) para. 30.

[62] *Kalimanzira* (n. 2).

[63] Ibid para. 512 (emphasis added).

[64] *Hategekimana* (n. 2).

[65] Ibid para. 644, citing the cases of *The Prosecutor v Ephrem Setako*, Judgment, Case No. ICTR-04-81, T. Ch. I, 25 February 2010, Para. 447; *Nahimana* et al (n. 23) (TC) para. 480; *The Prosecutor v Hormisdas Nsegimana*, Judgment, Case No. ICTR-01-69, T. Ch. I, 17 November 2009, Para. 797.

a crime or, at a minimum, 'the awareness of the substantial likelihood that a crime will be committed in the execution of the acts or omissions instigated'.[66]

The Trial Chamber in *Bikindi*[67] appeared to have made a slight departure from established jurisprudence. The accused, standing trial for the sole charge of direct and public incitement to commit genocide, was found guilty and convicted. The Trial Chamber, having examined the totality of his musical compositions as a singer and entertainer,[68] their political context within which they were disseminated and the prevailing ethnic tensions in Rwanda, did not limit its findings to the right and perils of free speech. The Trial Chamber discussed hate speech as a form of incitement that would amount to persecution as a crime against humanity.[69] The Trial Chamber held that if hate speech is discriminatory in nature and advocates for the perpetration of crimes in a discriminatory way, then, that would qualify as instigation under Article 2(3)(c).[70] The requirement of a substantial role in the commission of crimes for criminal responsibility to be imposed under Article 6(1) was overlooked by the Trial Chamber.

The above cases that have been tried by the Trial Chambers of the ICTR have repeatedly and consistently stipulated that criminal responsibility can be imposed under Article 6(1) only where the individual's mode of participation substantially contributes to the commission of the crime. This requirement of a substantial contribution is what I critique in the following paragraphs. I commence with a critical review of the wording of Article 6(1).

5.3 Changing the Approach to Construing Article 6(1)

The requirement of a substantial contribution to the commission of crimes for an accused to incur criminal responsibility is illogical, stemming first, from the erroneous construction of Article 6(1). In the following discussions, I show how the 'substantial contribution' requirement is the outcome of an illogical construction of Article 6(1) of the Statute of the ICTR.

66 *Hategekimana* (n. 2) para 644. See also *Setako* (n. 65) para 447.
67 *Bikindi* (n. 26).
68 *Bikindi* (n. 26) paras. 186–255.
69 *Bikindi* (n. 26) paras. 390–97.
70 Ibid paras. 417–26.

5.3.1 *The Bifurcated and Inchoate Character of Article 6(1) of the Statute of the ICTR*

Article 6(1) of the Statute of the ICTR imposes criminal responsibility on any person who 'planned, instigated, ordered, committed or otherwise aided and abetted *in the planning, perpetration or execution of a crime'* over which the Tribunal has jurisdiction.[71]

A simple construction of the wording of Article 6(1) dictates that Article 6(1) is bifurcated. First, for criminal responsibility to be imposed, it must be proved that the accused participated through any of the enlisted modes. These modes cover those who 'planned, instigated, ordered, committed or otherwise aided and abetted'. Secondly, the accused person's mode of participation must be at, or lead to any of the stages of any of the crimes over which the ICTR has jurisdiction. These stages, as provided in Article 6(1), range from planning, preparation to execution of any of the crimes. Third, Article 6(1) makes use of a disjunctive word ('or'), rather than a conjunction ('and'). This suggests that any mode of participation must lead to, or be present at any of the stages of the criminal activity, and not necessarily all. So, where instigation leads to the planning of, or preparation for any of the crimes, the instigator ought to incur criminal responsibility. The Trial Chamber in *Kajelijeli*[72] took this line of reasoning when it established that

> Article 6(1) reflects the principle that criminal responsibility for any crime in the Statute is incurred not only by individuals who physically commit that crime, but also by individuals who participate in and contribute to the commission of a crime in other ways, ranging from its initial planning to its execution, as specified in the five categories of acts in this Article: planning, instigating, ordering, committing or aiding and abetting.[73]

The Trial Chamber in *The Prosecutor v Paul Bisengimana*[74] stayed this line of reasoning when it held that 'the accused's participation may take place at the planning, preparation or execution stage of the crime....'[75]

In the above two cases, the Trial Chambers construed Article 6(1) correctly. They held that an accused's mode of participation may take place at any of the stages (planning, preparation or execution) of any of the crimes

---

[71] Emphasis added.

[72] *Kajelijeli* (n. 2).

[73] *Kajelijeli* (n. 2) para. 989. See also *Semanza* (n. 2) para. 377; *Kayishema and Ruzindana* (n. 2) (AC) para. 185; *Musema* (n. 2) para. 114; *Rutaganda* (n. 2) para. 33; *Kayishema and Ruzindana* (n. 2) (TC) paras. 196–97; *Akayesu* (n. 2) para. 473.

[74] Judgment, Case No. ICTR-00-60, T. Ch. II, 13 April 2006.

[75] *Bisengimana* (n. 74) para. 33.

over which the ICTR has jurisdiction. This statutory construction of Article 6(1) depicts its bifurcated character: first, the accused must participate through any of the modes enlisted in Article 6(1), and second, such a mode of participation must lead to any of the stages (planning, preparation or execution) of any of the crimes (genocide, crimes against humanity and violations of Article 3 common to the Geneva Conventions and of Additional Protocol II). However, in most cases, the Trial and Appeal Chambers' construction of Article 6(1) required that for criminal responsibility to be imposed under Article 6(1), it must be proved that the accused's mode of participation 'substantially contributed' to the commission of a crime. By introducing this substantial contribution requirement, both the Trial and Appeal Chambers have focused on the last stage of the crime: execution. They have disregarded the other two stages: planning and preparation.

The Trial and Appeal Chambers' substantial contribution requirement neither squares with a strict and correct construction of Article 6(1) nor with the Statute of the ICTR. Instigation, like any other enlisted mode of participation, ought to lead to the imposition of criminal responsibility if it resulted in the planning, preparation or execution of any of the crimes. The wording of Article 6(1) requires a two-stage test: first, proof that the accused participated through any of the stipulated modes, and second, that it resulted in any of the stages (planning, preparation or execution) of any of the crimes (genocide, crimes against humanity and violations of Article 3 common to the Geneva Conventions and of Additional Protocol II).

5.3.2 *The Intersection Between Articles 6(1) and 2(3)(c): The 'Kalimanzira Principles'*

As discussed earlier, instigation appears twice in the Statute of the ICTR: first, as a mode of participation that would lead to the imposition of criminal responsibility for *inter alia*, crimes against humanity;[76] and second, where it directly and publicly incites the commission of the crime of genocide.[77] The prosecutors have indicted persons under these two separate Articles.[78] However, where there is this confluence, their attitude has been to limit incitement to the crime of genocide. In some earlier cases, even

[76] Statute of the ICTR, Article 6(1).

[77] Ibid Article 2(3)(c).

[78] Examples include the (Amended) Indictments in the following cases: *Kalimanzira* (n. 21) para. I(I), (III); *Akayesu* (n. 21) paras. 5–11, 14–15.

when instigation met the requirements of Article 2(3)(c), and resulted in the commission of genocide, the prosecutors never considered the possibility of having those same facts found a charge of crimes against humanity. To them, incitement is limited to the crime of genocide. Even where such an incitement, being direct and public, and leads to the commission of crimes committed within the framework of an attack (as well as the other definitional elements of crimes against humanity), they have not reasoned it this way. As noted above, this is a problem because instigation has been narrowed down to the inchoate crime of direct and public incitement to commit genocide under Article 2(3)(c). Furthermore, the jurisprudence on instigation as a mode of participation in crimes against humanity has been undeveloped because of two main reasons: first, the strict limitation of instigation or incitement to genocide only under Article 2(3)(c) which punishes the inchoate crime of direct and public incitement to commit genocide; and secondly, the imposition of a requirement that criminal responsibility can only be imposed under Article 6(1) when it is proved that the accused participated through any of the enlisted modes and such participation substantially contributed to the commission of the crime.

In the recent case of *Kalimanzira*,[79] the Trial Chamber discussed the intersection between Article 6(1) (where instigation is a mode of participation that would lead to the imposition of criminal responsibility) and Article 2(3)(c) (which is the inchoate crime of direct and public incitement to commit genocide). Holding that instigation is synonymous with incitement, the Trial Chamber articulated the 'Kalimanzira Principles', which are a set of guidelines on how to approach instigation in such cases. The 'Kalimanzira Principles' are evident from the following statement:

- Incitement resulting in the commission of a genocidal act is punishable under the combination of articles 2(3)(a) and 6(1) of the Statute as genocide by way of instigation;
- Incitement resulting in the commission of a genocidal act and which may be described as 'direct' and 'public' is punishable either under Article 2(3)(c) of the Statute as Direct and Public Incitement to Commit Genocide, or under the combination of Articles 2(3)(a) and 6(1) of the Statute as genocide by way of Instigation;
- Incitement not resulting in the commission of a genocidal act but which may be described as 'direct' and 'public' is only punishable under Article 2(3)(c) of the Statute; and,

[79] *Kalimanzira* (n. 2) para 516.

- Incitement not resulting in the commission of a genocidal act, and which may not be described as 'direct' and 'public', is not punishable under the Statute.[80]

These guidelines, though a major step in the identification and resolution of this legal puzzle, are flawed for the following reasons. First, incitement is limited to the crime of genocide only. This ignores the possibility of laying a charge of incitement to commit crimes against humanity. In this regard, the 'Kalimanzira Principles' obfuscate Article 6(1), which, as has been discussed before, covers every crime over which the ICTR has jurisdiction including crimes against humanity. It also perpetuates the mistake of construing instigation under Article 6(1) as applying only to genocide. Secondly, the 'Kalimanzira Principles' make repeated use of the phrase 'resulting in the commission of'. The use of this phrase propagates the 'substantial contribution' requirement established by previous Trial and Appeal Chambers. Thirdly, it makes use of the word 'commission' (synonymous with execution) of a crime. It therefore limits the instigation under Article 6(1) to the commission of a crime, whereas Article 6(1) stipulates other stages (planning and preparation) in the disjunctive (as evidenced by the use of 'or') rather than a conjunction (use of the word 'and'). The 'Kalimanzira Principles' ought to have considered instigation as an inchoate crime in respect of crimes against humanity.

These guidelines, as well as the jurisprudence of the Trial and Appeal Chambers seem to establish that genocide and crimes against humanity are mutually exclusive. I hold a contrary view: genocide and crimes against humanity, as discussed below, though defined differently, are often constituted by similar actions. An act that amounts to a genocidal act may also amount to a crime against humanity. Therefore, instigation to genocide can still be instigation to crimes against humanity if it led to the planning, preparation or execution of a crime against humanity.

5.3.2.1 *Instigation Under Article 6(1) and Article 2(3)(c): Mutually Exclusive?*

There are no reasons why Article 6(1) and 2(3)(c) are not mutually exclusive. First, incitement under Article 2(3)(c) must be 'direct and public' and 'to commit genocide'. Its application is limited to the crime of genocide. On the other hand, instigation under Article 6(1) must be to any of the crimes over which the ICTR has jurisdiction, including crimes against humanity. The crimes of genocide and crimes against humanity share many

80 Ibid.

commonalities. In other words, criminal conduct may amount to both crimes against humanity and genocide.

This discussion is required to prove that what amounted to direct and public incitement to commit genocide may as well have qualified as instigation to crimes against humanity; and conduct that led to a charge of genocide may qualify as a crime against humanity. Therefore, directly and publicly inciting the commission of genocide under Article 2(3)(c) may also be instigation to crimes against humanity under Article 6(1).

5.3.2.2 *Genocide and Crimes Against Humanity: The Commonalities*

There are similarities between genocide and crimes against humanity. I discuss each to demonstrate these similarities.

The word genocide did not exist before 1945.[81] This word only came into existence after the Second World War. It became an international crime in 1948 following the adoption of the Genocide Convention by the United Nations General Assembly.[82] The Statute of the ICTR's defines genocide as follows:

> ...any of the following acts committed with intent to destroy, in whole or in part, a national, ethnical, racial or religious group, as such:
> a. Killing members of the group;
> b. Causing serious bodily or mental harm to members of the group;
> c. Deliberately inflicting on the group conditions of life calculated to bring about its physical destruction in whole or in part;

[81] Genocide (both its term and concept) was developed by a Polish lawyer of Jewish descent. He defined it as a hybrid word comprising the Greek *genes* (meaning race, nation or tribe) and Latin *cide* (meaning killing). Coined to reflect the realities of European life between 1933 and 1945, it later became the formulation of a legal concept referring to the destruction of human groups. As Lemkin wrote, 'the crime of genocide involves a wide range of actions, including not only deprivation of life but also the prevention of life (abortions, sterilizations) and also devices considerably endangering life and health (artificial death in special camps, deliberate separation of families for depopulation purposes and so forth). All these actions are subordinated to the criminal intent to destroy or to cripple permanently a human group. The acts are directed against groups, as such, and individuals are selected for destruction only because they belong to these groups. In view of such a phenomenon the terms previously used to describe an attack upon nationhood were not adequate. Mass murder or extermination wouldn't apply in the case of sterilization because the victims not murdered, rather a people was killed through delayed action by stopping propagation. Moreover mass murder does not convey the specific losses to civilization in the form of the cultural contributions which can be made only by groups of people united through national, racial or cultural characteristics.' Raphael Lemkin, 'Genocide as a Crime under International Law' (1947) 41*American Journal of International Law* 145, 145–51.

[82] The Genocide Convention was adopted by the United Nations General Assembly on 9 December 1948 (see n 6 above).

d. Imposing measures intended to prevent births within the group;
e. Forcibly transferring children of the group to another group.[83]

The following acts shall be punishable:
a. Genocide;
b. Conspiracy to commit genocide;
c. Direct and public incitement to commit genocide;
d. Attempt to commit genocide;
e. Complicity in genocide.[84]

The Statute of the ICTR defines crimes against humanity as follows:

> ...the following crimes when committed as part of a widespread or systematic attack against any civilian population on national, political, ethnic, racial or religious grounds:
>
> a. Murder;
> b. Extermination;
> c. Enslavement;
> d. Deportation;
> e. Imprisonment;
> f. Torture;
> g. Rape;
> h. Persecutions on political, racial and religious grounds;
> i. Other inhumane acts.[85]

From the definitions above, it is clear that the key difference between genocide and crimes against humanity lies in the requirement of a *dolus specialis* (specific intent) required for the crime of genocide. The *dolus specialis* of genocide is the intention to destroy a people, in whole or in part. These people must be a national, ethnical, racial or religious group.[86] It is this special intent, accompanying or coinciding with any of the *actus reus* that leads to the commission of the crime of genocide.

On the other hand, the definitional elements of crimes against humanity require that any of the enlisted crimes must be committed within the framework of an attack that is waged against any civilian population, widespread or systematic in pattern, and on any of the discriminatory grounds (national, ethnic, racial, religious or political).[87]

These two crimes require different *mens rea*. In the crime of genocide, the *dolus specialis* (specific intent) is that the accused's act must be

[83] Statute of the ICTR, Article 2(2).
[84] Ibid Article 2(3).
[85] Ibid Article 3.
[86] *Bikindi* (n. 26) para. 409; *Akayesu* (n. 2) para. 498.
[87] Statute of the ICTR, Article 3.

perpetrated with intent to destroy a people, in part or in whole.[88] On the other hand, crimes against humanity require that the accused's act be committed with knowledge that there is a widespread or systematic attack directed against any civilian population on any of the discriminatory grounds (namely, national, political, ethnic, racial or religious).[89]

Despite the different *mens rea* requirement, the same conduct may lead to either crime. For example, 'killing of the members of a group' as a genocidal act is not different from murder or extermination depending on the mass nature of the killings as a crime amounting to crimes against humanity.[90] 'Causing serious bodily or mental harm to members of the group' as a genocidal act is similar to torture as a crime against humanity.[91] Rape as a crime against humanity also qualifies as causing serious bodily or mental harm to members of the group as a genocidal act (if committed with genocidal intent). Almost every criminal act listed under the definition of crimes against humanity can fit into the crime of genocide, and vice-versa. They are only differentiated by the accompanying intent. So, where a Tutsi family was killed during the atrocities in Rwanda, that particular killing is a genocidal act if the intention was to destroy, in whole or in part, the Tutsis as an ethnic group. It would also qualify as extermination as a crime against humanity if the killings were committed as part of a widespread or systematic attack perpetrated against any civilian population on any of the discriminatory grounds. Similarly, where a radio journalist exhorted the Hutus to kill the Tutsis because of their ethnic origin, or a newspaper publisher urged the Hutus to take up machetes and eliminate the enemy (referring to Tutsis), these would qualify as both instigation to crimes against humanity and direct and public incitement to commit genocide – direct and public incitement to commit genocide (and it becomes irrelevant if the Hutus actually heeded the call and killed the Tutsis) because they constitute a direct and public instigation to commit genocide. If after, or based on such instigation, the Hutus were to plan or prepare an attack to be waged against the Tutsis (based on their ethnicity), such instigation would lead to the imposition of criminal responsibility under Article 6(1) of the Statute because it has led to the planning and/or preparation for crimes under the

88 *Kajelijeli* (n. 2) para 803; *Nahimana* et al (n. 26) (TC) para 969; *Musema* (n. 2) paras 154, 164; *Akayesu* (n. 2) paras 498, 498–524.

89 *Kajelijeli* (n. 2) para. 880; *Semanza* (n. 2) para. 332; *Ntakirutimana and Ntakirutimana* (n. 2) para. 803; *Bagilishema* (n. 2) para. 94; *Musema* (n. 2) para. 206; *Kayishema and Ruzindanda* (n. 2) (TC) para. 134.

90 See generally the Statute of the ICTR, Article 3(a) and (i), and Article 2(2)(a)–(c).

91 Ibid.

jurisdiction of the ICTR (either in the form of genocide, crimes against humanity, or both). Such calls would qualify as instigation to commit the crime of genocide (given the fact that the killing is done with the intent to destroy the Tutsis, an ethnic group, in part or in whole). These acts would also qualify as instigation to commit crimes against humanity given the fact that they are perpetrated within the framework of an attack, widespread and systematic in nature, and are directed against a civilian population (the Tutsis) based on their ethnicity. From the above analysis, it is clear that direct and public incitement to commit genocide under Article 2(3)(c) is not different from instigation to crimes against humanity under Article 6(1). Incitement and instigation are synonymous with each other. Furthermore, genocide and crimes against humanity share similarities. Thirdly, Article 2(3)(c) and Article 6(1) are not mutually exclusive.

Therefore, instigation is not limited to a genocidal act under Article 6(1). A statement that qualifies as direct and public incitement to commit genocide under Article 2(3)(c) may also qualify as instigation to commit crimes against humanity under Article 6(1). In cases where such instigation leads to the planning, preparation or execution of crimes against humanity, then, criminal responsibility must be imposed.

As discussed above and evidenced by the jurisprudence of the Trial Chambers, instigation under Article 6(1) has been limited to the crime of genocide. While it is correct to include genocide under Article 6(1) analysis, it is erroneous to limit instigation under Article 6(1) to the crime of genocide.

If instigation that amounts to genocide can still qualify as instigation to commit crimes against humanity under Article 6(1), then, the question that must be answered is whether this does not violate the principle of cumulative charges. In other words, is it legally permissible to use the same facts to found different charges against an accused? The Trial and Appeal Chambers of the ICTR have answered this question.

5.3.2.3 *The Issue of Cumulative Convictions*

A given set of facts that amounts to instigation as an inchoate crime under Article 2(3)(c) may have given rise to instigation to commit crimes against humanity under Article 6(1) of the Statute.For the reasons discussed below, this does not constitute cumulative charging.

According to *Kalimanzira*,[92] instigation may attract criminal responsibility under Article 6(1) and Article 2(3)(c). If there is a direct and public

---

[92] *Kalimanzira* (n. 2).

incitement to commit genocide, which actually results in the commission of genocide and crimes against humanity, then, the instigator will be criminally responsible under Article 6(1) and Article 2(3)(c). Therefore, where a statement, made in public, directly calling for the commission of acts which would qualify as genocide and crimes against humanity, resulted in the perpetration of both genocide and crimes against humanity (or just one of them), the individual must become criminally responsible under Article 6(1) for having instigated one or both crimes under the jurisdiction of the ICTR; as well as under Article 2(3)(c) of the Statute (for the inchoate crime of direct and public incitement to commit genocide even if the crimes were not committed). In such cases where the same statement qualifies to attract criminal responsibility under different statutory crimes, debates have developed regarding the permissibility of such a practice.[93] The Trial Chambers have addressed this issue on numerous occasions.

In *Akayesu*,[94] the question was whether the ICTR may find the accused guilty of all the crimes charged based on the same set of facts. The concern was that cumulative charging offends the principle of double jeopardy or the *non bis in idem* principle.[95] An accused person found guilty of both genocide and crimes against humanity may argue that he has twice been judged for the same crime, which, generally, is considered impermissible in criminal law. To resolve this issue, the Trial Chamber considered the reasoning of the International Criminal Tribunal for the Former Yugoslavia in some cases. First, in *The Prosecutor v Duško Tadić*,[96] the Trial Chamber ruled as follows:

> In any event, since this is a matter that will only be relevant insofar as it might affect penalty, it can best be dealt with if and when matters of penalty fall for consideration. What can, however, be said with certainty is that penalty cannot be made to depend upon whether offences arising from the same conduct are alleged cumulatively or in the alternative. What is to be punished by penalty is proven criminal conduct and that will not depend upon technicalities of pleading.[97]

---

[93] *The Prosecutor v Zoran Kupreškić, Drago Josipović, Vladimir Šantić, Mirjan Kupreškić, Vlatko Kupreškić, Dragan Papić*, Judgment, Case No. IT-95-16, T. Ch., 14 January 2000, Paras 637–748; *Akayesu* (n. 2) paras 462–70.

[94] *Akayesu* (n. 2) paras. 462–70.

[95] *Akayesu* (n. 2) para. 462.

[96] Judgment, Case No. IT-94-1, T. Ch. II, 7 May 1997.

[97] *The Prosecutor v Duško Tadić*, Decision on Defence Motion on Form of the Indictment, Case No. IT-94-1, T. Ch. II, 14 November 1995, Para. 10, cited by the Trial Chamber in *Akayesu* (n. 2) para. 463.

In *Tadić*,[98] at the sentencing stage, the Trial Chamber dealt with the issue of cumulative criminal charges by imposing *concurrent* sentences for each cumulative charge. For example, in relation to one particular beating, the accused received seven years' imprisonment for the beating as a crime against humanity, and a six-year concurrent sentence for the same beating as a violation of the laws or customs of war.[99]

This practice has been followed consistently by the ICTY. Citing the French *Barbie Case*,[100] the Trial Chamber held that this practice was followed as the French *Cour de Cassation* held that a single event could be qualified as both a crime against humanity and a war crime.[101]

The practice of imposing concurrent sentences ensures that the accused person is not punished twice for the same acts.[102] A few reasons justify this prosecutorial practice of accumulating criminal charges on the same facts. Civil systems, including Rwanda, have a principle called *concours idéal d'infractions*. This permits multiple convictions for the same act under certain circumstances, which, as articulated by the Trial Chamber, are:

a. where the crimes have different elements; or
b. where the provisions creating the crimes protect different interests; or
c. where it is necessary to record a conviction for both crimes in order to fully describe what the accused did.[103]

On the bases of these exceptions, the Trial Chamber concluded that it would be unjustifiable to convict an accused person of two crimes in relation to the same set of facts where:

a. One crime is a lesser crime included in the other, such as murder and grievous bodily harm or assault, rape and indecent assault, theft and robbery; or,
b. Where one crime charges accomplice liability and the other charges the accused as principal offender, such as in genocide and complicity in genocide.[104]

---

98 *Tadić* (n. 96).
99 *Akayesu* (n. 2) para. 464.
100 *Jugement, Cour de Cassation*, 20 Décembre 1985, *Bulletin des arrêts de la Cour de Cassation*, 1985, p. 1039 e.s).
101 *Akayesu* (n. 2) para. 463.
102 Ibid para. 467.
103 *Akayesu* (n. 2) para. 468.
104 Ibid.

The crimes over which the ICTR has jurisdiction have different elements. They also protect different interests. The crime of genocide was created to protect certain groups from extermination. These groups could be national, racial, ethnic or religious.[105] The crime of crimes against humanity protects civilian populations from widespread or systematic attacks committed on a discriminatory ground.[106] The underlying idea of Article 3 common to the Geneva Conventions and of Additional Protocol II is to protect non-combatants from war crimes in civil war. As the Trial Chamber held, 'these crimes have different purposes and are, therefore, never co-extensive.'[107] It is therefore in keeping with the underlying policy of these crimes to charge these crimes in relation to the same set of facts.

Additionally, as the jurisprudence shows, it may be necessary to record a conviction for more than one of these crimes in order to reflect what crimes an accused actually committed. In an example given by the Trial Chamber, where a military general ordered the killing of prisoners of war belonging to a particular ethnic group with the intent to destroy that group, this would be both genocide and a violation of common Article 3. Convictions for both genocide and violations of common Article 3 would accurately reflect the accused general's course of conduct.[108] This analogy also applies to cases of instigation.

The Trial Chamber refused to entertain the opinion that there exists a hierarchy of the crimes over which it has jurisdiction.[109] It held that none

---

[105] Statute of the ICTR, Article 3.

[106] Ibid. The Rome Statute of the ICC removed this element from the definition of crimes against humanity (Article 7(1)).

[107] *Akayesu* (n. 2) para. 469.

[108] Ibid. The Trial Chamber held: 'Having regard to its Statute, the Chamber believes that the offences under the Statute – genocide, genocide, crimes against humanity, and violations of article 3 common to the Geneva Conventions and of Additional Protocol II – have different elements and, moreover, are intended to protect different interests. The crime of genocide exists to protect certain groups from extermination or attempted extermination. The concept of crimes against humanity exists to protect civilian populations from persecution. The idea of violations of article 3 common to the Geneva Conventions and of Additional Protocol II is to protect non-combatants from war crimes in civil war. These crimes have different purposes and are, therefore, never co-extensive. Thus it is legitimate to charge these crimes in relation to the same set of facts. It may, additionally, depending on the case, be necessary to record a conviction for more than one of these offences in order to reflect what crimes an accused committed. If, for example, a general ordered that all prisoners of war belonging to a particular ethnic group should be killed, with the intent thereby to eliminate the group, this would be both genocide and a violation of common article 3, although not necessarily a crime against humanity. Convictions for genocide and violations of common article 3 would accurately reflect the accused general's course of conduct.'

[109] *Akayesu* (n. 2) para. 470.

of these crimes is superior or inferior to another.[110] The Statute of the ICTR does not establish a hierarchy of crimes, and all three crimes are presented on an equal footing. Genocide may be considered the gravest crime, yet, there is no legal differentiationof justification under the Statute of the ICTRfor holding that crimes against humanity or violations of Article 3 common and of Additional Protocol II are in all circumstances alternative charges to genocide and thus lesser crimes. These are different crimes. They all have different elements. They protect different interests. Consequently, it is permissible to have multiple convictions for the same set of facts.[111]

The issue of cumulative convictions arose again before the Appeals Chamber in *Musema*.[112] The question again was whether or not an accused person can be convicted of multiple crimes based on the same set of facts. The question in *Musema*[113] on the issue of cumulative conviction was not different from *Akayesu*'s:[114] whether it was permissible to convict the accused of both genocide and extermination (as a crime against humanity) based on the same set of facts. The Appeals Chamber approved and adopted the test in the case of *Zdravko Mucić, Hazim Delić, Esad Landžo, Zejnil Delalić v The Prosecutor* (commonly known, and hereinafter referred to as the *Čelebići* case).[115] The Appeal Chamber held that it was permissible to convict the accused on multiple crimes given the same set of facts.[116] After acknowledging the different approaches expressed on the issue of cumulative convictions both within the Tribunal and other jurisdictions, the Appeals Chamber was of the opinion that for reasons of fairness to the accused and the consideration that only distinct crimes may justify multiple convictions,

> multiple criminal convictions entered under different statutory provisions but based on the same conduct are permissible only if each statutory provision involved has a materially distinct element contained in the other. An element is materially distinct from another if it requires proof of a fact not required by the other.
>
> Where this test is not met, the Chamber must decide in relation to which offence it will enter a conviction. This should be done on the basis of the principle that the conviction under the more specific provision should be

110 Ibid.
111 Ibid.
112 *Musema* (n. 9).
113 Ibid.
114 *Akayesu* (n. 2).
115 Judgment, Case No.IT-96-21, Appeal Chamber, 20 February 2001, Para. 370 (known as *Mucić* et al, but commonly, and hereinafter, referred to as (the) '*Čelebići Case*').
116 *Musema* (n. 9) paras. 358–70.

> upheld. Thus, if a set of facts is regulated by two provisions, one of which contains an additional materially distinct element, then a conviction should be entered only under that provision.

In *Musema*,[117] the Appeal Chamber noted that the multiple convictions entered under Article 3 and Article 5 of ICTY Statute are permissible because each Article contained a distinct element requiring proof of a fact not required by the other Article.

The reasoning adopted by the Appeals Chamber in the *Čelebići* case was approved in its entirety by the ICTR Appeals Chamber in *Musema*[118] where it was held that the ruling 'reflects general, objective criteria enabling a Chamber to determine when it may enter or affirm multiple convictions based on the same acts'.[119]

Applying the foregoing analysis to the issue in *Musema*,[120] the Appeals Chamber of the ICTR held as follows:

> Applying the provisions of the test articulated above, the first issue is whether a given statutory provision has a materially distinct element not contained in the other provision, an element being regarded as materially distinct from another if it requires proof of a fact not required by the other....
>
> As a result, the application test with respect to double convictions for genocide and extermination as a crime against humanity is satisfied; these convictions are permissible.[121]

The above extracts clearly establish that the same set of facts can be used to bring multiple charges against an individual if the criteria discussed above are met. Therefore, the same set of facts that amount to instigation under Article 2(3)(c) can be used as instigation (a mode of participation) to commit genocide or crimes against humanity under Article 6(1) of the Statute of the ICTR.

Though this area of the law is well-settled, a worrying issue that needs to be addressed is whether it was correct to charge, try and convict an accused for the crime of direct and public incitement to commit genocide. As the jurisprudence of both the Trial and Appeal Chambers states, direct and public incitement to commit genocide is an inchoate crime: criminal responsibility would be incurred whether such incitement successfully led to the commission of genocide or not. In Rwanda, the crimes were

---

117 *Musema* (n. 9).
118 Ibid.
119 Ibid para. 363.
120 *Musema* (n. 9).
121 *Kajelijeli* (n. 2) para. 751.

committed. Given the nature of inchoate crimes, the question that needs to be answered is whether the inchoateness of this crime was lost, and therefore whether it is wrong to charge, try and convict individuals of it.

5.3.3 *Debating the Inchoateness of Article 2(3)(c) Within the Rwandan Context*

As discussed earlier, the Statute of the ICTR imported the definition of genocide from the Genocide Convention. It also imported other punishable acts listed in the Genocide Convention. One of these punishable acts is direct and public incitement to commit genocide.[122] The Genocide Convention did not define the words 'direct and public incitement to genocide'.[123] The jurisprudence on the meaning of these words has been developed extensively by both the Trial and Appeal Chambers of the ICTR. The Trial and Appeal Chambers have construed the meanings of the words 'direct', 'public', and 'incitement'.[124] In construing these words, the Trial and Appeal Chambers recognised the work of the delegates who drafted the Genocide Convention, whose underlying reason for the inclusion of this mode of participation in the perpetration of genocide was to punish individuals who use media portals to incite others to commit genocidal acts.[125] In addition, they have characterised the crime as inchoate, for which criminal responsibility would be incurred irrespective of whether the incitement is successful in leading to the commission of genocide or not.[126]

The importation of direct and public incitement to commit genocide (and other punishable acts) into the Statute of the ICTR and the inclusion of instigation as a mode of participation under Article 6(1) have confused the understanding of Article 6(1) which deals with the imposition of criminal responsibility; and Article 2(3)(c), which is the inchoate crime of direct and public incitement to commit genocide. As an inchoate crime, the Trial Chambers of the ICTR have firmly established that genocide does not need to occur for there to be criminal liability.[127]

---

122 See Statute of the ICTR, Article 2(3)(c); Genocide Convention, Article 3(c).

123 *Kalimanzira* (n. 2) para. 510.

124 For example, see generally the judgments in the following cases: *Hategekimana* (n. 2); *Muvunyi* (n. 26); *Kalimanzira* (n. 2); *Nahimana* et al (n. 26) (AC); *Nahimana* et al (n. 26) (TC); *Akayesu* (n. 2).

125 See *Akayesu* (n. 2) para. 551, where the Trial Chamber construed this inchoate crime by looking at the intention of the drafters of the Genocide Convention.

126 *Akayesu* (n. 2) paras. 561–63.

127 *Akayesu* (n. 2) paras. 561–63.

However, as in every inchoate crime, the perpetration of the full crime places the inchoateness into abeyance.[128] In other words, it is lost. This is applicable to cases of attempt and conspiracy. Liability for the inchoate crime of attempted murder would cease if the defendant proceeds to kill the victim. In such case, the defendant would be guilty of murder as a principal offender, or a co-offender if he, in agreement with another, perpetrated any of the *actus reus* elements of the crime.[129] The same can be said of conspiracy. Liability for the inchoate crime of conspiracy exists when an agreement to do an unlawful act is reached.[130] If two persons, X and Y, agreed to kill V, the agreement itself is sufficient to impose liability for the inchoate crime of conspiracy to murder. However, if in furtherance of such agreement to murder V, X and Y killed V, then, liability for the inchoate crime of conspiracy to kill would cease, and they would become criminally responsible for the crime of murder as co-offenders or principals in the first degree.[131] In incitement, the inchoate crime is committed once an inciter reaches another with the intention of encouraging him to commit a crime. If X encouraged Y to kill V, then, X would have committed the crime of incitement to murder. If Y goes ahead to kill V because of X's encouragement, then, X becomes liable as an accessory to murder (and in some jurisdictions, principal to the second degree). Once the crime is committed, then, liability would be imposed on him as an accessory.[132] From the above hypothetical analyses, it is evident that criminal liability for inchoate crimes changes when the full crime is committed. The accused in the above examples would incur criminal liability for the completed crimes, and not the inchoate crimes. Inchoate crimes are crimes that are still at the preparatory or initial stages, and when the crime in question is completed, then, it is incorrect to talk of criminal liability for inchoate crimes.[133]

These analytical discussions on the nature and limits of inchoate crimes are necessary to understand the inchoateness of the crime of direct and public incitement to commit genocide. The Trial and Appeal Chambers have repeatedly reiterated its inchoateness, holding that the imposition of criminal responsibility for direct and public incitement to commit

---

128 Ormerod (n. 3) 379–470; Dressler (n. 3) 379; Allen and Cooper (n. 3) 438–502; Heaton (n. 3) 401–39.

129 Ormerod (n. 3) 379; Dressler (n. 3) 380 -419; Allen and Cooper (n. 3) 438–63; Heaton (n. 3) 403–14.

130 Allen and Cooper (n. 3) 463–82; Heaton (n. 3) 415–33.

131 Heaton (n. 3) 367–400.

132 See generally Ormerod (n. 3) 379–470; Heaton (n. 3) 367–400.

133 Ormerod (n. 3) 379; Dressler (n. 3) 379–465; Allen and Cooper (n. 3) 438–99; Heaton (n. 3) 401–39.

genocide has no bearing on whether the crime of genocide is committed or not.[134] This line of reasoning squares with the intention of the drafters of the Genocide Convention, who created this inchoate offence as a result of the role played by persons who directly and publicly incite the commission of genocide.[135]

However, if liability for an inchoate crime ceases when the crime itself is completed (or committed), then, the question arises: why charge anyone for the inchoate crime of direct and public incitement to commit genocide when genocide is committed? My view is that this is further reflected in the definition of criminal responsibility under Article 6(1).[136] Instigation is one of the modes contemplated in Article 6(1), and it must lead to any of the stages (planning, preparation or execution) of any of the crimes (genocide, crimes against humanity or violations of Article 3 common to the Geneva Conventions and of Additional Protocols II). The killing of Tutsis (an ethnic group) by the Hutus (another ethnic group) was done with the intention to destroy them in whole. This amounted to genocide, per the definition articulated in the Statute of the ICTR and the Genocide Convention.[137] In my view, the inchoateness of Article 2(3)(c) ought to be lost. Criminal responsibility for every person who incited genocide (even directly and publicly) ought to be imposed under Article 6(1) given the fact that such instigation contributed to either the planning, preparation or execution of genocide.

5.3.4 *Joint Criminal Enterprise Approach*

The basis of criminal liability is an important domain in criminal law. Its primary goal is to identify specifically on whom criminal responsibility ought to be imposed. The law recognises different categories of perpetrators of crimes, and as discussed below, the rules on the imposition of criminal responsibility are different. In my view, and as illustrated in the discussions below, the requirement that criminal responsibility can be imposed under Article 6(1) only when it is proved that the accused's mode of participation substantially contributed to the crime does not square

134 *Kalimanzira* (n. 2) para. 515; *Bikindi* (n. 26) para. 419; *Nahimana* et al (n. 26) (AC) paras. 678–79; *Nahimana* et al (n. 26) (TC) para. 1013 ; *Kajelijeli* (n. 2) para.. 855; *Niyitegeka* (n. 26) para. 431; *Musema* (n. 2) para. 120; *Rutaganda* (n. 2) para. 38; *Akayesu* (n. 2) para. 562.

135 *Akayesu* (n. 2) para 551. See also *Nahimana* et al (n. 26) (AC) para 978; *Nahimana* et al (n. 26) (TC) para 678.

136 Article 6(1) defines the imposition of criminal responsibility for crimes over which the ICTR has jurisdiction.

137 See the definitions as articulated in the Statute of the ICTR, Article 2(2) the Genocide Convention, Article 2.

with the basic principles of criminal liability in cases of joint criminal enterprise. Before I expose the incongruity of this substantial contribution requirement with the basic principles of criminal participation, it is important to distinguish the different forms of criminal participation.

The basis of imposing criminal responsibility in criminal law is that the accused, by his act or omission, brought a result (consequence such as murder, or state of affairs such as public disorder) which is prohibited by law, and with the accompanying prescribed *mens rea*. In criminal law, a crime can be committed by a person acting solo, or a group of persons acting in agreement. The imposition of criminal responsibility varies accordingly: where one person is the principal offender of the crime, criminal responsibility is imposed upon him or her without any difficulty. However, in cases where a multitude of persons are involved in a criminal activity, there exist some rules on the imposition of criminal responsibility. This would depend on whether the accused persons are joint principal offenders, or acted within a joint criminal enterprise. It is important to examine the distinction between cases of joint principal offenders and cases of joint criminal enterprise.

Joint principal offenders are cases where two or more persons are jointly involved in the perpetration of a crime: that is, they all commit the *actus reus* of the crime in question. If A1, A2, A3 and A4 jointly attack the victim, V, with the intention to kill him, and all unleash punches against him resulting in V's death, then, all four accused persons (A1, A2, A3, and A4) are joint principal offenders. With the requisite *mens rea* (the intention to cause the death of V), they perpetrated the *actus reus* of murder (punching V). The position is not different even in cases where the principal offender is not present when the crime is completed. For example, if A1, A2, and A3 conspire to commit a crime, and agree that they would hire an innocent agent, I. It is immaterial that only A1 met the innocent agent (I) to hire him. All accused persons are liable to the inchoate crime of conspiracy because he (A1) acted in furtherance of their agreement. It is irrelevant that the other two accused persons (A2 and A3) were not present when A1 hired the innocent agent.

On the other hand, cases of joint criminal enterprise are different. 'Joint criminal enterprise' is descriptive of a case where numerous persons act with a common purpose. That purpose is to commit a crime. The imposition of criminal responsibility on individuals who are part of a joint criminal enterprise is simple: they are all considered as principal offenders.[138]

---

[138] This is the case in most common law countries. Australia is an example. See *Osland v R* (1998) 73 ALJR 173, HC of A. Joint criminal enterprise or joint unlawful enterprise has been

Furthermore, the capacity in which one of the persons acted in a joint criminal enterprise is immaterial. In cases where it is necessary to make a distinction, the test is this: did the accused by his or her own act (as distinct from anything done by the other accused persons) contribute to the *actus reus*? If in the affirmative, then, the accused is a principal offender. If the accused did not, then, some difficulties arise. If the accused is innocent, then, there is no crime the accused could have aided or abetted because of

---

a debatable doctrine as to whether it carries a distinct form of liability. However, it is used to describe cases where two or more persons embark on a joint enterprise to commit a crime or crimes. They would obviously have planned and agreed beforehand to commit such crimes. While this remains the clearest case, it is however possible to have such an agreement made immediately before or even during the commission of the crimes(s). The key and distinguishing ingredient of cases of joint criminal enterprise is the presence of a shared common purpose, or 'a shared common intention': in other words, each individual participating in the commission of the crime has the same intention as the others, and each individual knows that the others do intend the same thing (usually the result). As a consequence, each individual is criminally responsible for any (or whatever) crimes that the others commit which come within the scope of the common purpose or design. See Heaton (n. 3) 386. The doctrine of joint criminal enterprise has been the subject of numerous academic papers by many experts in the field of international criminal law. Their discussions, however, focus on where to draw a precise line as to which persons to hold responsible for the crimes committed by a joint criminal enterprise. This has been a recurrent issue ever since the Nuremberg Tribunals, but gathered much momentum after some landmark decisions rendered by both the Trial and Appeal Chambers of the *ad hoc* Tribunals (the ICTY and the ICTR). The points raised and approaches advanced by these scholars are very significant and eloquent, yet, remain different from the way I approach joint criminal enterprise in this book. Whereas their issue is on where to draw a line in holding persons responsible, my focus is the bigger picture of a joint criminal enterprise as it reflects the different roles played by different individuals at different times. In other words, it asks and answers the 'how' question: the role played towards the planning, preparation or execution of the crimes. Putting this into play, instigators should have been perceived as having played a role towards any of the stages of any of the crimes over which the ICTR has jurisdiction. Inasmuch as there is a cornucopia of literature on the issue of joint criminal enterprise, it is important that the approaches and focus are distinguished from what I do in this Chapter particularly and in the entire book generally. For an understanding of the approaches raised by some leading academic experts, see generally See generally Allison Marston Danner and Jenny S. Martinez, 'Guilty Associations: Joint Criminal Enterprise, Command Responsibility, and the Development of International Criminal Law' (2005) Vol. 93, 1 *California Law Review*, 75–169; Antonio Cassese, 'The Proper Limits of Individual Responsibility under the Doctrine of Joint Criminal Enterprise' (2007) Vol. 5, 1 *J Int Criminal Justice* 109–133; Elies van Slierdregt, 'Joint Criminal Enterprise as a Pathway to Convicting Individuals for Genocide' (2007) Vol. 5, 1 *J Int Criminal Justice* 184–207; Harmen van der Wilt, 'Joint Criminal Enterprise Possibilities and Limitations', (2007) Vol. 5, 1 *J Int Criminal Justice* 91–108; Jens David Ohlin, 'Three Conceptual Problems with the Doctrine of Joint Criminal Enterprise' (2007) Vol. 5, 1 *J Int Criminal Justice* 69–90; Kai Ambos, 'Joint Criminal Enterprise and Command Responsibility', (2007) Vol. 5, 1 *J Int Criminal Justice* 159–183; Kai Hamdorf, 'The Concept of a Joint Enterprise and Domestic Modes of Liability for Parties to a Crime: A Comparison of German and English Law' (007) Vol. 5, 1 *J Int Criminal Justice* 208–226; Rebecca L. Haffajee, 'Prosecuting Crimes of Rape and Sexual Violence at the ICTR: The Application of Joint Criminal Enterprise Theory' (2006) 29 *Harv. J. L. & Gender* 201–221; Steven Powles, Joint Criminal Enterprise – Criminal Liability

the accused's lack of *mens rea* and also knowledge that the accused aided and abetted the crime. The accused ought to be seen as an innocent agent in such cases.

In cases where the *actus reus* is a state of affairs, the question to be asked in determining who is a principal offender is: ignoring the accused, does the statutory definition of the state of affairs constituting a crime fit the principal offender?

From the above illustrations, it is clear that in cases where persons act with a common purpose, they are all considered as principal offenders. Two reasons are advanced for this: first, they all desire that the crime in question should be committed. Secondly, they play different roles towards the realisation of their purpose (the commission of the crime). It would be difficult to assign different degrees of blame to the different persons. How difficult would it be for the law to try to know whose act was more substantial than the other in the commission of the crime. Therefore, where it is evidenced that numerous persons acted with a common criminal purpose, they all incur criminal responsibility as principal offenders, and they are convicted as such without any distinction as to whose act was more substantial or trivial in causing the commission of the crime.

5.3.4.1 *The Formulation and Incorporation of the Joint Criminal Enterprise in the Charter of Nuremberg*

With these clear-cut principles of the imposition of criminal responsibility in cases of joint criminal enterprise, little difficulty was experienced by Prosecution at Nuremberg where the entire history of the activities of the Nazi Regime was examined. In a letter addressed to President Franklin D. Roosevelt on 22 January, 1945, the United States' Secretaries of State, War, and the Attorney-General wrote:

> The criminality of the German leaders and their associates does not consist solely of individual outrages, but represents the result of a systematic and planned reign of terror...We are satisfied that these atrocities were perpetrated in pursuance of a premeditated criminal plan or enterprise which either contemplated or necessarily involved their commission.[139]

In the discussions that preceded the establishment of the Nuremberg Charter, United States' Colonel Murray Bernays propounded a two-phased

by Prosecutorial Ingenuity and Judicial Creativity' (2004) 2 *J. Int'l Crim. Just.* 606–619; Verena Han, 'The Development of the Concept of Joint Criminal Enterprise at the International Criminal Tribunal for the Former Yugoslavia' (2005) 5 *Int'l Crim. L. Rev.* 167–201.

[139] Dept. of State, *Report of Robert H. Jackson, United States Representative to the International Conference on Military Tribunals* (1949) 4–5; Nina H.B. Jorgensen, *The Responsibility of States for International Crimes* (Oxford University Press Inc. 2000) 59.

solution to the problem.[140] First, an international tribunal would need to establish firmly that the Nazi Government engaged in a criminal conspiracy to commit the crimes that the Nuremberg Tribunal would be empowered to try and punish. There was an agreement to commit crimes (this made it a criminal conspiracy). This agreement was formulated and developed by members of the Nazi Regime. The Nazi Regime, broadly speaking, included the Nazi Party, its affiliates such as the Gestapo, the *Schutzstaffel* (SS), the *Sturmabteilung* (SA), and other governmental agencies. The members of the Nazi Regime partook in the planning (including design, preparation and provision of resources) of the crimes. Some instigated, some ordered and some provided the materials needed for the realisation of the plan. By so doing, they incurred criminal responsibility as part of a joint criminal enterprise. Representatives and members of these organisations labelled as criminal by the Nuremberg Tribunal would have guilt imputed to them and be subsequently prosecuted based on membership alone. The second phase of his proposal required that every member of an organisation held to be criminal would be subject to arrest, trial, and if found guilty, punishment in the national courts of the Allied Powers. This meant that proof that an individual was a member of any of these organisations was sufficient for such an individual to be charged.[141]

On 16 May 1945, the United Nations War Crimes Commission, prepared and delivered the following report:

> ...having ascertained that countless crimes have been committed during the war by organized gangs, Gestapo groups, SS or military units, sometimes entire formulations, in order to secure the punishment of all the guilty, makes the following recommendation to the member of Governments:
>
> a. to seek out the leading criminals responsible for the organization of criminal enterprises including systematic terrorism, planned looting and the general policy of atrocities against the peoples of the occupied states, in order to punish all the organizers of such crimes;
> b. to commit for trial, either jointly or individually all those who, as members of these criminal gangs, have taken part in any way in the carrying out of crimes as committed collectively by groups, formations or units.[142]

---

140 Jorgensen (n. 139).

141 President Franklin D. Roosevelt did not approve the two-phased plan, but his successor, President Harry Truman endorsed it in further deliberations preceding the establishment of the Tribunal. The French, however, held an alternative view. Guided by its law, they proposed a reversal of the burden of proof to invoke a presumption of guilt. Second, individuals could be held guilty of voluntary membership in an 'association' of criminals as provided for in the French Penal Code (Articles 265–67). See Jorgensen (n. 139) 60.

142 UNWCC, *History of the United Nations War Crimes Commission and the Development of the Laws of War* (1948) 296.

Based on the recommendations of the Commission, the Nuremberg Charter and Tribunal addressed the issue of criminal organisations in the following provisions:

> At the trial of any individual member of any group or organization the Tribunal may declare (in connection with any act of which the individual may be convicted) that the group or organization of which the individual was a member was a criminal organization.[143]
>
> After the receipt of the Indictment the Tribunal shall give such notice as it thinks fit that the prosecution intends to ask the Tribunal to make such declaration and any member of the organization will be entitled to apply to the Tribunal for leave to be heard by the Tribunal upon the question of the criminal character of the organization. The Tribunal shall have power to allow or reject the application. If the application is allowed, the Tribunal may direct in what manner the applicants shall be represented and heard.
>
> In cases where a group or organization is declared criminal by the Tribunal, the competent national authority of any Signatory shall have the right to bring individual to trial for membership therein before national, military or occupation courts. In any such case the criminal nature of the group or organization is considered proved and shall not be questioned.[144]
>
> Any person convicted by the Tribunal may be charged before a national, military or occupation court, referred to in Article 10 of this Charter, with a crime other than of membership in a criminal group or organization and such court may, after convicting him, impose upon him punishment independent of and additional to the punishment imposed by the Tribunal for participation in the criminal activities of such group or organization.[145]

The Nuremberg Charter empowered the Nuremberg Tribunal to declare that an indicted 'group or organization' was criminal. In subsequent proceedings, the criminality of a group or organisation would not be challenged. An individual who had acquired membership in such a group or organisation could be prosecuted for the crime of membership in such a criminal group or organisation. The intention of the provisions of the Nuremberg Charter was not to criminalise every member of every group or organisation that was labelled criminal. Such a possibility, however, was not expressly excluded by the same provisions. At the conclusion of the specific contents of the Nuremberg Charter, six groups and organisations were indicted by the Prosecutors of the Allied Powers. They were labelled

143 Charter of the IMT, Nuremberg, Article 9.
144 Charter of the IMT, Nuremberg, Article 10.
145 Charter of the IMT, Nuremberg, Article 11.

criminal groups and organisations that had been part of a wider conspiracy to commit the crimes the Nuremberg Tribunal was empowered to try and punish.[146]

The conduct of the Nuremberg trials, and the judgments rendered in all cases recognised the basic principles of joint criminal enterprise: every participant was considered a principal offender. The Charter of the IMT, Nuremberg, did not require that an accused's mode of participation articulated in Article 6(c) must substantially contribute to the commission of any of the crimes over which the Nuremberg Tribunal had jurisdiction. In my view, this was in accordance with the letter of the law: Article 6(c) of the Charter of the IMT, Nuremberg, imposed criminal responsibility on

> leaders, organizers, instigators and accomplices participating in the formulation or execution of a common plan or conspiracy to commit any of the foregoing crimes [crimes over which the Nuremberg Tribunal had jurisdiction].

The Prosecution recognised the existence of a joint criminal enterprise. Within this criminal enterprise, a plan or conspiracy to commit atrocities was developed. This plan was materialised, resulting in unspeakable atrocities which formed the bases of the crimes created by the Charter of the IMT, Nuremberg. There was no substantial contribution requirement for the imposition of criminal responsibility. The commission of the crimes in furtherance of the plan or conspiracy *ipso facto*evidenced the existence of a joint criminal enterprise. In addition, imposing criminal responsibility on the members of this joint criminal enterprise did not require proof that such a member's mode of participation substantially contributed to the commission of the crimes. In my view therefore, the Nuremberg trials were strictly in line with the principles of criminal liability in cases of joint criminal enterprise; and the judgments rendered therein recognised these principles without making any further requirement that an accused's mode of participation must have substantially contributed to the commission of a crime.

In retrospect, looking at the atrocities of the Nazi Regime unfolds a template: first, there existed a plan or conspiracy to commit the atrocities;

---

[146] These groups and organisations were the Cabinet of the Nazi Government (Reich Cabinet), the Leadership Corps of the Nazi Party, the *Schutzstaffel* (SS), the Gestapo, the *Sturmabteilung* (SA), and the General Staff and High Command of the German Armed Forces. However, due to the unease in precisely defining and developing the concept of collective guilt, the Nuremberg Tribunal proceeded with caution and declared criminal only the Leadership Corps of the Nazi Party, the Gestapo and the SS. See Jorgensen (n. 139) 62–65.

secondly, the involvement of the broader German citizenry in the perpetration of these atrocities; thirdly, the atrocities were widespread and systematic; and fourthly, the primary targets of these atrocities were either racial (Jews) or national (citizens of occupied territories). About half a century later, Rwanda would be the theatre of genocide where the Nazi Regime template with the key elements discussed above would be perpetrated against an ethnic group because of their ethnicity and political dissidents because of their political beliefs. To better understand this, it is important to look at the history of Rwanda's ethnic problems.

5.3.4.2 *Background to Rwanda's Ethnic Divisions*

As of 1994, Rwanda was a good example of a country with unresolved ethnic problems.[147] With an artificial ethnic distinction imposed on Rwandans by their colonial masters, the majority Hutus and minority Tutsis lived side by side with a profound animosity that resulted in intermittent and internecine (armed) conflicts.[148] In April 1994, a massacre aimed at the elimination of an ethnic group, the Tutsis (simply because they were Tutsis), and Hutu political dissidents (for their political opinions and beliefs), began in the capital city of Kigali, and quickly spread across the country. Within a period of one hundred days, almost a million people had been killed.[149]

A careful examination of the country's rough and unstable past reveals deep and unresolved ethnic tensions; a stalled agrarian economy; a history of political upheavals and a frightening pattern of organised mass killings in one of the most densely populated countries in the world.[150]

Colonised between 1897 and 1916 by Germans, the Belgians took control of Rwanda after the First World War and ruled the country until 1962. The lack of manpower and resources forced the Belgians to allow Rwandans govern themselves. In search of political stability, they accepted the monarchy, which was the existing institution at the time, headed by a divine king.[151]

---

[147] Christian P. Sherrer, *Genocide and Crisis in Central Africa: Conflict Roots, Mass Violence, and Regional War* (Praeger 2002); Edward L. Nyankanzi, *Genocide: Rwanda and Burundi* (Schenkam Books 1998); Linda Melvern, *Conspiracy to Murder: The Rwandan Genocide* (Verson 2004) 49.

[148] Sherrer (n. 147); Nyankanzi (n. 147).

[149] See generally Roméo Dallaire, *Shake Hands with the Devil: The Failure of Humanity in Rwanda* (Arrow Books 2004).

[150] Sherrer (n. 147), Nyankanzi (n. 147).

[151] Like most other African countries at independence, Rwanda had no experience in democracy, but centuries of tradition of organised statehood. This took the form of an oligarchy, headed by a king accorded divine status. Chukwuma Obidegwu, 'Rwanda:

The King's subjects were divided into three principal social groups; firstly, the Hutus, who were the majority (made up to about eighty five per cent of the population), comprised of mostly poor peasants; secondly, the Tutsis, who were more prosperous, owned land and cattle, being the traditional indicators of wealth in Rwandan society.[152] By 1990, the Tutsis made up about fourteen per cent of the country's population. The last were the peripheral Twas; who made up the remaining one per cent. They comprised groups of nomads and hunters who lived in forested areas. Despite the differences, the Hutus and Tutsis lived and worked together in their respective communities, with their huts juxtaposed in villages throughout the countryside. The two ethnic groups spoke the same language, practised the same culture and lived under the same rulers. Their primary distinctions were purely artificial.[153] The ethnic divide between the Hutus and Tutsis is neither attributable to cultural differences nor natural atavism as the exact origin of these three groups remains unknown. The Hutus and Tutsis are not separated by history, language, religion or territory, nor even distinguished by the often-cited physical traits.[154]

During the Belgian control of Rwanda, the disparities between the two ethnic groups were exploited by giving the Tutsis educational and other preferences. An identity card system was instituted (which later became a tool in the hands of the genocidists) whereby the ethnic identity of a person and his or her family was mentioned on the identity card. Movements between the Hutu and Tutsi ethnic groups were prohibited.[155] The Belgians believed that the easily identified more superior and malleable Tutsi aristocrats would be better in instituting European reforms. This belief led to widespread resentment. It generated profound animosity by the Hutus of first, the Belgian colonists for creating favouritism; and second, of their Tutsi neighbours for being the beneficiaries.[156]

The Search for Post-Conflict Socio-Economic Change, 1995–2001' (2003) *African Region Working Paper Series* No. 59, 1.

152 Obidegwu (n. 151).

153 The colonial masters adopted and institutionalised a rigid ethnic classification, based on class distinctions that existed in the pre-colonial kingdom of Rwanda. Colonial policies accorded the minority Tutsis social and economic privileges, while creating an underclass of the majority Hutu. Religious, racial and historical factors, as well as physical appearances, were evoked to justify the classifications and the implied superiority of Tutsis over Hutus. Obidegwu (n. 151).

154 Helen Nygren Krug, 'Genocide in Rwanda: Lessons Learned and Future Challenges to the UN Human Rights System' (1998) 67 *Nordic Journal of International Law* 165, 165–213.

155 Sherrer (n. 147).

156 Ibid.

Popular sentiment toward Belgian colonial rule among both ethnic groups changed from compliance to fervid opposition in the late 1950s.[157] Each ethnic group sought for both the establishment of an independent Rwandan nation and total control of the nation's government.[158] Hutu and Tutsi political parties were formed.[159] The struggle for independence of the Rwandan nation grew and was accelerated by the increasing distaste with the Belgian administration at the United Nations.[160] The colony obtained its independence in 1962. Through elections, the Hutus, for the first time in Rwandan history, came to power with Grégoire Kayibanda as President.[161]

The existing resentment between the Hutus and the Tutsis heightened. The transition to Republican government was anything but peaceful and cooperative. In early 1961, vengeful violence by Hutus led to the killings of over one hundred Tutsis; the burning of over three thousand homes and the displacement of about twenty two thousand persons. A report by the United Nations Trusteeship Commission concluded that 'an oppressive system has been replaced by another one', and predicted ominously that 'it is quite possible that some day we will witness violent reactions on the part of the Tutsi.'[162]

In the 1990s, Rwanda's economy experienced a crisis. It became stagnant. This was exacerbated by the anti–Tutsi sentiment.[163] The grim circumstances prevalent in the country pushed the Rwandan Minister of Defence at that time, Juvénal Habyarimana, to overthrow the shaky regime of President Kayibanda. An authoritarian and nepotistic government was set up, dominated by the Hutu political party.[164] The government gradually and systematically worked to weaken and isolate the Tutsis. It required Rwandans to carry identity cards that labelled them either Hutu or Tutsi.[165] Through discriminatory policies accompanied with open harassment, the Hutu-led government gradually weeded out Tutsis from positions in the military, civil service and local governments.

---

157 Ibid.

158 Ibid.

159 Ibid.

160 Ibid.

161 Ibid.

162 UN Trusteeship Commission Report of March 1961, quoted by Prunier Gerard, *The Rwanda Crisis: History of a Genocide* (Columbia University Press 1995) 53.

163 Rwanda's economy experienced a rapid growth and stability between 1960 and the 1970s. Growth rates began to decline in the 1980s and deteriorated drastically in the early 1990s with the commencement of a full-scale civil war in October 1990. Obidegwu (n. 151) 4.

164 Sherrer (n. 147).

165 Ibid.

In the early 1990s, the Tutsi rebels in Uganda established a united military organisation. One of its aims was to re-establish Tutsi rule in Rwanda. It was named the Rwandan Patriotic Front (RPF).[166] It launched numerous military incursions, which oft plunged the country into civil war. With the intervention and encouragement of international entities like the Organization for African Unity and the United Nations, the Rwandan Patriotic Front and the Habyarimana regime officially concluded a cease–fire in 1991.[167] However, this was broken on many occasions.[168] In August 1993, at Arusha, Tanzania, the two sides finally reached an agreement (the Arusha Accord) on a power–sharing arrangement that would return the country to multi–party rule in Rwanda.[169] In October 1993, the Security Council passed Resolution 872.[170] This created the United Nations Assistance Mission in Rwanda (hereinafter referred to as UNAMIR).[171]

166 Ibid.

167 Ibid.

168 Ibid.

169 The Arusha Accord attempted to address the fundamental problems behind the conflict: the institutional exclusion in the country, the rights of Rwandese to return to Rwanda, and the transition process to an inclusive, democratic and stable Rwanda. It set a good model for power-sharing, but lacked the incentives and sanctions for compliance by all the signatories and their political parties. Obidegwu (n. 151) 7.

170 United Nations Security Council Resolution 872, U.N. SCOR, 3288th meeting, U.N. Doc. S/RES/872 (1993) of 5October 1993.

171 Ibid. UNAMIR was established by Security Council Resolution 872 of 5 October 1993, to help implement the Arusha Peace Agreement signed by the Rwandese parties on 4 August 1993. Its mandate was: to assist in ensuring the security of the capital city of Kigali, monitor the ceasefire agreement, including establishment of an expanded demilitarized zone and demobilisation procedures, monitor the security situation during the final period of the transitional Government's mandate leading up to elections, assist with mine-clearance, and assist in the coordination of humanitarian assistance activities in conjunction with relief operations. It was adjusted by United Nations Security Council Resolution 912 (United Nations Security Council Resolution 912, U.N. SCOR, 3368th meeting, U.N. Doc. S/RES/912 of 21 April 1994), expanded by United Nations Security Council Resolution 918 (United Nations Security Council Resolution 918, U.N. SCOR, 3377th meeting, U. N. Doc. S/RES/918 of 17 May 1994), further adjusted by United Nations Security Council Resolution 997 (United Nations Security Council Resolution 997, U.N. SCOR, 3542nd meeting, U.N. Doc. S/RES/997 of 9 June 1995). By Resolution 965 (United Nations Security Council Resolution 965, U.N. SCOR, 3473rd meeting, U.N. Doc. S/RES/965 of 30 November 1994), it was specifically asked to contribute to the security in Rwanda of personnel of the ICTR and of human rights officers; and to assist in the establishment and training of a new, integrated, national police force. On 12 December 1995, the United Nations Security Council, by its Resolution 1029 (United Nations Security Council Resolution 1029, U.N. SCOR, 3605th meeting, U.N. Doc. S/RES/1029 of 12 December 1995), further adjusted its mandate to focus primarily on facilitating the safe and voluntary return of refugees, and, as an interim measure, contributing, with the agreement of the Government of Rwanda, to the protection of the ICTR. Its mandate officially came to an end on 8 March 1996. The withdrawal of the Mission was completed in April 1996.

It was based in Kigali, and under the command of General Roméo Dallaire. It hoped to assist in the implementation of the Arusha Accord.

In the first few months of UNAMIR's mission, the peace agreement established between the Hutus and the Tutsis was far from being implemented. The tension intensified and the bitterness that existed between the two groups worsened. On 6 April 1994, two surface-to-air missiles brought down the plane carrying the Presidents of Rwanda and Burundi as it approached the runway at the Kigali airport. Immediately, the systematic, premeditated and merciless killings of Tutsis and Hutu moderates in Kigali began. Ten Belgian paratroopers, part of the Belgian contingent of the United Nations' force, were disarmed and brutally murdered in cold blood by Rwandan government troops as they sought to protect the Rwandan Prime Minister who was assassinated.[172]

Starting in Kigali, the Rwandan capital, widespread and systematic slaughter of the Tutsis was spread with a ferocity that even its sinister organisers could not have hoped for. Aimed at completely eliminating the Tutsis (because of their ethnicity) perceived as the enemies in the country, in about a hundred days, almost a million Tutsis and Hutu-moderates had been consigned to death. The perpetrators, high within government circles, had made meticulous plans as well as set up a structure to execute them. A radio station under their control, *Radio Télévision Libre des Milles Collines* (hereinafter referred to as *RTLM*),[173] had been created for the purpose of whipping up anti-Tutsi sentiment. The peacekeeping force monitored most of the radio broadcasts, but hardly took them as serious, authoritative, or credible due to their extreme nature. The Tutsis were fully demonised in an incredible and unrealistic manner; and likened to cockroaches that needed to be exterminated.[174] The Belgians were not spared in the propaganda tactic. UNAMIR and the United Nations failed to analyse these broadcasts to determine the specificity of the threats and the ultimate consequences that could follow, like predicting who could be the next targets for assassination or massacre. UNAMIR became aware of the seriousness of the hate propaganda only in the early stages of the genocide, as the death of the Belgian peacekeepers was advocated for over the radio for being perpetrators of the assassination of the President.[175] As the genocide

---

172 Alison Des Forges, *Leave No One to Tell the Story: Genocide in Rwanda* (Human Rights Watch), <http://www.hrw.org/reports/1999/rwanda>.

173 *The Prosecutor v Ferdinand Nahimana, Jean-Bosco Barayagwiza and Hassan Ngeze*, Judgment Summary, Case No. ICTR-99-52-T, T. Ch. I, 3 December 2003, Para. 30.

174 *Nahimana* et al (n. 173) paras. 25–29.

175 One of the Radio Broadcasts blandished 'these Belgian bandits have committed many atrocities that merit punishment. We Rwandans will never forget that these bandits killed

developed, the extremists used the airwaves to justify their actions and to assign blame on the Tutsis for the nation's shortcomings.[176] Outrageously cruel and inhuman broadcasts filled the airwaves.[177] Macabre lines were set to popular tunes, with chilling words set to a charming melody being sung in the air.[178] The Hutus used public rallies as other means of spreading propaganda, inciting violence, and preparing the Hutu majority to condone, if not, commit the atrocities that were to occur. Venomous speeches were followed by several massacres of Tutsi civilians.

In effecting the massacres, the Hutus made use of weapons that had been imported into the country and supplied to them. These weapons comprised of machetes, spears, clubs, spikes and even farm tools. The Hutu militia slaughtered the Tutsis and Hutu moderates. Neighbours and friends turned against one another based on ethnicity. Men were killed in front of their families. Tutsi women, most often, were stopped, brutalised, raped, underwent mutilation of their genital organs (which were at times displayed in the public). Some were taken as captives and hidden by the Hutu men for sexual gratification; asked to kill their children and other members of their families before being killed. As the Hutus embarked on their systematic and widespread plan to completely eradicate the Tutsis, they made no distinction between men, women and children. A well–planned and carefully executed genocide,[179] specifically targeted Tutsi and Hutu families were murdered in their homes. At times, these executions occurred in public places such as churches, schools and hospitals.

The humanitarian crisis in Rwanda was a product of planning and preparation devised and masterminded by almost every level of the Hutu community: governmental figures, administrative authorities such as *Bourgmestres*,[180] military personnel, journalists, businessmen, university

---

the President we loved. The red-skinned Belgians have behaved like beasts. They should pay for their acts.' *RTLM* broadcast replayed in part in 'Chronicle of a Genocide Foretold', Part 2, Video Series, written and directed by Danièle Lacourse and Yvan Patry, produced by Sam Grana and Yvan Patry, Alter-Cine (Montreal) and the National Film Board of Canada (Ottawa), 1995/1996.

176 *Nahimana* et al (n. 173).

177 Ibid.

178 Ibid paras. 25–29.

179 '...these killings were not spontaneous or accidental....The events grew from a policy aimed at the systematic destruction of a people. The ground for violence was carefully prepared, the airwaves poisoned with hate, casting the Tutsis as scapegoats for the problems of Rwanda, denying their humanity.' United States President Bill Clinton, 'The International Community Must Work Together to Build Rwanda', in Glassman Bruce, Szumski Bonnie and Barbour Scott (eds), *The Rwanda Genocide* (Greenhaven Press 2004) 90.

180 *Bourgmestre* is a key administrative official in Rwanda who heads a commune (an administrative district). Prior to, and during the genocide, the *Bourgmestre* had powers

lecturers, and armed militias created for this purpose. It went through different stages which included instigation, planning, preparation and execution. The instigators reached the minds of the Hutu majority, fuelling and deepening anti-Tutsi sentiments through publications[181] and radio broadcasts,[182] and at times university lecture halls, religious services, political rallies and musical compositions.[183] At public rallies in national stadia, key ranking Hutu officials whipped up the minds of the broader Hutu population, insinuating the imminence of the defeat and urging them collectively to rise against Tutsi incursion.[184] Preparation was evidenced by the importation and distribution of weapons to Hutus and Hutu militia groups. Machetes, clubs, spikes were imported from China. The planning and organisation required early identifications of who were Tutsis, and the moderate Hutus opposed to the system.[185] The final phase, the perpetration of the atrocities, was implemented in indescribable terms. In hospitals, schools, churches, roadsides and at roadblocks, identified persons were brutally murdered. Tutsi women were raped, their genital organs mutilated before being subjected to death. Witnessing the cruelty inflicted on the targeted victims, husbands and grandparents instituted merciful killing as a better alternative.[186]

similar to the Mayor of Paris, France. For a comprehensive discussion of the powers enjoyed by the *Bourgmestre* during these periods, see *Akayesu* (n. 2) para.s 57–77.

[181] Gerald Caplan, 'Rwanda: Walking the Road to Genocide' in Allan Thompson (ed), *The Media and the Rwanda Genocide* (Pluto Press 2007) 20–37; Alison Des Forges, 'Call to Genocide: Radio in Rwanda, 1994' in Allan Thompson (ed), *The Media and the Rwanda Genocide* (Pluto Press 2007) 41–54; Mary Kimani, 'RTLM: the Medium that Became a Tool for Mass Murder' in Allan Thompson (ed), *The Media and the Rwanda Genocide* (Pluto Press 2007) 110–24; Charles Mironko, 'The Effect of RTLM's Rhetoric of Ethnic Hatred in Rural Rwanda' in Allan Thompson (ed), *The Media and the Rwanda Genocide* (Pluto Press 2007) 125–35; Thomas Kamilindi, 'Journalism in a Time of Hate Media' in Allan Thompson (ed), *The Media and the Rwanda Genocide* (Pluto Press 2007) 136–42; Jean-Pierre Chrétien, 'RTLM Propaganda: the Democratic Alibi' in Allan Thompson (ed), *The Media and the Rwanda Genocide* (Pluto Press 2007) 55–61; Darryl Li, 'Echoes of Violence: Considerations on Radio and Genocide in Rwanda' in Allan Thompson (ed), *The Media and the Rwanda Genocide* (Pluto Press 2007) 90–109; Simone Monasebian, 'The Pre-Genocide Case Against Radio-Télévision Libre des Milles Collines' in Allan Thompson (ed), *The Media and the Rwanda Genocide* (Pluto Press 2007) 308–29; Charity Kagwi-Ndungu, 'The Challenges in Prosecuting Print Media for Incitement to Genocide' in Allan Thompson (ed), *The Media and the Rwanda Genocide* (Pluto Press 2007) 330–42; Jean-Marie Biju-Duval, '"Hate Media"– Crimes Against Humanity and Genocide: Opportunities Missed by the ICTR' in Allan Thompson (ed), *The Media and the Rwanda Genocide* (Pluto Press 2007) 343–61.

[182] Caplan (n. 181); Forges (n. 181); Mironko (n. 181).

[183] *Bikindi* (n. 26).

[184] Linda Melvern, 'Missing the Story: The Media and the Rwandan Genocide' in Allan Thompson (ed), *The Media and the Rwanda Genocide* (Pluto Press 2007).

[185] Sherrer (n. 147).

[186] Ibid. See also Jared Diamond, *Collapse* (Penguin Books 2005) 316.

The above is a partial silhouette of the atrocities perpetrated in Rwanda in 1994. Noteworthy is the fact that these atrocities were not accidental. They were the outcome of years of planning and preparation, engaging different members of the rank and file of Hutu-led Rwanda: civilian and military personnel, civil society actors, political leaders, artists, businessmen, and Hutu militias that were established, organised and trained for the purpose of furthering the criminal plans of the Hutu-led government.

These atrocities radiated some distinctiveness. First, the crimes were massive and wholesale in nature, measured not only by the quantum of victims but by the number of people perpetrating them. Second, they were systematic: organised in both the planning and perpetration. Third, the leadership of the country was very involved, which paint a picture of state-orchestrated crimes. Lastly, the perpetrators justified these crimes, which were motivated by the political and ideological tenets of Hutu-domination policies.

5.3.4.3 *Situating the Rwanda's Ethnic Crises Within the Framework of a Joint Criminal Enterprise*

The ICTR was established as a result of the atrocities that had been perpetrated in Rwanda.[187] The animosity between the Hutus and the Tutsis grew deeper, resulting in the perpetration of genocidal acts. The perpetration of these atrocities required months of planning, with support from the government in power.[188] Furthermore, it depicted the existence of an agreement to have these crimes committed. This made it a criminal conspiracy. The broader Hutu majority subscribed to this plan and conspiracy. They played different roles at different times, but shared a common goal: the elimination of all Tutsis because of their ethnicity. Their participation was part of a criminal plan; therefore, any crime committed in furtherance of such a plan ought to lead to the imposition of criminal responsibility on the participant.

Given the existence of a criminal conspiracy known to every person taking part in it, I argue that every statement that qualifies as instigation must not be limited to the crime of genocide: it also qualifies as instigation to crimes against humanity (and certainly, instigation to commit violations of Article 3 common to the Geneva Conventions and of Additional Protocol II).

---

[187] See Reports of the U.N. Commission prior to the establishment of the ICTR.

[188] See generally Paul Magnarella, *When Victims Become Killers: Colonialism, Nativism, and the Genocide in Rwanda* (Princeton University Press 2001); John A. Berry and Carol Pott Berry (eds), *Genocide in Rwanda: A Collective Memory* (Howard University Press 1999).

To better understand how a joint criminal enterprise was developed to perpetrate the crimes agreed upon, it is necessary to examine the history of Rwanda detailing the deep ethnic divisions and intermittent internecine conflicts that occurred in the country prior to the 1994 genocide.

5.3.4.4 *Planning, Preparation and Execution of Atrocities as Evidence of the Existence of a Joint Criminal Enterprise*

As evidenced by the previous discussion, the crimes committed by the Hutus in Rwanda went through the three different stages stipulated in Article 6(1) of the Statute of the ICTR. First, the Hutus formulated a clear plan with a specific objective: the elimination of the Tutsis and Hutu-moderates. An agreement was reached on how to realise this objective. This agreement comprised of the kinds of crimes that would be committed, and the specific targets. The Hutus agreed to this agreement, and played different roles and at different times. The conception, planning, preparation and execution of this saw the participation of political figures, governmental leaders,[189] university professors,[190] artists,[191] businessmen,[192] political parties[193] which oft had armed militia wings;[194] and the media (both audio

---

[189] Examples include Jean Kambanda, Prime Minister of the Interim Government of the Republic of Rwanda from 8 April to 17 July 1994 (see *The Prosecutor v Jean Kambanda*, Indictment, Case No. ICTR-97-23-DP, OTP, 28 October 1997, Para 2.1); Jean de Dieu Kamuhanda, Minister of Higher Education and Scientific Research from mid-May 1994, a position he held till mid-July of 1994. Prior to this position, he was the Director of Higher Education and Scientific Research (see *The Prosecutor v Jean de Dieu Kamuhanda*, Indictment, Case No. ICTR-95-54A-T, OTP, 15 November 2000, Para 4.2); Clément Kayishema, Prefect of Kibuye Prefecture from 30 July 1992, took office and assumed his duties till July 1994 when he left the country (see *Kayishemaand Ruzindana* (n. 2) (TC) para 23); Ignace Bagilishema, *Bourgmestre* of Mabanza Commune on 8 February 1980, and served and acted in that capacity till the end of July 1994 (see *Bagilishema* (n. 2) para 3); Juvénal Kajelijeli (*Kajelijeli* (n. 2) para 6); Laurent Semanza, *Bourgmestre* for the Bicumbi Commune for a period of twenty years until his replacement in September 1993 (see *Semanza* (n. 2) para 1.5); Jean-Paul Akayesu, *Bourgmestre* for the Taba Commune from April 1993 till June 1994 (*The Prosecutor v Jean-Paul Akayesu*, Indictment, Case No. ICTR-96-4-T, OTP, 13 February 1996, Para 3).

[190] For example, Ferdinand Nahimana was a university professor of History. See *Nahimana* et al (n. 173) para. 2.

[191] Simon Bikindi was an artist and composer of music in Kinyarwanda. See *Bikindi* (n. 26) paras. 40–48.

[192] A good example is Obed Ruzindana, who was a businessman in the city of Kigali, Rwanda. See *Kayishemaand Ruzindana* (n. 2) (TC) para. 24.

[193] A good example is the Coalition for the Defence of the Republic (CDR) formed by Jean-Bosco Barayagwiza. It was a political party formed for the express purpose of solidifying Hutu control over the political institutions in the country, uniting the Hutus in confronting and defeating the Tutsis considered to be the enemies within the state. See *Nahimana* et al (n. 26) (TC) para. 950.

[194] The CDR, to further its goals, created a youth wing, *Impuzamugambi*. Its members mounted and supervised roadblocks, sorted the Tutsis from the Hutus which was

such as *RTLM* and print such as *Kangura*).[195] Their participation took different modes: ordering, planning, instigating, aiding and abetting.

In *Kayishema and Ruzindana*,[196] the Trial Chamber recognised the existence of a plan as well as its precise objective. As set out in the judgment,[197] the clear objective of the atrocities in Rwanda was to destroy the Tutsi population. The perpetrators had a common intention. Citing *Čelebići*,[198] the Trial Chamber held that where

> ...a plan exists, or where there otherwise is evidence that members of a group are acting with a common criminal purpose, all those who knowingly participate in, and directly and substantially contribute to, the realisation of this purpose may be held criminally responsible...and...[d]epending upon the facts of a given situation, the culpable individual may, under such circumstances, be held criminally responsible either as a direct perpetrator of, or as an aider or abettor to, the crime in question.[199]

The planning, preparation and execution of these crimes against the Tutsis and Hutu-moderates in Rwanda could not have been so effective and successful without the existence of a joint criminal enterprise. The materialisation of a well-crafted plan required not just the use of resources, but a high level of coordination and supervision entailing a criminal conspiracy at the high levels of government. It would have been much easier and effective to tackle the different participants in this joint criminal enterprise,

---

facilitated by the identity cards. The acts of *Impuzamugambi* were supervised and directed by Jean-Bosco Barayagwiza, who supplied weapons to them to enable them perpetrate the crimes against the Tutsis. *Nahimana* et al (n. 26) (TC) paras 950–55.

194 The alliance between Hassan Ngeze of *Kangura*, and Jean-Bosco Barayagwiza of CDR for the purpose of furthering their political agendas, and subsequent use of *Kangura* to further the political philosophies and policies of CDR would not only translate *Kangura* into a criminal organisation that engaged in political activities but also corroborate the voluntary subscription of these individuals to the joint criminal enterprise which planned, prepared, and perpetrated the crimes against the Tutsis and Hutu-moderates. *Nahimana* et al (n. 26) (TC) paras. 950–51. Another example is the National Republican Movement for Democracy and Development (*MRND*) of President Juvénal Habyarimana, which created the *Interahamwe* (meaning 'those who attack together'), and made up of 'bands of unemployed young men', 'fashioned into a menacing force', 'sang at the top of their lungs, blew whistles, and wore colourful uniforms...hung machetes from their belts and grenades around their necks.' Dina Temple-Raston, *Justice on the Grass: Three Rwandan Journalists, Their Trial for War Crimes, and a Nation's Quest for Redemption* (Free Press 2005) xi–xii, 5.

195 *RTLM* was used to propagate anti-Tutsi sentiments. The *Kangura* was founded by Hassan Ngeze, and also played an important role in the anti-Tutsi campaign. See *Nahimana* et al (n. 26) (TC) paras. 949–50.

196 *Kayishema and Ruzindana* (n. 2) (TC).

197 *Kayishema and Ruzindana* (n. 2) (TC) ch. 5.1.

198 *Čelebići* (n. 115).

199 *Kayishema and Ruzindana* (n. 2) (TC) para. 203, citing *Čelebići* (n. 115) para. 328.

which led to the perpetration of the atrocities they clearly agreed to. If that were done, then, the requirement of substantial contribution to the commission of a crime for the imposition of criminal responsibility under Article 6(1) becomes completely unnecessary and redundant.

In the joint criminal enterprise in Rwanda, different persons played different roles. Some perpetrated the material elements of the crimes, such as those who carried out the killings and raped women. Some were present at the scenes where the crimes were committed, and intentionally assisted their commission by supplying weapons to the perpetrators. Others ordered the commission of the crimes, mindful of their leadership and political positions.

Of special interest is the role played by the instigators: individuals who influenced the minds of others to commit these crimes. Instigators played a huge role in polarising the Rwandan communities. They did these by poisoning the minds of the Hutus through publications and sounding unpleasant and incredible narrations over the airwaves. They also urged the Hutus to engage in the massive onslaught in order to defeat the enemies.

In order to better appreciate the roles of instigators in the Rwandan atrocities and how they were part of a joint criminal enterprise, it is necessary to examine what they said.

5.3.4.5 *The Role of Instigators in the Rwandan Genocide*

In the atrocities that took place in Rwanda, the role of instigators cannot be ignored. The amplification of the worsening tensions between the Hutus and Tutsis became the principal occupation of print media like the *Kangura* and *RTLM*. Artists produced musical compositions which, when examined within the political context and cultural realities of Rwanda, helped inflated rather than deflate the animosity. Key political figures such as governmental leaders and military personnel in public places reached out to Hutus, urging them to enjoin in the efforts to stop and defeat the enemies. Print and audio-visual media depicted Tutsis as snakes, assigned blame on them for the difficulties of the country, and made the attack against them imminent.

These statements amounting to instigation filled the airwaves before the genocide. They were consumed by the broader Hutu public, who would hunt for new releases of newspapers in which Tutsis were demonised. With prominent Hutu personalities making intermittent appearances on radio and television, the Hutu majority lent credibility to their allegations, had their minds instigated, and ultimately became part of the agreement to perpetrate the crimes the instigators asked them to.

This narrative account gives just a partial silhouette of the role of instigators, which can be better appreciated if their words are examined given the ethnic tension that existed in the country.

In the case of *Akayesu*,[200] the Trial Chamber found that in the early hours of 19 April, 1994, the accused joined a crowd of over a hundred people which had gathered around the body of a young member of *Interahamwe* in Gishyeshe.[201] The accused took the opportunity to address the people, urged them to unite in order to eliminate the enemy.[202] During this meeting, the accused also received from the *Interahamwe* documents containing the names of Rwandan Patriotic Front (RPF) accomplices, which he read out.[203]

In *Ruggiu*,[204] the accused was charged, *inter alia*, with direct and public incitement to genocide, and crimes against humanity, he pleaded guilty, and admitted he broadcast some of the following over *RTLM*:

- he condemned the attitude of Agathe Uwilingiyimana, the Prime Minister, who was compromising the Rwandan political institutions and, further, demanded that she leave office;
- he congratulated the valiant combatants who were engaged in a battle against the 'Inyenzi' at Nyamirambo, including civilians, Interahamwe militiamen, members of political parties and military combatants;
- there would be a reward offered by the government for any one who killed or captured a white man fighting on the side of the RPF;
- they were having a 'good time' killing the Inyenzi and the population was determined to fight and chase the Inyenzi-Inkotanyi out of the country. He further called on the youth to 'work' with the Army;
- the population should be mobilised and the youth should 'work' throughout the country with the Army and the government to defend the country....[205]

The accused admitted that over *RTLM*, he intermittently played songs. His intention was to encourage the population to fight the enemy. One such song is entitled 'Naanga Abakwtie', which means 'I do not like the Tutsi'.[206] The accused acknowledged that 'RTLM broadcasts reflected the political ideology and plans of extremist Hutus, particularly members of MRND and the Coalition for the Defence of the Republic'.[207] The accused further

200 *Akayesu* (n. 2).
201 Ibid para. 673 (i).
202 *Akayesu* (n. 2) para. 673 (ii).
203 *Akayesu* (n. 2) para. 673 (v).
204 *Ruggiu* (n. 30).
205 Ibid para. 44 (v).
206 *Ruggiu* (n. 30) para. 44 (x).
207 *Ruggiu* (n. 30) para. 44 (xi).

admitted that his broadcasts over *RTLM* 'incited young Rwandans, *Interahamwe* militiamen and soldiers to engage in armed conflict against the "enemy" and its accomplices and to kill and inflict serious bodily and mental harm to Tutsis and moderate Hutus'.[208]

The Trial Chamber found him guilty of direct and public incitement to genocide[209] and persecution as crimes against humanity.[210]

In *Niyitegeka*,[211] some of the charges against the accused included genocide,[212] complicity in genocide,[213] conspiracy to commit genocide,[214] direct and public incitement to commit genocide,[215] crimes against humanity (murder),[216] crimes against humanity (extermination),[217] crimes against humanity (rape),[218] crimes against humanity (other inhumane acts).[219]

The Trial Chamber found that on May 13, 1994, sometime between 7.00 am and 10.00 am, the accused 'was one of the leaders of a large-scale attack by thousands of armed attackers against Tutsi refugees at Muyira Hill.'[220] These attackers comprised *Interahamwe*, soldiers, policemen, and Hutu civilians. They chanted 'Tuba Tsemba Tsembe', which means 'Let's exterminate them', a reference to the Tutsis.[221] The Trial Chamber found that the accused, at this incident, was armed with a gun during the attack, in the course of which he shot at Tutsi refugees.[222] The attack resulted in the death of thousands of Tutsis. During this attack, the accused instructed the attackers, showed them where to go and how to wage the attacks against the Tutsis.[223]

---

208 Ibid.

209 *Ruggiu* (n. 30) para. 44 (Section IV: 'Verdict').

210 Ibid.

211 *Niyitegeka* (n. 26).

212 Count one, under Article 2 (3) (a) of the Statute of the ICTR. See *Niyitegeka* (n. 26) para. 408.

213 Count two (as an alternative to count one), under the Statute of the ICTR. See *Niyitegeka* (n. 26) para. 421.

214 Count three, under Article 2 (3) (b) of the Statute of the ICTR. See *Niyitegeka* (n. 26) para. 422.

215 Count four, under Article 2(3)(c) of the Statute of the ICTR. See *Niyitegeka* (n. 26) para. 430.

216 Count five, under Article 3 (a) of the Statute of the ICTR. See *Niyitegeka* (n. 26) para. 441.

217 Count six, under Article 3 (b) of the Statute of the ICTR. See *Niyitigeka* (n. 26) para. 448.

218 Count seven, under Article 3 (g) of the Statute of the ICTR. See *Niyitigeka* (n. 26) para 455.

219 Count eight, under Article 3 (i) of the Statute of the ICTR. See *Niyitigeka* (n. 26) para 459.

220 *Niyitegeka* (n. 26) para 413.

221 Ibid.

222 Ibid.

223 Ibid.

The Trial Chamber also found that the accused directly and publicly incited persons, including but not limited to local administrative officials, soldiers, civilian militias, communal police and local residents, 'to kill or cause serious bodily or mental harm to members of the Tutsi population with intent to destroy, in whole or in part, a racial or ethnic group'.[224] The charge of direct and public incitement was supported by evidence indicating that the accused held a meeting at Kucyapa after the large-scale attack on May 13, 1994 at Muyira Hill.[225] The purpose of this meeting was to decide the programme of killings for the next day, and to organise the killings of Tutsis in Bisesero.[226] The Trial Chamber found that the accused thanked the attackers for their participation in attacks.[227] He commended them for a 'good work', which was a reference to the killing of Tutsi civilians.[228] The accused told them 'to share the people's property and cattle, eat meat so that they would be strong to return the next day to continue the "work", that is, the killing.'[229] The following day, attacks were launched against the Tutsis in Bisesero throughout the day.[230] Having construed the meaning of the word 'work' used by the accused to mean the killing of Tutsis, the Trial Chamber found that the accused had the requisite intent to destroy, in whole or in part, the Tutsi ethnic group.[231] Its judgment stated:

> The Chamber finds that in urging attackers to work, and to eat meat so that they would be strong to return the next day to continue the 'work', the Accused is individually criminally responsible, pursuant to Article 6(1) of the Statute, for inciting attackers to cause the death and serious bodily and mental harm of Tutsi refugees in Bisesero, as provided in Article 2(3)(c). Accordingly, the Chamber finds that the Accused is guilty of direct and public incitement to commit genocide as charged in Count 4 of the Indictment.[232]

In *Kajelijeli*,[233] the accused was charged on multiple counts, amongst which was direct and public incitement to genocide.[234] The Trial Chamber found that on the morning of 7 April, 1994, the accused instructed the *Interahamwe* at Byangabo Market and incited an assembled crowd there to 'kills and

224 Ibid para 430.
225 Ibid para 433.
226 Ibid.
227 Ibid.
228 Ibid.
229 Ibid.
230 Ibid.
231 Ibid para 436.
232 Ibid para 437.
233 *Kajelijeli* (n. 2).
234 Ibid para 848.

exterminate all those people in Rwankeri' and to 'exterminate the Tutsis'.[235] Furthermore, the accused ordered the *Interahamwe* to dress up and 'start to work'.[236]

On the basis of these statements made by the accused to the crowd, the Trial Chamber found it proved beyond reasonable doubt that the accused 'is criminally responsible, pursuant to Article 6(1) of the Statute, for inciting directly and publicly the *Interahamwe* and the crowd to commit genocide by killing or causing serious bodily or mental harm to members of the Tutsi population in Rwankeri, Mukingo *Commune*.'[237]

In *Nahimana* et al,[238] the Trial Chamber found that the statements and publications of all three accused persons whipped up anti-Tutsi sentiments, and played a role in the atrocities perpetrated against the Tutsis and Hutu-moderates in Rwanda.[239]

In one of the publications carrying *The Ten Commandments* of the Bahutu people, its introduction warned its readers:

> The enemy is still there, among us, and is biding his time to try again, at a more propitious moment, to decimate us.
> Therefore, Hutu, wherever you may be, wake up! Be firm and vigilant. Take all necessary measures to deter the enemy from launching a fresh attack.[240]

The second part of the article was entitled 'The Tutsi ambition', in which Tutsis were described as 'bloodthirsty'.[241] It referred to their continuing ideology of Tutsi domination over Hutus, and to the 'permanent dream of Tutsi' to restore Tutsi minority rule in the country.[242] In another article, the Hutus were exhorted to wake up 'now or never' and be aware of a new Hutu ideology.[243] Hutu readers were urged to 'be prepared to defend themselves against this scourge', and to 'cease feeling pity for the Tutsi!'[244]

The Trial Chamber found that *The Appeal to the Conscience of the Hutu* and *The Ten Commandments* of the Hutu included within it, published in *Kangura* No. 6 in December 1990, conveyed both contempt and hatred for the Tutsi ethnic group, and for Tutsi women in particular as enemy

---

235 Ibid para 856.
236 Ibid.
237 Ibid para 860.
238 *Nahimana* et al (n. 26) (TC).
239 See generally *Nahimana* et al (n. 26) (TC) paras 949–1045.
240 *Nahimana* et al (n. 173) para 12.
241 *Nahimana* et al(n. 173) para 13.
242 Ibid.
243 Ibid.
244 Ibid.

agents.[245] Another publication conveyed Tutsi women as a 'ruthless enemy, determined to conquer the Hutu, and called on the Hutu to take all necessary measures to stop the enemy.'[246]

The Trial Chamber found that numerous articles and editorials in *Kangura*, such as *The Appeal to the Conscience of the Hutu*, conveyed hatred and contempt for the Tutsi ethnic group, and for Tutsi women in particular who were portrayed as enemy agents.[247] It called on readers to take all necessary measures to stop the enemy, which was defined to mean the Tutsi population.[248] The cover of *Kangura*, edition No. 26, promoted violence by conveying the message that the machete should be used to eliminate the Tutsis once and for all.[249] It was a direct and public call for the destruction of the Tutsi ethnic group. Through hate propaganda and fear-mongering, *Kangura* paved the way for the preparation and perpetration of genocide and other atrocities in Rwanda. It did this by 'whipping the Hutu population into a killing frenzy'.[250]

The Trial Chamber found that Ngeze manned and supervised roadblocks in Gisenyi in 1994 that identified targeted Tutsi civilians who were subsequently taken to and killed at the *Commune Rouge*.[251] He often drove around with a megaphone in his vehicle, mobilising the population to come to CDR meetings and spreading the message that the *Inyenzi* would be exterminated, *Inyenzi* meaning, and understood to mean, the Tutsi ethnic minority.[252] The Trial Chamber found that these words amounted to instigation to kill Tutsi civilians.[253]

Ferdinand Nahimana, in a Radio Rwanda broadcast on 25 April 1994, said he was happy *RTLM* had played an instrumental role in awakening the Hutu majority, and that the population had stood up with a view to halting the enemy.[254] He equated the enemy with the Tutsi ethnic group.[255] As the mastermind of *RTLM*, the Trial Chamber found that Ferdinand Nahimana 'set in motion the communications weaponry that fought the war of media,

245 *Nahimana* et al (n. 173) para 16.
246 Ibid.
247 Ibid.
248 Ibid.
249 *Nahimana* et al (n. 173) para 17.
250 *Nahimana* et al (n. 173) para 64.
251 *Nahimana* et al (n. 173) para 68.
252 Ibid.
253 Ibid.
254 *Nahimana* et al (n. 173) paras 1–78.
255 Ibid.

words, newspapers and radio stations' he described in his Radio Rwanda broadcast of 25 April as a complement to bullets.[256]

Jean-Bosco Barayagwiza said in public meetings 'let's exterminate them', with 'them' meaning the Tutsi population.[257] After separating the Tutsi from the Hutu and humiliating the Tutsi by forcing them to perform the *Ikinyemera* (a traditional dance), at several public meetings, he threatened to kill them and said it would not be difficult.

In *The Prosecutor v Joseph Serugendo*,[258] the charges against the accused 'concern the *Interahamwe* and the killing campaign, and RTLM re-installation and operation in July 1994. With regard to the first of these issues, Serugendo [the accused], as a member of the *Interahamwe*, is alleged to have planned with other leaders of the MRND between 1992 and 17 July 1994 political meetings and rallies in order to indoctrinate, sensitize, and incite members of the *Interahamwe* to kill or cause serious bodily or mental harm to members of the Tutsi population, with the aim of destroying the Tutsi ethnic group'.[259]

The accused acknowledged these allegations, stating that between early 1992 and 1994, he, as a member of *Inherahamwe*, 'planned with the leaders of the MRND, and the *Interahamwe* militias, political meetings and rallies aimed at inciting members of the *Interahamwe* to kill or cause serious harm to members of the Tutsi population with the goal of destroying the Tutsi ethnic group'.[260]

In *Bikindi*,[261] the accused broadcast over loudspeakers statements such as 'the majority' to 'rise up and look everywhere possible' and not to 'spare anybody' (referring to the Tutsis as the minority). The Trial Chamber held that this 'unequivocally constitutes a direct call to destroy the Tutsi ethnic group'.[262] The Trial Chamber found that the accused's address to the population while returning from Kayove, asking 'Have you killed the Tutsis here?' and whether they had killed the 'snakes' was a 'direct call to kill Tutsis, pejoratively referred to as snakes'.[263]

In *Kalimanzira*,[264] the Trial Chamber found that the accused attended a public meeting at the Nyabisagara football field 'where he thanked the

256 Ibid.
257 Ibid.
258 Judgment, Case No. ICTR-2005-84-I, T. Ch. I, 12 June 2006.
259 *Serugendo* (n. 258) para 20. See also *Serugendo* (n. 21) para 8.
260 *Serugendo* (n. 258) para 21.
261 *Bikindi* (n. 26).
262 Ibid para 423.
263 Ibid.
264 *Kalimanzira* (n. 2).

audience for their efforts at getting rid of the enemy, but warned them not to grow complacent, to remain armed at all times, and exhorted the crowd to keep searching for enemies hidden in the bush or in other persons homes, which they did'.[265] The Trial Chamber also found that the accused instructed them to destroy the homes of dead Tutsis and plant trees in their place. The Trial Chamber held that 'by instructing the people present to kill any surviving Tutsis, demolish their homes, and wipe out any traces of their existence, there is no reasonable doubt that the accused intended to incite the audience present to commit acts of genocide'.[266]

In *The Prosecutor v TharcisseMuvunyi*,[267] the accused was charged with inciting the local population to perpetrate massacres against the Tutsis at the Butare prefecture.[268] The Trial Chamber found that during this meeting, the accused said that the Hutus had made a mistake in marrying the young Tutsi girls and hiding them. One witness mentioned that the accused said that such Hutus had to hand over the Tutsis. The accused used proverbs such as 'when a snake wraps itself around a calabash, you have to kill the snake and break the calabash'.[269]

Given these different recitations of what the different accused persons said, and as the Trial Chambers found them to amount to instigation, it is important to look at how they fit into that group of persons (collective individuals) who agreed, planned and perpetrated crimes against humanity in Rwanda.

5.3.4.6 *Fitting the Instigators into the Definition of Crimes Against Humanity*

The requirement that crimes against humanity be committed as part of a widespread or systematic attack waged against a civilian population implies the existence of both a plan and structure in place to realise such an attack that meets these definitional requirements.[270] A widespread attack targeting a large number of civilians must require a plan. Such a plan details the various crimes to be committed, its target, the means and the individuals to perpetrate them. An attack is systematic when it is well

265 *Kalimanzira* (n. 2) para 613.
266 Ibid.
267 *Muvunyi* (n. 26).
268 Ibid para 2.
269 *Muvunyi* (n. 26) para 63.
270 Guénaël Mettraux, *International Crimes and the ad hoc Tribunals* (Oxford University Press 2005) 170–72.

organised.[271] The establishment of a structure to define what criminal activities would be perpetrated, by whom and the means to perpetrate them are key components of the requirement of 'systematicity'.[272] It is therefore logical to postulate that though these adjectives are alternative in application, they are not exclusive as an attack that is widespread (large scale of victimisation) is more than likely to be systematic (organised).[273]

In Rwanda, the Hutu-led government formulated a plan to eliminate the Tutsis. Their ethnicity was the main reason for such formulations. They were scapegoated for the economic problems and political instability of the country. Hutus with moderate political views were targeted for victimisation simply because of their political opinions.

These narratives depict acts which can be legally characterised as a conspiracy: there existed an agreement by two or more persons to commit crimes against the Tutsis and Hutu-moderates. This criminal conspiracy was voluntarily subscribed to by numerous individuals. This made it a joint criminal enterprise: an agreement by two or more persons to engage in criminal activity.[274] The persons making this joint criminal enterprise played different roles such as planning, instigating, ordering, aiding and abetting and committing the crimes. These different roles were performed in different stages: some at the planning stage, some at the preparation stage, and others at the perpetration stage. The crimes were committed, which, *ipso facto*, serve as eloquent evidence that they were in furtherance of an attack, widespread and systematic in nature, and waged against a civilian population on one of the discriminatory grounds.

The existence of a joint criminal enterprise having as its purpose the commission of the crimes it had planned, and the commission of these crimes as planned by the joint conspirators establish a causal link. There is

[271] Mettraux suggests a list of factors to be taken into consideration when determining whether an attack is 'systematic' for the purpose of the definitional elements of crimes against humanity: the number of criminal acts; the existence of criminal patterns; the logistics and financial resources involved; the number of victims; the existence of public statements or political views underpinning the events; the existence of a plan or policy targeting a specific group of individuals; the means and methods used in the attacks; the inescapability of the attack; the foreseeability of the criminal occurrences; the involvement of political or military authorities; temporarily and geographically repeated and coordinated military operations which all led to the same result or consequences; alteration of the ethnic, religious, or racial composition of the population; the establishment and implementation of autonomous political or military structures at any level of authority in a given territory; adoption of various discriminatory measures. See Mettraux (n. 270) 171.

[272] Ibid.

[273] Ibid.

[274] Ormerod (n. 3) 206–21, 402–16; Heaton (n. 3) 386–91.

an inseparable relationship here, which, *ipso facto*, suggests different modes of participation and the resulting planning, preparation and execution of the crimes. Without the various modes of participation in the different stages of the criminal activity, it is arguable that these crimes would not have been committed. There is a clear causal relationship here between each individual's mode of participation and the resulting crimes. The execution of these crimes was preceded by planning and preparation, all being stages articulated in Article 6(1) of the Statute. By analogy, it becomes unnecessary to require that the prosecution must prove that the individual's mode of participation contributed substantially to the commission of the crime. Article 6(1) is not limited only to the commission of the crime (which is the final stage of a criminal activity). It covers planning and preparation.

Furthermore, in cases of a joint criminal enterprise, it might become difficult for the prosecution to ascertain what particular crime is attributable to a particular individual. At Nuremberg, the prosecutors did not consider the contribution of every single accused person to the atrocities of the Nazi Regime. Rather, it considered the Nazi Regime as a joint criminal enterprise because of its criminal objectives. Every member thereof was considered to have shared in the criminal objectives of the Nazi Regime, and consequently, contributed in some way to the atrocities of the Nazi Regime. So, where the accused in *Akayesu* asked the militias to 'go to work and defeat the enemy', that would amount to instigation to commit both genocide and crimes against humanity if it can be established that such a statement led to the planning, preparation or execution of any of those crimes; and the statement was understood to lead to the destruction of a people based on their ethnicity and the perpetration of atrocities committed within the framework of an attack against a civilian population.[275]

Instigation as a mode of participation under the Statute of the ICTR fits squarely into the Rwandan atrocities. The above statements were made by the instigators as part of planning an agreement that the crimes would be committed. The instigators had knowledge of their actions: that it

275 This is a correct construction of Article 6(1) of the Statute of the ICTR. It is sufficient to prove that the accused made such a statement, as it would be interpreted in that context to mean to kill. It is not necessary to prove that such a statement led to the commission of the crimes the accused instigated: as long as crimes were committed within the broader framework of the existence of a plan, it suffices. Otherwise, the Trial Chambers would be suggesting that despite the existence of a joint criminal enterprise, the prosecution still has the duty to prove the contribution of each individual, which seems illogical and almost impractical.

would contribute to the perpetration of the crimes which they wanted to have committed. Through instigation, they contributed to the planning, preparation and execution of these crimes. They all operated within the framework of a joint criminal enterprise, within which the plan was conceived and developed, and a structure put in place to materialise their objectives.

Given that their participation in such a criminal enterprise was through the mode of instigation, it is obvious that the instigators did not intend to instigate only the crime of genocide. They made those statements which were considered to be instigation with the hope that the broader Hutu population would do whatever was necessary to perpetrate the crimes. Their intention was to have the crimes committed. Characterising acts as genocide and crimes against humanity is the task of a legal practitioner. The instigators know little of the fine differences between these crimes. In instigating the planning, preparation or execution of these crimes, they made no distinction as to whether they wanted genocide or crimes against humanity or both to be committed. They simply wanted their objectives to be met: the commission of crimes.

Therefore, in performing the task of classifying these crimes, the international law scholar must exercise caution in not assuming an intimate understanding of these fine legislative differences by the instigator. The acts of instigation as stated above were all done within the framework of a plan to extinguish the Tutsis, and such acts of instigation must lead to the imposition of criminal responsibility where it is established that it led to either the planning, preparation or execution of any of the crimes. To suggest that instigation is limited to the crime of genocide is simply an indirect way of juxtaposing both crimes and making one take a higher position over the other.

In my analysis, I have argued that while it is correct to construe instigation to genocide as mode of participation that would lead to the imposition of criminal responsibility under Article 6(1), it is incorrect not to do the same for crimes against humanity because instigation (as well as the other modes of participation) to commit crimes against humanity is clearly covered by Article 6(1). Furthermore, the 'substantial contribution' requirement is the outcome of an illogical understanding of Article 6(1), which is both bifurcated and inchoate, and covers the different stages of the crimes. Criminal responsibility ought to be imposed where it is proved that the accused's mode of participation contributed to any of the stages of the crimes, rather than it being a substantial contribution to its commission.

Factual allegations that led to a charge of direct and public incitement to genocide ought to have been used to found a charge of instigation to crimes against humanity given the fact that incitement is synonymous with instigation, instigation under Article 6(1) must not be direct, public or to commit the crime of genocide only, and the similarity of conduct that arises to genocidal act and crimes against humanity.

CHAPTER SIX

BEYOND THE STATUTE OF THE ICTR: INSTIGATION AS A MODE OF PARTICIPATION IN CRIMES AGAINST HUMANITY

6.1 Introduction

Instigation, as it exists in international law, is a mode of participation in international crimes. The critique of the jurisprudence of the Trial and Appeal Chambers of the ICTR, even though it comes at a time when the Tribunal (ICTR) is about to wind-down, is of immense value for the future of international criminal justice. Given the dramatic turnaround in the definition of crimes against humanity as articulated in the Statute of the ICTR and the way the crimes were committed in Rwanda, the jurisprudence on crimes against humanity has evolved significantly, which lays the foundation for other criminal justice systems to tap from this reservoir.

6.2 Appraising the Jurisprudence on Instigation

As discussed in the previous chapters, the Statute of the ICTR defines the imposition of criminal responsibility in the following words:

> A person who planned, instigated, ordered, committed or otherwise aided and abetted in the planning, preparation or execution of a crime referred to in articles 2 to 4 [genocide, crimes against humanity and violations of Article 3 common to the Geneva Conventions and of Additional Protocol II] of the present Statute, shall be individually responsible for the crime.[1]

Instigation is one of the modes of participation stated in Article 6(1). However, under this same mode of participation features under Article 2(3)(c), which makes punishable direct and public incitement to commit genocide.

In the previous Chapters, I have looked at instigation as a mode of participation, and how the Trial and Appeal Chambers of the ICTR have construed the wording of Article 6(1) as well as Article 2(3)(c).

---

[1] Statute of the ICTR, annexed to United Nations Security Council Resolution 955, U.N. SCOR, 3453rd meeting, U.N. Doc. S/RES/955 (1994), Article 6(1).

As established by the jurisprudence of both the Trial and Appeal Chambers, criminal responsibility would be imposed under Article 6(1) only where the accused's mode of participation substantially contributes to the commission of a crime over which the ICTR has jurisdiction.[2] On the other hand, direct and public incitement to commit genocide exists as an inchoate crime. As an inchoate crime, responsibility is incurred irrespective of whether it leads to genocide or not.[3]

Every case dealing with any or both of these Articles has been examined. I extrapolated the approach the Trial and Appeal Chambers took in construing these Articles. I have argued and critiqued their construction of Article 6(1): the substantial contribution requirement is the result of an erroneous understanding and construction of Article 6(1). As I stated in Chapter Four, Article 6(1) is bifurcated in nature: any of the five modes must lead to any of the stages (planning, preparation or execution) of any of the crimes over which the ICTR has jurisdiction. The bifurcated character of Article 6(1) further reveals its inchoate nature: a mode of participation that leads to planning or preparation and falls short of execution is inchoate (at the initial, embryonic or preparatory stages). In drafting Article 6(1), a disjunctive word ('or') rather than a conjunctive word ('and') was used in the different stages of the crimes. A logical construction of this choice of words points authoritatively that where any of the modes leads to any of the stages

[2] *The Prosecutor v Idelphonse Hategekimana*, Judgment, Case No. ICTR-00-55, T. Ch. II, 6 December 2010, Para.. 644; *The Prosecutor v Callixte Kalimanzira*, Judgment, Case No. ICTR-05-88-T, T. Ch. III, 22 June 2009, Para. 512; *The Prosecutor v Juvénal Kajelijeli*, Judgment, Case No. ICTR-96-44-T, T. Ch. II, 1 December 2003, Para. 759; *The Prosecution v Laurent Semanza*, Judgment, Case No. ICTR-97-20, T. Ch. II, 15 May 2003, Para. 379; *The Prosecutor v Gérard Ntakirutimana and Elizaphan Ntakirutimana*, Judgement, Case No. ICTR-96-17-T, T. Ch. I, 21 February 2003, Para. 787; *Clément Kayishema and Obed Ruzindana v The Prosecutor*, Judgement, Case No. ICTR-95-1A, Appeal Chamber, 1 June 2001, Paras. 186; *The Prosecutor v Ignace Bagilishema*, Judgement, Case No. ICTR-95-1-A, T. Ch. I, 7 June 2001, Paras. 30, 33; *The Prosecutor v Alfred Musema*, Judgment, Case No. ICTR-96-13-T, T. Ch. I, 27 January 2003, Para. 115; *The Prosecutor v Georges Rutaganda*, Judgment, Case No. ICTR-96-3-T, T. Ch. I, 6 December 1999, Para. 43; *The Prosecutor v Clément Kayishema and Obed Ruzindana*, Judgment, Case No. ICTR-95-1-T, T. Ch. I, 21 May 1999, Paras. 199–207; *The Prosecutor v Jean-Paul Akayesu*, Judgment, Case No. ICTR-96-4, T. Ch. I, 2 September 1998, Para. 477.

[3] *The Prosecutor v Tharcisse Muvunyi*, Judgment, Case No. ICTR-00-55A-T, T. Ch. III, 11 February 2010, Paras. 24–25; *Kalimanzira* (n. 2) para. 510; *The Prosecutor v Simon Bikindi*, Judgment, Case No. ICTR-01-72, T. Ch. III, 2 December 2008, Para. 419; *Ferdinand Nahimana, Jean-Bosco Barayagwiza and Hassan Ngeze v The Prosecutor*, Judgment, Case No. ICTR-99-52-A, Appeal Chamber, 28 November 2007, Paras. 678–79; *The Prosecutor v Ferdinand Nahimana, Jean-Bosco Barayagwiza and Hassan* Ngeze, Judgment, Case No. ICTR-99-52-T, T. Ch. I, 3 December 2003, Paras. 678, 720; *Kajelijeli* (n. 2) para. 855; *The Prosecutor v Eliézer Niyitegeka*, Judgment, Case No. ICTR-96-14-T, T. Ch. I, 16 May 2003, Para. 431; *Musema* (n. 2) para. 120; *Rutaganda* (n. 2) para. 38; *Akayesu* (n. 2) para. 562.

(rather than all of them), it would suffice to lead to the imposition of criminal responsibility. Therefore, the Trial and Appeal Chambers' requirement of a substantial contribution to the commission of the crime is an obvious limitation to just one stage (execution as synonymous with commission) which is incongruous with the wording of Article 6(1).

I have also examined the crime of direct and public incitement to commit genocide as stated in the Statute of the ICTR. As mentioned earlier, the jurisprudence of the ICTR has established it as an inchoate crime and criminal responsibility would be imposed irrespective of whether it successfully leads to the commission of genocide or not.[4] The jurisprudence of the Trial and Appeal Chambers is correct, especially when construed in light of the rationale behind its inclusion in the United Nations' Convention on the Prevention and Punishment of the Crime of Genocide (hereinafter referred to as the Genocide Convention).[5] In criminal law, specific crimes fall under the rubric of inchoate crimes.[6] They are attempt,[7] conspiracy[8] and incitement.[9] The phrase 'inchoate crimes' is a jurisprudential jargon used to refer to crimes that are at the initial, preparatory, or embryonic stage.[10] They are still being developed, and have not been fully completed. When the full crime is completed, criminal responsibility is imposed for the full crime. For example: in the crime of attempted murder, an accused person will incur responsibility if, with the requisite *mens rea*, he or she transcends the borders of mere preparation and goes ahead to commit a crime, but is intercepted by an act independent of his or her will. So, if an accused,

---

4 *Muvunyi* (n. 3) paras. 24–25; *Kalimanzira* (n. 2) para. 510; *Bikindi* (n. 3) para. 419; Judgment, Case No. ICTR-01-72, T. Ch. III, 2 December 2008, Para. 419; *Nahimana* et al (n. 3) (AC) paras. 678–79; *Nahimana* et al (n. 3) (TC) para 678, 720; *Kajelijeli* (n. 2) para 855; *Niyitegeka* (n. 3) para 431; *Musema* (n. 2) para 120; *Rutaganda* (n. 2) para 38; *Akayesu* (n. 2) para 562.

5 The *Convention on the Prevention and Punishment of the Crime of Genocide*, United Nations General Assembly Resolution 260(III), U.N. GAOR, 3rd Session, 179th meeting, U.N. Doc. A/RES/260A (1948) of 9 December 1948. It was adopted on 9 December 1948 and went into force on 12 January 1951.

6 David Ormerod, *Smith and Hogan Criminal Law* (12th edn., Oxford University Press 2008) 379; Joshua Dressler, *Understanding Criminal Law* (5th edn., LexisNexis 2009) 379; Michael J. Allen and Simon Cooper, *Elliott & Wood's Cases and Materials on Criminal Law* (9th edn., Sweet & Maxwell 2006) 438; Russell Heaton, *Criminal Law Textbook* (Oxford University Press 2004) 401–2.

7 Ormerod (n. 6) 380–99; Dressler (n. 6) 379–419; Allen and Cooper (n. 6) 438–63; Heaton (n. 6) 403–14.

8 Ormerod (n. 6) 399–437; Dressler (n. 6) 429–64; Allen and Cooper (n. 6) 463–82; Heaton (n. 6) 415–33.

9 Ormerod (n. 6) 438–46; Dressler (n. 6) 421–28; Allen and Cooper (n. 6) 482–88; Heaton (n. 6) 433–39.

10 Ormerod (n. 6) 379; Dressler (n. 6) 379; Allen and Cooper (n. 6) 438; Heaton (n. 6) 401–2.

A, intending to murder his or her victim, V, went to a shop, bought a rifle, travelled to the city where his or her victim, V, lives, opens fire at V (the victim) but misses because he or she is a poor shooter, the accused would be guilty of attempted murder. However, if he or she shot at his or her victim, and actually got and killed the victim (V), the accused would be guilty of murder or capital murder (depending on the legal system). It would be illogical to charge, try and convict the accused (the perpetrator) of the inchoate crime of attempted murder because the accused has actually committed the crime. In the case of conspiracy, the crime is committed when two persons agree to commit a crime.[11] Once an agreement is reached, the inchoate crime of conspiracy is committed. However, if the parties to the agreement were to go further and perpetrate the crime they agreed to, then, criminal responsibility would be imposed for the crime committed. If two persons, A and B, agreed to rob a bank, that suffices as conspiracy to robbery. If they both robbed the bank, then, both would be charged as co-offenders or principal and accessory depending on what roles they each play and at what time.[12] In the inchoate crime of incitement, the crime is committed once a person reaches to another and urges the incited person (or incite) to commit a crime, and the inciter does so with the knowledge or intention that the person incited would commit the crime.[13] Once the crime is committed, he or she is responsible as an inciter, which falls under aiding and abetting in most jurisdictions.

From the above examples, it is obvious that the inchoateness of a crime can be lost. In the cases of attempt, conspiracy and incitement discussed above, their inchoate character is lost once the full crime is committed.

With this analysis, I have debated the question as to whether the inchoateness of Article 2(3)(c) (direct and public incitement to commit genocide) was lost in Rwanda due to the fact that the crimes incited were committed. In my opinion, though the Trial and Appeal Chambers did much work in developing the jurisprudence of direct and public incitement to commit genocide under Article 2(3)(c), they made fundamental errors in understanding the purpose underlying its inclusion in the Genocide Convention.[14] Recognising the role of inciters was not a new

---

[11] Ormerod (n. 6) 399–437; Dressler (n. 6) 429–64; Allen and Cooper (n. 6) 463–82; Heaton (n. 6) 415–33.

[12] Ormerod (n. 6) 180, 182, 189–93.

[13] Ormerod (n. 6) 441–43; Dressler (n. 6) 421–28; Allen and Cooper (n. 6) 482–88; Heaton (n. 6) 433–39.

[14] *Akayesu* (n. 2) para. 551, where the Trial Chamber quoted a statement by one of the delegates to the Genocide Convention: 'It was impossible that hundreds of thousands of people should commit so many crimes unless they had been incited to do so and unless the

concept: the drafters sought to expand the scope of criminal responsibility to include individuals who directly and publicly incite the commission of genocide. Therefore, even though incitement is an inchoate crime, the imposition of criminal responsibility was broadened to cover different classes of participants such as articulated in the Genocide Convention and the Statute of the ICTR.[15] Like other inchoate crimes under the Statute of the ICTR and Genocide Convention, responsibility is incurred irrespective of whether the crime of genocide is committed or not.[16] However, in the case of direct and public incitement to commit genocide, as documented in the preparatory works of the drafters of the Genocide Convention, it was included as an acknowledgement of the role inciters play in the perpetration of genocide.[17] It is logical to argue that even though direct and public incitement to commit genocide is an inchoate crime, the primary reason underlying its inclusion was to expand the scope of criminal responsibility and impose it on individuals who participate via incitement. It would have been much better to depict it as a standalone crime under the Statute of the ICTR. Furthermore, in developing the jurisprudence of this crime, the Trial Chambers looked at the discussions of the delegates when drafting the Genocide Convention.[18] As discussed by the Trial Chamber in *Akayesu*,[19] the essence of including direct and public incitement to genocide was because mass involvement in the perpetration of genocide was impossible without individuals inciting the masses to take part therein.[20] Therefore, the delegates sought to hold responsible such individuals. By identifying and imposing criminal responsibility on such persons, the delegates expanded the scope of those bearing responsibility for the commission of genocide. They did not characterise direct and public incitement to genocide as an inchoate crime.

---

crimes had been premeditated and carefully organized. He asked how in those circumstances, the inciters and organizers of the crime could be allowed to escape punishment, when they were the ones really responsible for the atrocities committed.' See Summary Records of the Meetings of the Sixth Committee of the General Assembly, 21 September–10 December 1948, Official Records of the General Assembly, statements by Mr Morozov, p. 241.

15 Ibid.

16 *Muvunyi* (n. 3) paras. 24–25; *Kalimanzira* (n. 2) para. 510; *Bikindi* (n. 3) para. 419; *Nahimana* et al (n. 3) (AC) paras. 678–79; *Nahimana* et al (n. 3) (TC) para. 678, 720; *Kajelijeli* (n. 2) para. 855; *Niyitegeka* (n. 3) para. 431; *Musema* (n. 2) para. 120; *Rutaganda* (n. 2) para. 38; *Akayesu* (n. 2) para. 562.

17 *Akayesu* (n. 2) para. 551.

18 *Akayesu* (n. 2) para. 561.

19 *Akayesu* (n. 2).

20 *Akayesu* (n. 2) para. 561.

Furthermore, the Trial and Appeal Chambers, though they developed their jurisprudence on direct and public incitement to commit genocide by looking at the preparatory work of the delegates to the Genocide Convention, they failed to identify a key difference between the Genocide Convention and the Statute of the ICTR. The Genocide Convention simply defined the crime of genocide and articulated further the list of punishable acts.[21] The Statute of the ICTR is not different in this regard.[22] However, a key distinction is that under the Statute of the ICTR, there is a separate Article that deals with the imposition of criminal responsibility. The Genocide Convention did not have any such provision. Article 6(1) stipulates five traditional forms of participation which, if resulting in any of the stages of any of the crimes over which the ICTR has jurisdiction, would lead to the imposition of criminal responsibility. Instigation is one of these modes of participation.[23]

Unfortunately, by focusing on the rationale behind the inclusion of direct and public incitement to commit genocide as deliberated by the delegates to the Genocide Convention, the analysis and construction of instigation as a mode of participation to the crimes over which the ICTR has jurisdiction became blurred. Instigation became limited to the crime of genocide, and to direct and public incitement to genocide.

In the preceding chapter (Chapter Five), I argued that the Trial and Appeal Chambers have been mistaken in their appreciation of instigation under both Articles. As mentioned earlier, the intention of the delegates in making direct and public incitement to genocide punishable was to hold responsible such individuals. That ought to be the same guideline to be adopted by the Trial and Appeal Chambers. Even if their characterisation of direct and public incitement to genocide as inchoate was novel, its inchoateness was lost as a result of the commission of genocide in Rwanda. Unless the word inchoate was incorrectly used, it is difficult to understand why criminal responsibility ought to be imposed for an inchoate crime when the crime was actually committed.

It would have been more logical to hold that direct and public incitement to genocide, in line with the spirit behind its inclusion in the Genocide Convention, is a standalone crime and a mode of participation that would lead to the imposition of criminal responsibility for such individuals. Furthermore, the Statute of the ICTR defines the imposition of criminal

21 Genocide Convention, Article 2(c) and Article 3(a)–(e).
22 See Statute of the ICTR, Article 2(2) and Article 2(3)(a)–(e).
23 Statute of the ICTR, Article 6(1).

responsibility under Article 6(1). Instigation features as one of the modes of participation. As the jurisprudence of the Trial Chambers establishes, the words instigation and incitement are synonymous with each other, and can be used interchangeably.[24]

There are however, some key differences between instigation under Article 6(1) and incitement under Article 2(3)(c). Instigation under Article 2(3)(c) must meet the following criteria: first, it must be direct; secondly, it must be public; and third, it must be only to commit the crime of genocide. On the other hand, under Article 6(1), instigation (like any other enlisted mode) must lead to any of the stages (planning, preparation or execution) of any of the crimes. It is therefore not limited to any crime, and it must not meet any criterion or criteria such as direct and public.

Instigation that is direct and public, and to commit the crime of genocide, also qualifies as instigation to genocide under Article 6(1). This is so because what amounts to instigation under Article 2(3)(c) would also amount to instigation under Article 6(1). Genocide is one of the crimes over which the ICTR has jurisdiction. Therefore, individuals charged with direct and public incitement to commit genocide ought to be charged also with instigation to genocide under Article 6(1).

Given this analysis, it is obvious that there are cases where instigation under Article 6(1) intersects with instigation under Article 2(3)(c). In fact, this occurred since the first case of *Akayesu*.[25] However, it remained unnoticed until the case of *Kalimanzira*[26] where the Trial Chamber took notice and outlined a set of guidelines on how to approach such cases.[27] The 'Kalimanzira Principles', I argue, are a major step towards fixing this problem.[28] However, they remain fundamentally flawed. Two main reasons explain this: first, they repeat the wrong language of the jurisprudence of the Trial Chambers. By saying 'instigation that results in the commission of', the 'Kalimanzira Principles' are predicated upon recognition of only one of the stages articulated in Article 6(1): commission. Secondly, they are limited to genocide. This is an odd restriction to Article 6(1), which states numerous modes of participation that must lead to any of the crimes over which the ICTR has jurisdiction. The 'Kalimanzira Principles' therefore serve as an eloquent testimony that instigation, both under Articles 6(1) and 2(3)(c), have been limited to the crime of genocide.

---

24 *Kalimanzira*, (n. 2) para 511; *Akayesu* (n. 2) para 481.
25 *Akayesu* (n. 2).
26 *Kalimanzira* (n. 2).
27 *Kalimanzira* (n. 2) para. 516.
28 *Kalimanzira* (n. 2) para. 516. See also Chapter Four above.

The Trial and Appeal Chambers' limitation of instigation to genocide is inconsistent with the wording of Article 6(1). Furthermore, such limitation depicts some dichotomy between genocide and crimes against humanity. I have argued in this book that though no individual was indicted for instigating crimes against humanity, instigation to genocide also qualifies as instigation to crimes against humanity. Under the Statute of the ICTR, these two crimes have different definitional elements.[29] The legal characterisations given to the acts amounting to them are different too. However, they share much resemblance. A good example is the killing of a people. That would be a genocidal act if it was perpetrated with the intention to destroy a people, in part or in whole, and such people met any of the distinct criteria: race, religion, nationality or ethnicity.[30] That same killing would amount to murder or extermination (mass murder) as a crime against humanity if it were perpetrated as part of a widespread or systematic attack, directed against any civilian population, and such population can be characterised as religious, national, ethnic, political or racial.[31] Examples abound. Furthermore, when the instigators instigated these atrocities to be committed, they did not make a distinction as to whether they wanted or preferred genocide or crimes against humanity to be committed. They simply wanted the crimes committed. Characterising these acts into different crimes based on the definitions contained in international instruments is the work of the jurist, and the similarities of these elements must not be ignored.

The ICTR is in its final days as it is winding down. Given this state of affairs, the question that is asked is this: why this study at this time? I have undertaken this project for a few reasons.

First, even though the ICTR is closing down, international criminal justice is still evolving. In fact, the ICTR has been a major development in international criminal law, and given the nature and trend of events in Rwanda leading to the perpetration of atrocities and the involvement of key figures in the planning, preparation and commission of these crimes, much can be borrowed from the ICTR. The jurisprudence of the ICTR is rich. Though dotted by flaws in interpretation, current and future international criminal justice institutions have much to learn from this jurisprudence, and also take a monumental step further in improving and perfecting it. One of such institutions is the International Criminal Court.

29 See Statute of the ICTR, Articles 2(2) and 3.
30 Statute of the ICTR, Article 2(2).
31 Statute of the ICTR, Article 3(a) or (b).

6.3 Instigation Under the Rome Statute of the International Criminal Court

Like most institutions prior to the establishment of the International Criminal Court, it has recognised instigation as a mode of participation. It also has the standalone crime of direct and public incitement to commit genocide.[32] Interestingly, this standalone crime comes under the sub-head of 'Individual Criminal Responsibility'.

> In accordance with this Statute, a person shall be criminally responsible and liable for punishment for a crime within the jurisdiction of the Court if that person:
> a. Commits such a crime, whether as an individual, jointly with another or through another person, regardless of whether that other person is criminally responsible;
> b. Orders, solicits or induces the commission of such a crime which in fact occurs or is attempted;
> c. For the purpose of facilitating the commission of such a crime, aids, abets or otherwise assists in its commission or its attempted commission, including providing the means for its commission;
> d. In any other way contributes to the commission or attempted commission of such a crime by a group of persons acting with a common purpose. Such contribution shall be intentional and shall either:
> i. Be made with the aim of furthering the criminal activity or criminal purpose of the group, where such activity or purpose involves the commission of a crime within the jurisdiction of the Court; or
> ii. Be made in the knowledge of the intention of the group to commit the crime;
> e. In respect of the crime of genocide, directly and publicly incites others to commit genocide...[33]

It is noteworthy that despite the differences in wording the Rome Statute of the ICC, criminal responsibility under Article 25(3) is broadly defined: for the most part, it does not specify the modes of participation, but uses unrestrictive phrases.[34]

Secondly, the definition of crimes against humanity under the Rome Statute of the ICC is not so different from that of the Statute of the ICTR.[35] As discussed in Chapter Four, the Statute of the ICTR introduced elements

---

[32] See the Rome Statute of the ICC, Article 25(3)(e).

[33] Article 25(3) of the Rome Statute of the ICC (sub-article punishes 'direct and public incitement to genocide' as an inchoate crime).

[34] See for example the phraseology '...in any other way contributes to the commission or attempted commission...' (Article 25(3)(d)).

[35] See Rome Statute of the ICC, Article 7(1) and Statute of the ICTR, Article 3.

which, hitherto, did not exist in any previous international instrument. The definitional element of a widespread or systematic attack that is directed against any civilian population as has been discussed requires a multiplicity of persons. Crimes against humanity are group crimes. The Rome Statute of the ICC imposes criminal responsibility on any individual who participates in any of the stipulated ways in any of the crimes. Therefore, no mode of participation ought to be limited to any crime. This must be emphasised because the Trial Chambers of the ICTR have been consistent in limiting instigation to the crime of genocide, a practice which is contrary to Article 6(1).

Thirdly, the inclusion of direct and public incitement to genocide under Article 25(3)(e) as a mode of incurring individual criminal responsibility raises much interest. As discussed above, it is very possible to have cases where instigation under this standalone crime intersects with instigation as a mode of participation. In such cases, the 'Kalimanzira guidelines' are useful, but must be carefully read because they are a repetition of the interpretative flaws of the Trial and Appeal Chambers.

With situations referred to the International Criminal Court, instigation featuring as a mode of participation in the crimes over which the Court has jurisdiction added to the inclusion of the inchoate crime of direct and public incitement to commiti genocide, it would be interesting to see how the International Criminal Court contributes to the evolution of the jurisprudence of crimes against humanity when committed through instigation.

BIBLIOGRAPHY

Affidavits at Nuremberg Trials.

African Charter on Human and Peoples' Rights, 27 June 1981, OAU Doc. CAB/LEG/67/3 rev. 5; 1520 U.N.T.S. 217.

Alexander L, *Is There a Right to Freedom of Expression?* (Cambridge Studies in Philosophy and Law 2006).

Allen M J and Cooper S, *Elliott & Wood's Cases and Materials on Criminal Law* (9th edn., Sweet & Maxwell 2006).

Allied Control Council Law No. 10.

Ambos K, 'Joint Criminal Enterprise and Command Responsibility', (2007) Vol. 5 1 *J Int Criminal Justice* 159–183.

Arusha Accord 1993.

Arusha Peace Agreement, 4 August, 1993.

Arzt D E, 'Nuremberg, Denazification and Democracy: The Hate Speech Problem at the International Military Tribunal'(1995) Vol. XII, 3 *N. Y. L. Sch. J. Hum. Rts.*, 689.

Atkins R and Mintcheva S, (eds), *Censoring Culture: Contemporary Threats to Free Expression* (Free Press 2006).

Baker E, *Human Liberty and Freedom of Speech* (Oxford University Press 1989).

Bassiouni C M, *Crimes against Humanity in International Criminal Law*, (Martinus Nijhoff Publishers 1992).

——, *Crimes against Humanity in International Criminal Law* (Kluwer Law International 1999).

——, *Editor's Note*, in Bassiouni C M (ed), 3 *INTERNATIONAL CRIMINAL LAW*, Vol I (3rd edn., Martinus Nijhoff Publishers 2008).

Berlin Protocol 1945.

Berry J A and Berry C P (eds), *Genocide in Rwanda: A Collective Memory* (Howard University Press 1999).

Bierzanek R, '*War Crimes: History and Definition*', in Bassiouni M C (ed), *International Criminal Law*, Vol III (Dobbs Ferry 1987).

Biju-Duval J, 'Hate Media'–Crimes Against Humanity and Genocide: Opportunities Missed by the International Criminal Tribunal for Rwanda' in Alan Thompson (ed), *The Media and the Rwanda Genocide* (2007).

Bill of Rights 1689 (England).

Blayney M S, 'Herbert C. Pell, War Crimes and the Jews' (1976) 65 *American Jewish Historical Quarterly* 335.

Bloxham D, *Genocide on Trial: War Crimes Trials and the Formation of Holocaust History and Memory* (Oxford University Press 2001).

Bollinger L C and Stone G R, *Eternally Vigilant: Free Speech in the Modern Era* (University of Chicago Press 2003).

Bosmajian H, *Freedom Not to Speak* (New York University Press 1999).

Braun S, *Democracy off Balance: Freedom of Expression and Hate Propaganda Law in Canada* (University of Toronto Press 2004).

Breitman R, *The Architect of Genocide: Himmler and the Final Solution* (The Bodley Head 1991).

British India Act No. 30 of 1836 (United Kingdom).

Bulletin des arrêts de la Cour de Cassation, 1985.

Canadian Law Reform Commission, *Secondary Liability: Participation in Crime and Inchoate Offences*, Canada Working Paper No 29, 1982.

Caplan G, 'Rwanda: Walking the Road to Genocide' in Alan Thompson (ed), *The Media and the Rwanda Genocide* (Pluto Press 2007).

Cassese A, Gaeta P and Jones J R W D, *The Rome Statute of the International Criminal Court: A Commentary* (Oxford University Press 2002).

Cassese A, 'The Proper Limits of Individual Responsibility under the Doctrine of Joint Criminal Enterprise' (2007) Vol. 5 1 *J Int Criminal Justice* 109–133.

Charter of the International Military Tribunal for the Far East, Tokyo.

Charter of the International Military Tribunal, Nuremberg.

Charter of the United Nations.

Chrétien J, 'RTLM Propaganda: the Democratic Alibi' in Alan Thompson (ed), *The Media and the Rwanda Genocide* (Pluto Press 2007).

'Chronicle of a Genocide Foretold', Part 2, Video Series, written and directed by Danièle Lacourse and Yvan Patry, produced by Sam Grana and Yvan Patry, Alter-Cine (Montreal) and the National Film Board of Canada (Ottawa), 1995/1996.

Clark R S, 'Crimes against Humanity' in George Ginsburgs and V.N. Kudriavtsev (eds), *The Nuremberg Trial and International Law* (Martinus Nijhoff 1990).

Clinton B, 'The International Community Must Work Together to Build Rwanda', in Bruce G, Bonnie S, and Scott B (eds), *The Rwanda Genocide* (Farmington Hills 2004).

Commission of Experts established pursuant to United Nations Security Council Resolution 935 (1994).

Commission on the Responsibility of the Authors of the War and on Enforcement of Penalties, *Report Presented to the Preliminary Peace Conference, March 29, 1919, reprinted in* 14 *AJIL* 95, 144 (1920).

Convention on the Elimination of All Forms of Racial Discrimination, United Nations General Assembly Resolution 2106A (XX), U.N.G.A. 1406th Plenary Meeting, U.N. Doc. A/RES/20/2016 of 20 December 1965; 660 U.N.T.S. 195.

Convention on the Prevention and Punishment of the Crime of Genocide, United Nations General Assembly Resolution 260(III), U.N. GAOR, 3rd Session, 179th meeting, U.N. Doc. A/RES/260A (1948) of 9 December 1948.

Convention Respecting the Laws and Customs of War on Land (Hague, IV), 18 October 1907.

Cryer R and Boister N, *The International Military Tribunal for the Far East: An Appraisal* (Oxford University Press 2008).

Dallaire R, *Shake Hands with the Devil: The Failure of Humanity in Rwanda* (Arrow Books 2004).

Danner A M and Martinez J S, 'Guilty Associations: Joint Criminal Enterprise, Command Responsibility, and the Development of International Criminal Law' (2005) Vol. 93 1 *California Law Review* 75–169.

Decision on Defence Motion on Form of the Indictment, *The Prosecutor v Duško Tadić* Case No. IT-94-1, T. Ch. II, 14 November 1995.

Decision on the Prosecutor's Motion for Joinder and Decision on Barayagwiza's Extremely Urgent Motion for Lack of Jurisdiction and for Waiver of Time Limits Under Rule 72(A) and (F) of the Rules, *The Prosecutor v Jean-Bosco Barayagwiza* ICTR-97-19-I.

Declaration of German Atrocities, 1 November 1943, 1943, reprinted in (1944) 38 AJIL (Supp.) 3, 7–8.

Declaration of the Rights of Man and of the Citizen (France).

Dept. of State, *Report of Robert H. Jackson, United States Representative to the International Conference on Military Tribunals* (1949).

'*Der Sturmer*'.

Despatch from the British Ambassador (Halifax) to the United States' Secretary of State, 19 August 1944, in *Foreign Relations of the United States,* Diplomatic Papers 1944, Vol. I, General, 1351, 1352.

Destexhe A, *Rwanda Genocide in the Twentieth Century* (New York University Press 1996).

Diamond J, *Collapse* (Penguin Books 2005).

Draft Code of Crimes Against the Peace and Security of Mankind 1996, adopted by the International Law Commission, 48th Session, 1996.

Draft Code of Offences against the Peace and Security of Mankind 1954, adopted by the International Law Commission, 6th Session, 1954.
Draft Criminal Code (Law Com. No. 177) (United Kingdom).
Dressler J, *Understanding Criminal Law* (5th edn., LexisNexis 2009).
'Elements of Crimes', ICC-ASP/1/3, p. 108, Art. 8 (2) (b) (xxii) - 1, Art. 8 (2) (e) (vi)–1.
English Law Commission, *Assisting and Encouraging Crime*, Consultation Paper No 131, 1993.
European Convention for the Protection of Human Rights and Fundamental Freedoms, 4 November 1950, 213 U.N.T.S. 222, 312 ETS 5, as amended by Protocol No. 11 of 11 May 1994.
Foreign Relations of the United States, *Diplomatic Papers 1944*, Vol. I, General, 1351, 1352.
Forges A D, 'Call to Genocide: Radio in Rwanda, 1994' in Alan Thompson (ed), *The Media and the Rwanda Genocide* (Pluto Press 2007).
Forges A D, *Leave No One to Tell the Story: Genocide in Rwanda* (Human Rights Watch), <http://www.hrw.org/reports/1999/rwanda>
Fourth Report of Mr. Doudou Thiam, Special Rapporteur, U.N. Doc. A/CN.4/398, reprinted in [1986] 2 *Y. B. INT'L. L. COMM'N.* 53.
French Penal Code.
German Penal Code 1871 (Germany).
Graven J, 'Les Crimes Contre l'Humanité' (1950–I) 76 *RECEUIL DES COURS* 427.
Haffajee R L, 'Prosecuting Crimes of Rape and Sexual Violence at the ICTR: The Application of Joint Criminal Enterprise Theory' (2006) 29 *Harv. J. L. & Gender* 201–221.
Hamdorf K, 'The Concept of a Joint Enterprise and Domestic Modes of Liability for Parties to a Crime: A Comparison of German and English Law' (2007) Vol. 5 1 *J Int Criminal Justice* 208–226.
Han V, 'The Development of the Concept of Joint Criminal Enterprise at the International Criminal Tribunal for the Former Yugoslavia' (2005) 5 *Int'l Crim. L. Rev.* 167–201.
Heaton R, *Criminal Law Textbook* (Oxford University Press 2004).
Herik L V D and Sliedregt E S, 'Removing or Reincarnating the Policy Requirement of Crimes against Humanity: Introductory Note' (2010) Vol. 23 4 *Leiden Journal of International Law* 825–826.
Inter-American Convention on Human Rights, 22 November 1969, 1144 U.N.T.S. 123.
International Covenant on Civil and Political Rights, 999 U.N.T.S. 171.
International Law Commission Report, 1996.
Jones P A and Card R, *Cross and Jones' Introduction to Criminal Law* (8th edn., Butterworths 1976).
Jorgensen N H B, *The Responsibility of States for International Crimes* (Oxford University Press 2000).
Kagwi-Ndungu C, 'The Challenges in Prosecuting Print Media for Incitement to Genocide' in Alan Thompson (ed), *The Media and the Rwanda Genocide* (Pluto Press 2007).
Kamilindi T, 'Journalism in a Time of Hate Media' in Alan Thompson (ed), *The Media and the Rwanda Genocide* (Pluto Press 2007).
Kangura.
Kimani M, 'RTLM: the Medium that Became a Tool for Mass Murder' in Alan Thompson (ed), *The Media and the Rwanda Genocide* (Pluto Press 2007).
Kirsch S, 'Two Kinds of Wrong: On the Context Element of Crimes against Humanity' (2009) Vol 22 3 *Leiden Journal of International Law* 525–541.
Kochavi A J, *Prelude to Nuremberg: Allied War Crimes Policy and the Question of Punishment* (University of North Carolina Press 1998).
Kress C, 'On the Outer Limits of Crimes against Humanity: The Concept of Organization within the Policy Requirement: Some Reflections on the March 2010 ICC Kenya Decision' (2010) Vol 23 4 *Leiden Journal of International Law* 855–873.
Krug H N, 'Genocide in Rwanda: Lessons Learned and Future Challenges to the UN Human Rights System' (1998) 67 *Nordic Journal of International Law* 165.
Lemkin R, 'Genocide as a Crime under International Law' (1947) 41 *American Journal of International Law* 145.

Letter of 9 February 1993, from the United Nations Secretary-General, addressed to the President of the United Nations Security Council, 10 February 1993, UN Doc. S/25274.
Letter of 24 May 1994, from the United Nations Secretary-General, addressed to the President of the United Nations Security Council, 27 May 1994, UN Doc. S/1994/674.
Letter of 5 October 1993, from the United Nations Secretary-General, addressed to the President of the United Nations Security Council, 6 October 1993, UN Doc. 2/26545.
Li D, 'Echoes of Violence: Considerations on Radio and Genocide in Rwanda' in Alan Thompson (ed), *The Media and the Rwanda Genocide* (Pluto Press 2007).
London Agreement Establishing the International Military Tribunal, Nuremberg, 1943.
London Agreement for the Prosecution and Punishment of the Major War Criminals of the European Axis, Aug. 8, 1945, 59 Stat. 1544, 82 UNTS 279.
Luban D, 'A Theory of Crimes Against Humanity' (2004) 29 *Yale J. Int'l L.* 85–167.
Magnarella P, *When Victims Become Killers: Colonialism, Nativism, and the Genocide in Rwanda* (Princeton University Press 2001).
Melvern L, *Conspiracy to Murder: The Rwandan Genocide* (Verson 2004).
Melvern L, 'Missing the Story: The Media and the Rwandan Genocide' in Allan Thompson (ed), *The Media and the Rwanda Genocide* (Pluto Press 2007).
Memorandum of Reservations Presented by the Representatives of the United States to the Report of the Commission on Responsibilities.
Mettraux G, *International Crimes and the ad hoc Tribunals* (Oxford University Press 2005).
Mironko C, 'The Effect of RTLM's Rhetoric of Ethnic Hatred in Rural Rwanda' in Alan Thompson (ed), *The Media and the Rwanda Genocide* (Pluto Press 2007).
Monasebian S, 'The Pre-Genocide Case Against Radio-Télévision Libre des Milles Collines' in Alan Thompson (ed), *The Media and the Rwanda Genocide* (Pluto Press 2007).
Morris V and Scharf M P, *The International Criminal Tribunal for Rwanda Vol. 1* (Transnational Publishers, Inc. 1998).
Moscow Declaration 1943.
Nahimana F, *Le Sang Hutu est-il rouge?(Is Hutu Blood Red?)*
Nowrojee B, 'A Lost Opportunity for Justice: Why Did the ICTR Not Prosecute Gender Propaganda?' in Alan Thompson (ed), *The Media and the Rwanda Genocide* (Pluto Press 2007).
Nyankanzi E L, *Genocide: Rwanda and Burundi* (Schenkam Books 1998).
Obidegwu C, 'Rwanda: The Search for Post-Conflict Socio-Economic Change, 1995–2001' (12 November, 2003) 59 *African Region Working Paper Series* 1.
Offences Against the Person Act 1861 (United Kingdom).
Ohlin J D, 'Three Conceptual Problems with the Doctrine of Joint Criminal Enterprise' (2007) Vol. 5 1 *J Int Criminal Justice* 69–90.
Ormerod D, *Smith and Hogan Criminal Law* (12th edn., Oxford University Press 2008).
Overy R, *Interrogations: The Nazi Elite in Allied Hands, 1945* (Penguin Group 2001).
Powles S, Joint Criminal Enterprise – Criminal Liability by Prosecutorial Ingenuity and Judicial Creativity' (2004) 2 *J. Int'l Crim. Just.* 606–619.
Preliminary Report on Violations of International Humanitarian Law in Rwanda, transmitted by the Secretary-General's Letter of 1 October 1994, UN Doc. S/1994/1125.
Principles of International Law Recognized by the Charter of the Nuremberg Tribunal and the Judgment of the Tribunal.
Proceedings of the IMT, pt. 8.
Prosecutor's Motion for Joinder of Trials of *The Prosecutor v Jean-Bosco Barayagwiza, The Prosecutor v Ferdinand Nahimana* and *The Prosecutor v Hassan Ngeze* of 10 April 2000.
Prunier G, *The Rwanda Crisis: History of a Genocide* (Columbia University Press 1995).
Report of the Secretary-General Pursuant to Paragraph 5 of United Nations Security Council Resolution 955 (1994), 13 February 1995, UN Doc. S/1995/134.
Reports of the Special Rapporteur for Rwanda of the United Nations Commission on Human Rights, UN Doc. S/1994/1157 (Annexes I and II).
Rome Statute of the International Criminal Court, U.N. Doc. A/CONF.183/9 (1998) reprinted in I.L.M. (1998).

Rutayisire J, Kabano J, and Rubagiza J, 'Curriculum Change and Social Cohesion in Conflict-affected Societies (July 2002–December2003): Proposal of Rwanda'<http://www.ibe.unesco.org/Regional/social_cohesion/sc_rwanda.htm>.
Rwandan Penal Code (Rwanda).
Schabas W A, *The UN International Criminal Tribunals: The Former Yugoslavia, Rwanda and Sierra Leone* (Cambridge University Press 2006).
Schwelb E, 'Crimes Against Humanity' (1946) 23 *Brit. Y. B. Int'l L.* 181.
Sherrer C P, *Genocide and Crisis in Central Africa: Conflict Roots, Mass Violence, and Regional War* (Praeger 2002).
Showalter D, *Jews, Nazis, and the Law: The Case of Julius Streicher 1997*, in the Museum of Tolerance on-line library at <<http://motlc.wiesenthal.com/site/pp.asp?c=gvKVLcMVIuG&b=395155>>.
Slierdregt E V, 'Joint Criminal Enterprise as a Pathway to Convicting Individuals for Genocide' (2007) Vol. 5 1 *J Int Criminal Justice* 184–207.
Smith Act 1940 (United States).
Smith B F, *The Road to Nuremberg* (Basic Books 1981).
Smith D, 'Timeline: A History of Free Speech' *The Guardian* (London: 2006), <<http://www.guardian.co.uk/media/2006/feb/05/religion.news>>. Retrieved on 2 May 2010.
Speeches of the Prosecutors.
Sprecher D A, *Inside the Nuremberg Trial: A Prosecutor's Comprehensive Account* (University Press of America 1999).
Statute of the International Criminal Tribunal for Rwanda, annexed to United Nations Security Council Resolution 955, U. N. SCOR, 3453rd meeting, U.N. Doc. S/RES/955 (1994) of 8 November 1994.
Statute of the International Criminal Tribunal for the former Yugoslavia, annexed to United Nations Security Council Resolution 827, U. N. SCOR, 3217th meeting, U.N. Doc. S/RES/827 (1993) of 25 May 1993.
Statute of the Special Court for Sierra Leone, annexed to the Agreement between the United Nations and the Government of Sierra Leone on the Establishment of a Special Court for Sierra Leone pursuant to United Nations Security Council Resolution 1315, U. N. SCOR, 4186th meeting, U.N. Doc. S/RES/1315 (2000) of 14 August 2000.
Summary Records of the Meetings of the Sixth Committee of the General Assembly, 21 September–10 December 1948, Official Records of the General Assembly, Statements by Mr Morozov.
Taylor T, *The Anatomy of the Nuremberg Trials: A Personal Memoir* (Alfred A. Knopf, Inc. 1992).
Temple-Raston D, *Justice on the Grass: Three Rwandan Journalists, Their Trial for War Crimes, and a Nation's Quest for Redemption* (Free Press 2005).
The Hague Conventions on the Laws and Customs of War.
The Situation of Human Rights in the Territory of the Former Yugoslavia, 3 September 1992, UN Doc. A/47/418-S/24516.
The Situation of Human Rights in the Territory of the Former Yugoslavia, 6 November 1992, UN Doc. A/47/635-S/24766.
Trial of German Major War Criminals: Speeches of the Prosecutors at the Close of the Case Against the Indicted Organizations (1946).
Trial of the Major War Criminals before the IMT, Nuremberg, 14 Nov. 1945–1 Oct. 1946, (1947), Nuremberg Judgment.
Triffterer O, *Commentary on the Rome Statute of the International Criminal Court: Observers' Notes, Article by Article* (2nd edn., Hart Publishing 2008).
United Nations General Assembly Resolution 174(II), U.N. GAOR, 2nd Session, 123rd meeting, U.N. Doc. A/RES/174(II), 21 November 1947.
United Nations General Assembly Resolution 1904 (XVIII), U.N.G.A. 1261st Plenary Meeting, U.N. Doc. A/RES/18/1904 (XVIII), 20 November 1963.
United Nations General Assembly Resolution 2106A (XX), U.N.G.A. 20th Session, 1406th Plenary Meeting, U.N. Doc. A/RES/20/2016, 20 December 1965.

United Nations Secretary-General's Report Pursuant to Paragraph 2 of the United Nations Security Council Resolution 808, 3 May 1993, UN Doc. S/25704.

United Nations Security Council Resolution 713, U.N. SCOR, 3009th meeting, U.N. Doc. S/RES/713 ((1991), 25 September 1991.

United Nations Security Council Resolution 780, U.N. SCOR, 3119th meeting, U.N. Doc. S/RES/780 (1992), 6 October 1992.

United Nations Security Council Resolution 808, U.N. SCOR, 3175th meeting, U.N. Doc. S/RES/808 (1993), 22 February 1993.

United Nations Security Council Resolution 827, U.N. SCOR, 3217th meeting, U.N. Doc. S/RES/827 (1993), 25 May 1993.

United Nations Security Council Resolution 872, U.N. SCOR, 3009th meeting, U.N. Doc. S/RES/872 (1993), 5 October 1993.

United Nations Security Council Resolution 912, U.N. SCOR, 3368th meeting, U.N. Doc. S/RES/912 (1994), 21 April 1994.

United Nations Security Council Resolution 918, U.N. SCOR, 3377th meeting, U.N. Doc. S/RES/918 (1994), 17 May 1994.

United Nations Security Council Resolution 955, U.N. SCOR, 3453rd meeting, U.N. Doc. S/RES/955 (1994), 8 November 1994.

United Nations Security Council Resolution 965, U.N. SCOR, 3473rd meeting, U.N. Doc. S/RES/965 (1994), 30 November 1994.

United Nations Security Council Resolution 997, U.N. SCOR, 3542nd meeting, U.N. Doc. S/RES/997 (1995), 9 June 1995.

United Nations Security Council Resolution 1029, U.N. SCOR, 3605th meeting, U.N. Doc. S/RES/1029 (1995), 12 December 1995.

United Nations Security Council Resolution 1315, U.N. SCOR, 4186th meeting, U.N. Doc. S/RES/1315 (2000), 14 August 2000.

United Nations Trusteeship Commission Report, March 1961.

United Nations' Universal Declaration of Human Rights, United Nations General Assembly Resolution 217A, U.N.G.A. 3rd Session, U.N. Doc. A/RES/3/217A (1948) of 10 December 1948.

United States' Constitution.

United States Sentencing Commission's Guidelines Manual, November 1998.

UNWCC, *History of the United Nations War Crimes Commission and the Development of the Laws of War* (1948).

Vansina J, *Antecedents to Modern Rwanda: The Nyiginya Kingdom* (University of Wisconsin Press 2004).

Wilt H V D, 'Joint Criminal Enterprise Possibilities and Limitations', (2007) Vol. 5 1 *J Int Criminal Justice* 91–108.

Wireless Telegraphy Act 1949 (United Kingdom).

Wright L, 'War Crimes Under International Law' (946) 62 *LAW Q. REV.* 40.

Yearbook of the International Law Commission, 1954, Vol. II.

Yearbook of the International Law Commission, 1996, Vol. II (Part Two).

INDEX

www.ingramcontent.com/pod-product-compliance
Lightning Source LLC
La Vergne TN
LVHW020652300926
849161LV00004B/915

* 9 7 8 9 0 0 4 2 5 4 1 2 1 *